Civil Passions

Civil Passions

MORAL SENTIMENT
AND DEMOCRATIC DELIBERATION

Sharon R. Krause

PRINCETON UNIVERSITY PRESS

PRINCETON AND OXFORD

Library of Congress Cataloging-in-Publication Data

Krause, Sharon R.
Civil passions : moral sentiment and democratic deliberation / Sharon R. Krause.
p.   cm.
Includes bibliographical references and index.
ISBN 978-0-691-13725-4 (cloth : alk. paper)
1. Political psychology. 2. Justice. 3. Fairness. I. Title.
JA74.5.K715 2008
320.01'9—dc22   2008016895

British Library Cataloging-in-Publication Data is available

This book has been composed in Palatino

Printed on acid-free paper. ∞

press.princeton.edu

Printed in the United States of America

10   9   8   7   6   5   4   3   2   1

FOR TAYHAS

my love, my heart's adventurer;

when I am lost,

you find me.

Contents

Acknowledgments

I HAVE ACCRUED a number of debts in writing this book, which I acknowledge with much gratitude. The National Endowment for the Humanities supported the research and writing of the book through a summer grant and a year-long faculty fellowship. For helpful commentary on various chapters and challenging conversation about the arguments, I thank Arash Abizadeh, Susan Bandes, Richard Bourke, Corey Brettschneider, Simone Chambers, Jack Crittendon, Joshua Dienstag, Patrick Dineen, Dave Estlund, Fonna Forman-Barzilai, Michael Frazer, Bill Galston, Bryan Garsten, Cheryl Hall, Don Herzog, Istvan Hont, David Kim, Charles Larmore, Mika LaVaque-Manty, Jacob Levy, Jane Mansbridge, Patchen Markell, Lida Maxwell, Kirstie McClure, Don Moon, Jenny Nedelsky, Tayhas Palmore, Davide Panagia, Carmen Pavel, Andy Sabl, John Scott, Hasana Sharp, Annie Stilz, Tracy Strong, Luke Swaine, Christina Tarnopolsky, Adam Tebble, John Tomasi, and Karen Zivi. Ian Malcom shepherded the book through the publication process with grace and wisdom; Jon Munk and Jack Amoureux provided excellent editorial assistance. Audiences at several universities offered valuable feedback and engaging discussion on different parts of the book, including Brown University; the Boalt School of Law at the University of California, Berkeley; the University of California, Davis; the University of California, Los Angeles; the University of California, San Diego; Columbia University; the University of London; McGill University; the University of Michigan; and the University of Toronto. Versions of three chapters have been published elsewhere and appear here in revised form. Chapter 1 appeared originally as "Desiring Justice: Motivation and Justification in Rawls and Habermas," *Contemporary Political Theory* 4 (4) (November 2005): 363–85; it is reproduced here with permission of Palgrave Macmillan. Chapter 3 appeared as "Passion, Power, and Impartiality in Hume," in Rebecca Kingston and John Ferry, eds., *Bringing the Passions Back In: The Emotions in Political Philosophy* (Vancouver: University of British Columbia Press, 2007); reprinted here with permission of the publisher, all rights reserved by the publisher. Chapter 6 appeared as "Moral Sentiment and the Authority of Law," *Culture and Politics* 1 (1) (December 2006): 17–38.

Civil Passions

Citizenship, Judgment, and the Politics of Passion

How do we distinguish, as citizens, between laws that are worthy of our allegiance and those we should reject or resist? Democratic procedural criteria are important here, but ostensibly democratic procedures sometimes go wrong, generating laws that endanger civil liberties or obstruct social justice. And while the principle of judicial review gives the courts a role in evaluating legislative outcomes, citizens in liberal democracies also have a responsibility in this regard. As citizens, our relationship to the laws should not be one of blind obedience, after all; it should reflect critical engagement and sound judgment. In fact, we have a political obligation as liberal-democratic citizens to evaluate the laws and to resist (or try to reform) laws that do violate liberty or obstruct justice. How do we carry out this evaluation? What faculties of heart and mind do we use? Americans today are in the process of publicly deliberating about the justice of gay marriage, for instance. In deliberating about an issue such as this one—which brings together questions of politics, morality, and law—what capacities do we employ? In particular, what is the right combination of thinking and feeling, of reason and passion, of cognition and affect, within such deliberation?

The common response to this question is to insist that there is *no* right combination of reason and passion, at least when it comes to deliberation about important political questions and matters of basic justice. The only way to achieve good deliberation, in other words, is to excise passions from the deliberative process entirely. The worry is that these affective modes of consciousness will cloud our reason and therefore impede the impartiality that is needed for sound moral judgment, equitable adjudication, and fair political deliberation. This is the dominant view (although certainly not the only one) in the history of political thought in the West. It is also the dominant view in political theory today. This book challenges that view. The practical deliberation that we use to assess laws and public policies inevitably incorporates emotions and desires—and these passions *can* contribute in a positive way to the impartial standpoint that makes public decisions legitimate. To be sure, passions also can impede impartiality, and when they do so they cause problems for the legitimacy of democratic decision making and the justice of its outcomes. Cruelty and bigotry, for instance, should never determine the direction our collective deliberation takes. And a spirit of civility, not jingoism or destructive rage, should guide it. Like civility, the ideal of impartiality is crucial to legitimate deliberation and to justice, and it should never be abandoned. Yet the real possibility of conflict between passion and impartiality does not tell the whole story of their very complex relationship. *Civil Passions* develops an account of affective but impartial judgment, loosely inspired by the moral sentiment theory of David Hume, and provides a systematic statement of the role the passions might properly play in moral judgment and public deliberation.

In articulating the affective dimensions of impartiality, the book addresses a problem that has plagued normative theories of democratic decision making for a generation. The rationalist models of deliberation and norm justification that predominate in political theory today (as represented, for instance, in the work of John Rawls and Jürgen Habermas) suffer from a motivational deficit. The ideal of reason as a faculty that abstracts from sentiment, which undergirds impartiality on this view, disconnects the deliberating subject from the motivational sources of human agency, which are found in the affective attachments and desires from which subjects are asked to abstract. The self as deliberator comes apart from the self as agent. To be sure, both Rawls and Habermas make a place for affect in their theories of justice. Specifically, both recognize the importance of engaging citizens' attachments and desires as a means of fostering allegiance to the rational procedures of norm justification and their results, thereby generating a feeling for justice that lends it stability. Yet both views aspire to limit the contributions of affect to the realm of application, while norm justification itself is conceived as a function of a form of reason that transcends affective influences. In effect, what they give us is a two-stage model: first, reason tells us what justice means and what it requires in terms of laws and public policies; then once this normative matter is settled, we move to the realm of application where we can begin to think about how to socialize citizens into the affective dispositions that support the norms that reason has justified. The forms of judgment modeled by Rawls's original position and Habermas's moral standpoint betray a familiar fear about affect, which is that our passions will impugn the impartiality on which deliberation in matters of justice ought to rest. So the dominant paradigms can accept that affective concerns help motivate right action but not that such concerns figure in the justification of action or the norms that guide it. They are reluctant to tie the content and authority of moral and political norms to the psychological states of individuals. The rationalists see affect as antithetical to impartiality, and they find the source of normativity in a form of reason that opposes passion. Yet to insulate deliberation from affect is to disconnect it from the passions that motivate action.

Action is not the only thing to suffer either, for decision making itself is hindered by efforts to abstract too fully from the influence of the passions. In the last fifteen years a revolutionary new literature has emerged in neuroscience and neuropsychology that calls into question the human ability to conduct practical reasoning in the absence of sentiments.[1] These studies, which involve patients who have impairments to regions of the brain associated with feeling, suggest that decision making depends on the affective experience of concern—specifically attachments, aversions, and desires. Patients with affective impairments may be perfectly capable of logical analysis; often they can reason effectively about the costs and benefits of various courses of action. What they cannot do effectively, the studies show, is *decide* on a course of action. The implication of these findings is that practical reasoning—deliberation that results in decisions about what to do—necessarily incorporates sentiments. Affect has a role in motivating decisions as well as actions, and therefore the motivational deficit associated with rationalist models of deliberation undermines not only compliance but the very process of deliberation itself. This new literature thus poses a fundamental challenge to the rationalist paradigms of deliberation and norm justification that dominate political theory today.

Political scientists have recently begun to explore the implications of these findings for political behavior in such areas as party identification, negative campaigning, the formation of social movements, and international conflict mediation.[2] The point they all press is that our analytical perspectives on political behavior should reflect the fact that sentiments are as essential to decision making as reason is. In fact, sentiments are a part of practical rationality itself. There is no faculty of practical reason that entirely stands apart from sentiment.[3] Among other things, sentiments set the basis for future decisions by providing a sense of what matters, based on prior learning and experience. In other words, sentiments constitute the horizons of concern within which practical judgment and deliberation transpire. What the empirical literature indicates, then, is that we cannot deliberate effectively about practical ends (in politics or anything else) without feeling. The implication is that sentiments must play a more important role in deliberation about justice than the dominant models in political theory acknowledge. What the empirical literature does not provide, however, is a normative account of how feeling *should* figure in practical deliberation if its conclusions are to be just, and specifically how sentiments might serve the important democratic ideal of impartiality.

Increasingly, normative theorists in moral philosophy, political theory, and the law are recognizing the importance of affect within judgment and deliberation. This recognition marks real progress, for it expands the conceptual framework within which judgment and deliberation are understood, but it has generated its own set of difficulties. Whereas the rationalists suffer from a motivational deficit, the theorists of affect too often suffer from a normative deficit. They frequently fail to provide clear criteria for the legitimate incorporation of sentiment. Not all feelings support sound judgment or fair public deliberation, after all. Consider Michael Walzer's discussion of how "our hostility to aggression is just as passionate as aggression itself."[4] Behind this hostility, he says, is not a faculty of reason that transcends sentiment but a form of reason infused with sentiment:

> Behind that hostility . . . is a mental picture of people like ourselves living quietly and peacefully in their own places, in their homes and homeland. They are attacked without legitimate cause (that's the definition of aggression), their families and friends, their cities and towns, their way of life, threatened with destruction, perhaps destroyed. Surely our rational condemnation of the attack cannot be understood without reference to that mental picture. In fact, it derives from that picture; it depends on our emotional identification with those people, who are the projected images of the men and women with whom we ourselves live, at home and in peace. Identifications of this sort are the work of the affiliative passions, and they shape our response to aggression as surely as the passion for triumph and domination shapes the aggression itself.[5]

Our judgments of good and bad, right and wrong, are therefore a function of feeling as much as intellectual understanding. Yet Walzer does not specify how we are to distinguish sound passionate judgments from unsound ones. Surely some affiliative passions can lead to poor judgments and unjust decisions. We need to know when and how feelings should be incorporated into the deliberative process; we need to know how far empathic (or "affiliative") concern should reach; and we need some standards or method for discriminating between sentiments that deserve our respect and those that do not.

Another problem is that theorists of affect sometimes defend affective judgment as an alternative to impartiality. The feminist "ethics of care" that emerged in the 1980s grounds judgment in concern for particular others.[6] It eschews impartiality, which it associates with rational respect for universal principles of justice. More recent proponents of this approach sometimes treat justice-oriented judgment and care-oriented judgment as complementary rather than competitive.[7] Yet, like the rationalists, they associate impartial deliberation about justice with a form of reason that transcends sentiment. In this respect, they concede far too much to the dominant paradigm. Iris Young and Martha Nussbaum have similarly championed emotional forms of judgment as alternatives to impartiality.[8] Although their approaches differ markedly from one another (and from the ethics of care), they share a certain skepticism about the ideal of impartiality, which they associate with an exclusive and untenable conception of human reason.

Yet democratic citizens cannot afford to give up on this ideal. Impartiality entails a deliberative perspective that is neither prejudiced nor fragmentary. It involves considering things in a way that is not determined by (or does not simply serve) one's own interests, narrow sympathies, or idiosyncratic convictions. It is also an inclusive, even comprehensive view, which incorporates the relevant perspectives of all those affected by the object under consideration. Impartiality admits of degrees insofar as our judgments may be more or less free of prejudice and more or less inclusive. Few of us achieve perfect impartiality on a regular basis, and cross-cultural impartiality is especially difficult. But for most of us the exercise of impartiality in varying degrees of (im)perfection is a familiar experience. The aspirational ideal that guides us in this exercise is extremely valuable. Among other things, impartiality helps to insulate our evaluations and decisions from the privileges of power. Without some degree of impartiality, public decisions would lack legitimacy and justice would prove elusive. This is one thing that the rationalists get right: impartial judgment *is* a crucial condition of just public decision making in liberal democracy. It protects citizens from the unadorned force of power on public matters having to do with justice.

Impartiality is also important in the context of individual moral judgment. It aids in social coordination, for one thing, because to coordinate our lives with others we need to be able to think beyond the limits of our own private views. A person whose deliberative perspective was determined exclusively by self-interest without any consideration of the interests or perspectives of others could not succeed in achieving even his own ends over time, much less collective ones. The fact that impartiality helps facilitate social coordination makes it prudent. Impartiality also manifests the virtue that Hume called "humanity," a reflective sensitivity to the sufferings and the joys of others, even a kind of respect for persons as morally significant. Without this virtue, as Hume saw, one's personal character would be marked by bigotry, incivility, and ignorance, and it could never bear its own survey. We can press beyond Hume, as well, to add that exercising impartiality in judgment is a way of treating others as ends in themselves, an obligation that can be justified by means of moral sentiment. One need not

recur to Kant to support the duty of equal respect—as we shall see—
and this duty makes impartiality important. So while we should be
skeptical about exclusive and untenable notions of reason, we should
not reject impartiality. To reject impartiality is to saddle affective forms
of judgment with a normative deficit. In short, our theories of moral
judgment and democratic deliberation have been caught on the horns
of a dilemma: they have either been too rationalist to motivate action
and decision, or they have been too indiscriminately rooted in the passions to carry normative weight. *Civil Passions* means to dissolve this
dilemma by articulating an ideal of affectively engaged impartiality,
and hence an account of judgment and deliberation that is both motivationally and normatively compelling.

The book thus addresses a lacuna that plagues contemporary theory
in the political, moral, and legal domains, but it also speaks to a serious
problem in American public life today. On the common view of political deliberation, which assumes a dichotomy between reason and
passion, one either deliberates from "impartial reason" or one's deliberation is driven by personal passions. And when passions drive deliberation, we think, the results can only be described as debased. Yet the
rationalist ideal of impartiality that pervades the public culture is an
idyll. It should therefore come as no surprise that public decision making in the United States today most often proceeds by means of interest-based competition, which is another name for the politics of untutored passion. Yet even as we give in to the politics of passion in its
lowest form, our elusive ideal of reason continues to engage our aspirations and to tell us that passion-driven deliberation is illegitimate
and likely to generate injustice. One result of trying and failing to live
up to this impossible ideal of deliberation is cynicism about politics.
The widely discussed lack of political participation in the United States
today is only partly a product of excessive individualism, the absence
of civic virtue, and the lack of social capital. This disengagement also
reflects the disillusionment that naturally follows from our attachment
to the false dichotomy between reason and passion, and from the absence of an achievable ideal of impartiality.

To make matters worse, widespread citizen disengagement undercuts the possibility of genuine impartiality in public deliberation. The
reason is that our deliberative process can only be fully impartial if it
reflects the legitimate concerns of all affected. But we can only know
the concerns of others if they tell us about them, which requires precisely the kind of active engagement in public life that the rationalist
ideal discourages. American politics therefore needs a new way of understanding public deliberation, one that answers to the noble aspiration of impartiality but that does not disparage the passions that inevi-

tably influence decisions and animate action. We must reject the false dichotomy between reason and passion in both political theory and American public life because this dichotomy undercuts our ability to advance the cause of justice. In its place we need a better understanding of the holistic nature of practical reasoning as a faculty that combines both cognitive and affective states of mind, both intellect and feeling. We need standards that inspire reflective and legitimate decision making but that are also practically viable and motivationally compelling, hence affectively engaged. The purpose of *Civil Passions* is to illuminate the nature of practical judgment in this respect, and to show why this more holistic vision of ourselves and our capacities promises a more vital—and more just—democratic politics.

But what, exactly, is "affect"? Psychologists typically define affect capaciously to include all mental states that take the form of feeling as opposed to mere belief or understanding. Specific emotions such as anger, sadness, and joy are forms of affect, but so are desires, aversions, and attachments. Many of these states involve beliefs, of course. Anger, for instance, depends on the belief that one has been wronged. Yet as a phenomenological matter, affective states cannot be reduced to belief or understanding; something beyond belief makes our experience of affective modes of consciousness distinctive. In recent years, technological innovations have allowed researchers to correlate this distinctive experience with specific regions of the brain, regions that differ from those that are activated during purely intellectual activities such as logical analysis. Although affective states have some common features, not all forms of affect are equally important for practical deliberation, or important in the same way. Emotions can, but need not, carry the motivating force that makes decision and action possible. I can be sad, for instance, without being motivated to do anything. Emotions do not always involve dispositions for action, nor do they necessarily suggest grounds for decision. By contrast, desires, aversions, and attachments are marked by a general tendency to motivate us. They have a special connection to the will because they are states of mind that involve a wish that the world be, or come to be, one way rather than another.

Simon Blackburn's language of "concern" is instructive here. Blackburn defines concerns as the "things that we care about, aspects of the situation that present themselves as reasons for or against action."[9] Like desires, concerns are affectively engaged and practically motivating. Concerns may be "backward-looking, forward-looking, self-centred, not self-centred, moral, [or] non-moral," but they always refer to things that *matter* to us, and they entail dispositions for decision and action rather than an orientation of disengaged understanding.[10] In contrast to common usages of the term "desire," however, which are often synonymous with unreflective impulse or appetite, concerns may be reflective and incorporate beliefs. The concern for justice and the desire for fair treatment clearly entail ideas about what justice and fairness mean and why they matter. Concerns combine affective and cognitive modes of consciousness, then, and they will include interests and reflective desires as well as attachments, personal convictions, and the things (whether persons or principles) to which we are emotionally committed. The term "concern" thus parallels Cheryl Hall's use of the word "passion," which on her definition involves a cognitive perception of the object of passion as valuable. Yet this perception has an affective valence as well as a cognitive one. As Hall puts it, "to value one thing over another *is* to care about it, not just to impassively think that it is better. Put the other way around, passion *is* the affective manifestation of value."[11] Concerns are affective states that involve reflective valuing and caring, and that dispose us to decision and action.

Concerns are often experienced in connection with specific emotions, such as anger or happiness or grief, but they need not be. It is possible to have a concern for justice, for instance, without (at the moment) experiencing anything other than the sense of its importance, the feeling that it matters, the desire to see it realized. In this sense, concerns may come apart from emotions, or the usual slate of emotions. Yet emotions do generally imply concerns, although the relationship may be indirect. The feeling of anger may not always engage the will in the direct way that desires and aversions do, but anger typically arises when one's concerns have been thwarted, when something one cares about has been violated. Emotions and concerns are conceptually distinct, then, but they are frequently intertwined in practice. Both involve the affective experience of caring in a way that goes beyond mere understanding, although they often include beliefs.

This book is interested partly in affect as concerns, which Hume (like Hall) called "passions." Concerns provide important conditions for practical judgment and deliberation in the sense that the latter always transpire within particular horizons of concern. I follow Hume, too, in using the term "sentiment" to refer to affective states in the widest sense, including not only emotions and concerns but also pleasures and pains. It is worth emphasizing that many (perhaps most) human sentiments, including pleasures and pains, include a cognitive component. Sentiments so conceived figure as inputs in the perspective-taking dimension of moral judgment and public deliberation, as described in the chapters that follow. *Civil Passions* thus focuses not only on affect as background concerns but also on the whole range of sentiments that may factor into a specific instance of perspective-taking properly conceived.

In holding affective concerns to be necessary conditions of judgment and deliberation, I dispute a central premise of the dominant neo-Kantian paradigm in moral and political theory today, which holds that reason as a faculty of the mind that transcends sentiment is perfectly capable, on its own, of motivating at least decisions if not also actions.[12] One way to see the limits of this view is to consider some examples. A recent theorist of deliberative democracy has offered the following illustration of how the intellect on its own supposedly directs decisions within individual moral deliberation:

> I once heard two men discussing whether it was right to use "she" and "her" instead of "he" or "his" when referring to generic persons. A was for, B was against. B did not feel that arguments concerning equality or fairness had any force. Having exhausted all other (and better) justifications, A said that, if nothing else, B should use feminine pronouns because B was "a gentleman!" B was cornered and found it hard to disagree. What does this exchange accomplish? First, it appeals to an image of the self that may be generally agreeable to the obstinate B. It further points out an inconsistency in preferences by forcing into the discussion the notion that if B wants to stick with his male-gendered vocabulary, he must argue against a shared male norm: "be kind to women." . . . Deliberation channels old norms to new cases: it restates an unassailable principle and then shows that the opponent's argument violates that principle; thus, out of consistency . . . the recalcitrant party is induced to revise his preferences or else recant the principle.[13]

The contribution of reason within B's deliberation, on this account, is to point out the supposed inconsistency involved in simultaneously wishing to be a gentleman and rejecting the generic use of the feminine pronoun. (For present purposes, we leave aside the question of whether these two positions are truly inconsistent.) Yet no conclusion is possible on the basis of the recognition of inconsistency alone. On the basis of this recognition, one is free to conclude in favor of either alternative, or to live with the inconsistency. Think of Whitman's famous lines: "Do I contradict myself? Very well then, I contradict myself, I am large, I contain multitudes."[14] B is brought to support the generic use of feminine pronouns only because he *cares* about being a gentleman and about acting in ways that are consistent with his professed principles (this "appeals to an image of the self that may be generally agreeable to the obstinate B").

The affective dimension of deliberation here is easy to miss because it is dressed up in the ostensibly rational garb of "norms" and "principle"—the rejection of feminine pronouns is said to violate the (to B) "unassailable principle" of gentlemanliness—but it should not be difficult to see through this rationalist language to the affective core beneath it. To be sure, B may have strong grounds for considering the ideal of gentlemanliness to be unassailable, but these grounds will not rest on intellect alone. As the passage indicates, there is also an appeal here to a self-image that is desirable. And the ideal of consistency itself must have some appeal. As the empirical research on practical reasoning canvassed in chapter 2 suggests, unless this principle connects up with things B cares about, it will not have the power to conclude his deliberation or determine his action. Because affective concerns such as the desire to be consistent are often widely held and because they may enter consciousness without the fiery blaze of some other desires, it may be easy to forget that they are indeed desires, albeit reflective ones. In fact, such concerns are often mistaken for "reason itself," generating the erroneous belief that (in this case) the mere cognition of logical inconsistency leads to the revision of one's views. A better way to understand the desire for consistency (or the desire to be a gentleman) is in terms of what Hume called a "calm passion." When affective concerns are experienced in a calm fashion "and cause no disorder in the soul, they are very readily taken for the determinations of reason, and are suppos'd to proceed from the same faculty, with that, which judges of truth and falsehood."[15] Calm passions such as the desire for consistency may be mistaken for "reason," but on reflection we can see that they differ from purely cognitive states in being a form of reflective caring, not merely a type of understanding.

Consider another example. Suppose that you find yourself inexplicably angry at an acquaintance, John, a feeling you cannot understand, as John has done nothing to warrant it. Still, you cannot shake the feeling, and because of your anger you repeatedly act in ways that generate conflict with John. After confiding in a friend, you come to see that John reminds you of your father, toward whom you have warranted but unresolved feelings of anger. Suddenly you *understand* that you have no *reason* to be angry with John. Your feeling of anger dissipates (perhaps even disappears), and you resolve to begin treating him more justly. It may seem here that reason has eradicated an affective state, or acted directly on your emotions so as to change them. Yet letting go of such misplaced emotions typically requires more than cognitive insight. It also involves the desire not to be dominated in the present by negative experiences from the past, as well as the desires to treat others justly, to avoid unwarranted conflict, and so on. Without these affective concerns, the cognitive insight would have little ability to conclude deliberation or affect action. The affective dimensions of this reflective process should not be thought to undercut its status as deliberative, however. Think again about the content of B's reflections, above. The force of the better argument may indeed have been the determining ground of his decision, but the reasons that made this argument appear to him to be the better one built in affective concerns (B's desires to be a gentleman and to be consistent) and hence they were not independent of his sentiments.

The nature and power of practical reason vis-à-vis sentiment has been the subject of much debate among philosophers in recent years. The dispute raises deep questions about moral psychology and about the nature and sources of normativity. At stake in this debate is the promise of impartial justice. The rationalists worry that impartial justice will be impossible if reason cannot transcend the passions; the sentimentalists worry that it will be impractical (because unmotivated) if reason does not engage the passions. I do not claim to have resolved the debate, but I do hope to press political theorists to venture outside the dominant, neo-Kantian paradigm in thinking about these matters, matters that underlie all our theorizing about justice and that ought to get more attention in political theory than they do. The point I mean to press is that sentiments are integral, not antithetical, to practical reasoning. I take the empirical literature from neuroscience and neuropsychology to be very suggestive in this regard. It may turn out to be wrong—future research could yield new results that are inconsistent with its findings—but there are good reasons to accept the new research as the best that empirical study can tell us at the moment about how practical reasoning works.[16] We look more closely at this literature in chapter 2. Still, *Civil Passions* is not a book of neuropsychology, and the view it advances does not rest solely—or even primarily—on the data collected by scientists. In disputing the rationalist ideal of practical reason that transcends sentiment, I draw also on work by moral philosophers operating in the Humean tradition such as Simon Blackburn and Bernard Williams. They offer conceptual arguments showing the limits of the neo-Kantian view, some of which are canvassed in the pages that follow. I introduce some additional considerations, as well. For instance, chapter 1 demonstrates the sometimes surreptitious ways in which affect inevitably contributes to deliberation even on the ostensibly rationalist models of Rawls and Habermas. Chapter 4 likewise investigates the "reasons" that supposedly motivate decision making in rationalist accounts of public deliberation, and shows that these reasons typically incorporate affective concerns. Chapter 3 addresses one of the most powerful Kantian critiques of the Humean position on practical reason and provides a Humean reply, thus disarming the critique.

While the work of moral philosophers such as Blackburn and Williams is illuminating, however, none of it has addressed from a normative perspective the political dimensions of affective judgment, or elaborated its political implications. To be fair, the moral philosophers are largely addressing debates within metaethics. Their work is not intended to answer the normative political questions raised here. *Civil Passions* means to bring insights from the work in philosophy to bear on normative political theory. I explore both the political dimensions and the political implications of affective judgment, and show how a Humean view about the limits of reason as a faculty that transcends sentiment can be compatible with an ideal of impartiality in public deliberation, and hence with the possibility of justice.

What makes the Humean approach so powerful in this respect is that, rightly understood, it can simultaneously acknowledge the importance of affect alongside intellect within practical reasoning and articulate standards for impartial judgment and deliberation. The generalized standpoint of moral sentiment enables us to make impersonal judgments on the basis of a reflective, impartial set of feelings. It disputes the common belief that to deliberate impartially means to deliberate without feeling. Hume's theory of moral sentiment thus shows how reflective feeling, when properly arrived at, can support rather than thwart impartiality. For this reason, my account of public deliberation for liberal-democratic societies takes Hume as a point of departure. I do not say that Hume had all the right answers. Part of the argument of the book is that affective deliberation needs the support of liberal rights and a contestatory democratic politics if it is to achieve impartiality. This argument goes well beyond anything Hume himself advocated, and in some ways stands in tension with his political views. But I look to Hume, and especially to his theory of moral sentiment, for inspiration in thinking beyond the boundaries of the contemporary, neo-Kantian paradigm. In contrast to the dominant theories of justice and democratic deliberation today, Hume treated moral judgment as a reflective passion, where thought and feeling are integrated at the deepest level. And even though he rejected the idea that the intellect on its own could motivate action, still he gave it an important role in judgment. He also insisted on the objectivity and the impartiality of judgment. In fact, judgment achieves its impartiality through the mechanism of a generalized standpoint, and in this respect it actually converges with contemporary accounts of justice and democratic deliberation. But there is this difference: the generalized standpoint in Hume grows out of, rather than abstracts from, the usual sources of human action and decision as they are found in affective attachments and desires. Indeed, Humean judgment gets both its motivational efficacy and its normative authority from its footing in these sentiments.

So Hume has much to teach us today. His account of moral judgment as reflective sentiment offers a powerful corrective to the rationalism of current liberal and democratic theory.[17] He gives us tools for incorporating empirical findings about the inevitably affective dimensions of practical reasoning into a normative theory of impartiality that has valuable implications for how we understand moral judgment, public deliberation, and the authority of law. Judgment and deliberation are distinct phenomena, to be sure. For one thing, judgment need not be practical, or action-guiding. Aesthetic judgments, for instance, may have no impact on what we do. Even moral judgments need not directly influence individual behavior. One can evaluate the actions or character of another person as good or bad without oneself being moved to act in any particular way. The point of deliberation, by contrast, is precisely to guide action; hence, deliberation is necessarily practical. Although in any particular case one may not act on one's decision (weakness of will may be a factor here), still one's purpose in undertaking deliberation always is to decide what to *do*. Yet if deliberation is distinct from judgment, it nevertheless builds on judgment. The values and principles that guide moral deliberation are (or should be) endorsable from the perspective of impartial moral judgment. Judgment helps us to identify what we should value; deliberation enables us to guide our action in light of these values. It is also important to mark the distinction between individual moral deliberation, on the one hand, and public deliberation about matters of law and social policy, on the other. At least in liberal democracies, public deliberation calls for additional criteria beyond what is required for individual impartiality in moral deliberation. It requires fair procedures, for example, as well as the constraint of sound constitutional principles and norms of equal access, accountability, publicity, and reciprocity. These additional requirements speak to the distinctive demands of political legitimacy. Still, sound public deliberation builds on the impartiality of individuals much as deliberation itself builds on judgment. Consequently, a theory of moral judgment can illuminate important aspects of public deliberation.

Even accepting the potential value of a moral sentiment approach to judgment and deliberation, however, one might wonder if Hume is the best source of inspiration. The eighteenth century saw many philosophers of moral sentiment, after all, some of whom were more democratic or more liberal in their political views than he was. Nor did Hume have the last word on moral sentiment. Adam Smith's elaboration of the Humean view, and his modifications to it, have struck many readers as a genuine improvement in moral sentiment theory. So why look to Hume? Hume's theory is certainly the most fully worked out version of the moral sentiment approach prior to that of Smith. It is superior to those of Shaftesbury and Hutcheson, for instance, in distinguishing between sympathy as a communicative faculty of the mind and benevolence as a moral virtue, and in grounding moral sentiment in empirically verifiable human responses rather than in a metaphysically questionable and politically controversial religious teleology. I shall argue, too, that Hume's approach to moral sentiment can stand up to Smith's, although Smith helps us see where Hume's theory needs further elaboration. A careful analysis of the differences between Hume and Smith in this regard is beyond the scope of my project, however—this book is not a study of the moral sentiment school. Yet in elaborating Hume's view it does mean to draw attention to moral sentiment theory more generally as a resource for political theory today. I take Hume as my point of departure because of the fruitful way in which his theory of judgment combines impartiality with affective engagement.

Nevertheless, I do depart from his views in some key respects. For one thing, I do not adopt Hume's specific theory of justice. His conception of justice is too narrow to be adequate, with its limited emphasis on the protection of property rights and the keeping of promises. Hume's theory of moral sentiment can help us in our personal and public deliberations about justice, but only if the meaning of justice is understood to go beyond Hume's own definition of it. Hume's theory of moral sentiment can come apart from his theory of justice, and *Civil Passions* draws inspiration from the former while largely disregarding the latter. Another departure I make is to take seriously the political context of judgment and deliberation. Hume was very sensitive to the fact that moral sentiment is an intersubjective phenomenon, and that our judgments reflect many layers of social communication. This is not to deny the possibility of individual judgment, even judgment that cuts against the grain of received opinion, but it does insist on the socially embedded character of judgment and on the idea that normative standards reflect shared concerns. Exactly how individual judgment can be socially embedded while allowing for social criticism is something I take up in chapters 3, 4, and 5. Despite Hume's attention to the intersubjective character of judgment, however, he was largely silent about the negative effects that the wrong social and political arrangements can have on the impartiality of judgment. Impartial judgment depends upon a faculty of moral sentiment that is sensitive to the widest possible range of human experience and that is well informed about the sentiments of affected others. Political inequalities and social exclusions, which marginalize particular groups and make their experience opaque to the majority, handicap moral sentiment. For this reason, impartiality in both individual judgment and public deliberation will be difficult, if not impossible, in the absence of liberal-democratic political institutions and practices. In developing this claim, my project truly breaks ranks with Hume. Not only did he not look to politics to support moral sentiment, he did not favor the democratic activism and the strong role for individual rights that are crucial to my own account of impartiality. Yet as I argue in what follows, there are good Humean grounds for pursuing the approach I take, even if Hume himself did not see them. In interpreting the history of political thought for the purposes of normative political theory today, we should look for insight and illumination but we should not be slaves to the sometimes limited vision of individual philosophers.

In part because I am not reluctant go to beyond Hume where I think necessary, and in part because I read Hume in ways that sometimes challenge received opinion, my account of moral sentiment escapes many of the worries that people commonly have about Humeanism. Hume is widely associated with political conservatism, for instance, and he is known to have been a racist.[18] I show that his theory of judgment can be decoupled from these other aspects of his thought. *Civil Passions* connects moral sentiment to the moral ideal of respect for persons, to democratic activism and social equality, and to a critical but progressively more inclusive form of impartiality in judgment. The fact that Hume may not have approved of the political dimensions of this project should undercut neither their value nor his value for us. Kant thought that women should be excluded from republican citizenship, after all, and that government should never be resisted.[19] These mistakes are rarely cited as reasons to ignore the very suggestive notions of autonomy, dignity, and freedom that his theory offers. On the contrary, these concepts are widely appropriated by moral and political theorists today. There is no reason to treat Hume differently from Kant in this respect.

Another common worry about Humeanism is that it cannot generate—is even incompatible with—the universal principles of right that play such an important role in the practices and the self-understanding of liberal democracy. Moral and political judgment on the Humean view are nothing more than rank conventionalism that ultimately issue in cultural relativism, or so the common complaint goes. My reading of Hume deflects this criticism by showing that there is more to judgment than mere conventionalism, even on Hume's own explicitly stated account. Hume himself connects sound judgment to a form of impartiality that reaches beyond the bounds of one's society and the prejudices of one's era. Moreover, drawing on broadly Humean insights we can go beyond Hume's own writings to find grounds that justify principles with universal scope, including the principle of equal respect, the value of liberal democracy, and the aspiration to impartiality itself.

Although this book adopts a broadly Humean approach, Hume himself plays a relatively small role in it. Most of the book engages a more contemporary set of literatures concerning judgment and deliberation, primarily in political theory but touching on moral philosophy, psychology, legal theory, and empirical political science. Chapter 1 ("Justice and Passion in Rawls and Habermas") begins the study by investigating the dominant, rationalist paradigm of deliberation within contemporary political theory. The chapter explores some of the ways in which affective concerns—especially attachments to the good—figure in the models of judgment and deliberation defended by Rawls and Habermas. Our conceptions of the good naturally engage affective modes of consciousness because to see something as good is to desire it, to care about it, or to hold it as an object of concern. The "good" differs from the "right" in this respect—that it naturally engages the passions.[20] And despite the fact that both theories mean for the right to take priority over the good in our judgments about justice, they both make a place for affect. Indeed, both acknowledge (not always wittingly) that the right itself may be infused with feeling. In this way they turn out to be somewhat more nuanced as representatives of the rationalist paradigm of judgment than first appears. Yet even their accommodations of passion tend to subordinate it to forms of reason that are intended to be immune to the actual sentiments of real persons. Ultimately, the rationalist account—even a nuanced rationalism—not only generates a motivational deficit but misrepresents the normative grounds of moral and political judgment. Consequently, we need to go beyond Rawls and Habermas to understand how sentiments properly contribute to our judgments about justice.

The rationalism that characterizes the dominant theories of justice has been challenged in recent years on a number of fronts. The critiques that concern us in chapter 2 ("Recent Alternatives to Rationalism") all make affect central to their accounts of moral and political judgment. The first group of theorists (Carol Gilligan, Joan Tronto, Nel Noddings) we consider argues for the ethics of care as opposed to the disinterested morality of abstract principle that is said to characterize rationalist models of justice. The second group (Martha Nussbaum, Antonio Damasio, Herbert Marcus, among others) includes those working on the role of emotions within practical judgment. The contributions here are both philosophical and empirical, the latter issuing from political science as well as neuropsychology. Finally, we consider several contemporary accounts (those of Simon Blackburn, Bernard Williams, Michael Smith) of moral judgment inspired by Hume, which specify the ways that sentiments and concerns interact with reason to generate judgment and to constrain it. As powerful and as important as these efforts are, each is subject to certain difficulties. As mentioned above, these accounts tend to give up on the important ideal of impartiality, which they (like the rationalists) regard as antithetical to affect. No theory that forsakes impartiality can hope to guide legitimate public deliberation, however, for in liberal democracies legitimacy and impartiality rightly go hand in hand. In some cases, the accounts canvassed here end up recurring to a traditional ideal of passion-free reason to provide the normative authority that is lost to judgment when the ideal of impartiality is abandoned. In these cases, the ostensibly emotion-based accounts run up against the same problems as the rationalist ones. In addition, none of the existing views of passion-inflected judgment attends adequately to the *politics* of judgment. This is especially true of the neo-Humean views, which neglect the ways in which the sentiments that figure in judgment reflect the prevailing balance of power within society. Again, the point here is not so much to criticize these views (which rarely set out to address normative political questions) as to indicate the kinds of issues they open up for political theory. Impartiality in affective judgment requires a political context of rights-supported activism and democratic contestation, which challenge prevailing power relations and incorporate the voices of excluded and marginalized members of the polity. Any viable account of affective judgment and deliberation needs a political theory of individual rights, democratic activism, and social equality to sustain it.

Chapter 3 ("Moral Sentiment and the Politics of Judgment in Hume") begins the process of articulating an alternative to both the rationalist and the existing affective accounts of judgment and deliberation. The chapter examines Hume's theory of evaluative judgment as a form of moral sentiment. Drawing mainly on Hume's *Treatise of Human Nature* and *An Enquiry Concerning the Principles of Morals*, I elaborate the operations of judgment as moral sentiment, showing how this concept of judgment achieves impartiality and avoids narrow subjectivism without sacrificing affective engagement. Impartial moral sentiment rests on two things: the adoption of an impersonal perspective that incorporates, via the faculty of sympathy and the practice of perspective-taking, the reflectively endorsable sentiments of those affected; and attentiveness to human nature, conceived as a cluster of common, empirically verifiable human concerns. Together these two features constitute the impartial standpoint of moral sentiment. At the same time, I offer a critical analysis of the politics of impartiality, or the ways in which the structure of the political order as well as informal power relations inevitably permeates the sentiments on which our judgments rest. Insofar as the moral sentiments are socially constituted and hence affected by existing laws and political practices, they may tend to reflect prevailing inequalities and exclusions, thus perpetuating rather than correcting prejudice. The limits of sympathy exacerbate this danger. For all its value in showing the importance of affective modes of consciousness within judgment and deliberation, then, Hume's account is incomplete on its own terms. In order to achieve its great promise of affectively engaged but impartial judgment, the Humean approach needs liberal-democratic politics. In answering to this need in later chapters, I move beyond Hume to articulate a new approach to individual judgment and public deliberation that is grounded in reflective sentiment and constrained by the duty of equal respect.

Chapter 4 ("Affective Judgment in Democratic Politics") explores the moral sentiment model of individual judgment in the context of contemporary liberal democracy. It shows how liberal-democratic politics can support the extension of sympathy and thereby enhance the impartiality of practical judgment and deliberation. Institutional mechanisms such as equal voting rights and representative government, as well as informal practices of public contestation and debate, are key here. At the same time, I examine the ways in which moral sentiment contributes to the judgments of individual citizens on important public issues that raise questions of justice. This chapter brackets the role of moral sentiment within public deliberation as "will-formation," the formal procedures of state decision making that generate coercively enforced laws and policies. Deliberation in this form requires additional criteria beyond individual impartiality for the justification of legitimate political decisions, and is considered in chapter 5. Here we examine instead public deliberation as "opinion-formation," including the exercise of impartial individual judgment on questions of public importance. The informal processes of public deliberation as opinion-formation rightly incorporate both individual and collective judgment. In deliberating about issues such as abortion, gay rights, or welfare reform, for instance, we move back and forth between the question of what is *right* and the question of what we, as citizens of this particular polity, can reasonably be expected to agree upon. Democratic legitimacy demands agreement among citizens in reaching decisions that are coercively enforced by the state, and this requires deliberation together with others in terms of commonly held, explicitly public values. Yet public values sometimes go wrong, and the agreement required for political legitimacy can obstruct the implementation of new and better visions for the future. Individual moral judgment can be a powerful corrective to collectivism, then, which makes it a valuable component of public deliberation understood in the widest sense. Thus a good deal of public deliberation does—and should—stimulate the exercise of individual moral judgment on the part of citizens.

Chapter 5 ("Public Deliberation and the Feeling of Impartiality") takes up the formal process of public deliberation as will-formation and the role of moral sentiment within it. Because public deliberation in this form issues in decisions that are coercively enforced on all citizens through law, it must build in mechanisms to ensure that those subject to its outcomes are also in some real way its authors and masters. Important as individual impartiality is, public deliberation will need to meet additional procedural criteria if it is to generate legitimate political decisions, including equal access, accountability, publicity, and reciprocity. Formal public deliberation also differs in structural ways from the judgments of individuals because it involves collective rather than individual decision making. And unlike individual moral judgment, public deliberation must answer to the fundamental political values that govern the exercise of power in the polity in which it arises. In a constitutional liberal democracy, this means that public deliberation is subject to the legal constraints of a constitution, a tradition of constitutional interpretation, and a set of basic rights, all of which establish in law the public values of the polity. Beyond that, political deliberation typically takes place in the context of the need for determinate decisions, usually on matters of some dispute, which will affect the lives of people who may disagree deeply about them. The need for determinate decisions and the fact of pluralism thus set additional constraints on public deliberation. Finally, public deliberation is subject to constraints arising from the particular institutional settings in which it takes place. The deliberative practices of legislators, for instance, will differ in some measure from those of judges, executives, and members of the general public. The institutional structure and function of each branch of government and those of civil society set different types of constraint on deliberation in each domain, although some core features will be consistent across domains.

The core features that establish impartiality in public deliberation are best characterized as aspects of "reciprocity." Deliberation guided by reciprocity is typically understood as a process of seeking "mutually justifiable reasons, and reaching a mutually binding decision on the basis of those reasons."[21] The ideal of reciprocity as usually conceived within theories of deliberative democracy is marred by an excessive rationalism, however, which ultimately renders these models untenable. Chapter 5 argues for an alternative understanding of reciprocity—and with it, democratic deliberation—that incorporates sentiments within the ideal of impartiality and provides principled criteria for the proper inclusion of sentiment but without subjugating it to a form of reason that transcends feeling. Reciprocity rightly conceived involves (a) the communication of politically legitimate sentiments through the practice of perspective-taking; and (b) an attachment to the common, affective concerns that are constitutive of the political order. Although previous accounts of reciprocity have incorporated the practice of perspective-taking, they have not adequately articulated the affective dimensions of this practice. The alternative view developed here also reconceives the "public-reason" dimension of reciprocity, casting it as a form of reflective concern. In short, reciprocity rests on civil passions.

Civil passions thus take two forms, consistent with the two dimensions of reciprocity. On the one hand, they include the many different sentiments of persons that are represented via perspective-taking within the generalized standpoint of impartial deliberation. When this standpoint is properly construed (as specified in chapter 5), it is affectively engaged yet "civil"—in the eighteenth-century sense of civilized, or free of prejudice and error, inclusive of the widest range of human experience, and marked by a refined sensitivity to human concerns. Yet civil passions so conceived are not to be identified with any fixed list of particular sentiments. It would be a mistake to think that civil passions are all pleasant, for instance. A refined faculty of moral sentiment will incorporate feelings of anger and shame—when they are justified—as well as gratitude and benevolence. The second sense of civil passions includes the attachments citizens have to their shared public values. These passions are "civil" in the political sense of the word, or tied to a particular public and its constitutive values. The list of civil passions in this sense will be more restricted because it refers to the specific values that shape the polity. Yet these passions are not necessarily tame. They may sometimes be unruly, generating justified civil resistance or pressure for political reform. If civil passions are not anemic, neither are they uncritical of the public values that orient them. Blind attachment to prevailing norms is no part of civil passion. We shall have more to say about all this in the course of the coming chapters. For now it is enough to note that the "civil-passions" account of reciprocity makes it possible to distinguish between sentiments that rightly have a place in the deliberative context and those that should be excluded. It provides further evidence that affect and impartiality need not be mutually exclusive.

Impartial public deliberation also trades on the authority of law. It depends on this authority to constrain the outcomes of deliberation in ways that are consistent with what reciprocity requires. Deliberation depends on law's authority for its implementation as well. At least at the level of will-formation, public deliberation imposes binding obligations on citizens, which can only be effective in practice if the law enjoys an authoritative status in society. The affective character of public deliberation raises a new set of questions here, however, because the leading accounts of law's authority today look for justification of this authority to an ideal of reason that transcends sentiment. How should we understand the obligatoriness of deliberation's results, as law, if these results arise instead through the exercise of reflective sentiment? What is the nature and basis of law's authority? Chapter 6 ("The Affective Authority of Law") investigates these questions. The authority of the law, in contrast to its strength, is a normative condition. Laws impose obligations on us; they tell us what we ought to do and not only what we must do. For the law to be authoritative in this way, it must elicit both the respect and the allegiance of its subjects. How it does so has been the subject of longstanding debate among legal theorists. This debate reflects the standard lack of interest in (or disparagement of) sentiment within jurisprudence in the history of the modern West, which has always associated law with a form of reason that transcends the passions. Indeed, the whole purpose of law, it is often thought, is to regulate unruly affect through the application of cool-headed cognition. As a result, the affective dimensions of law's authority are not well understood.

No one denies that the law must engage the affective concerns of its subjects if it is to motivate adherence. What most theorists overlook is the place of passions in establishing the normative force of law's authority. In the course of chapter 6 we shall see that the two dimensions of this authority—the law's right to obligate and its power to motivate—are both grounded in the reflective concerns of its subjects. To show how such concerns generate normativity and why we cannot conceive of obligations (whether moral, political, or legal) without affect, we return to the theory of moral sentiment. The moral sentiment approach suggests that for the law to have normative authority (that is, to justifiably generate obligations) it must be endorsable from within a generalized standpoint that rests upon the sympathetic communication of sentiments among those subject to it. When it is endorsable in this way, the law also has motivational authority (that is, the ability to animate allegiance). In this sense, the moral sentiments that enable us to justify law's authority also help generate allegiance to it, although the motivational authority of law depends upon other feelings as well, including mutual concern among citizens. I reiterate here the importance of a democratic political culture, which helps extend the moral sentiments of citizens so as to incorporate the concerns of all those subject to the law. The affective sources of law's authority are crucial to understanding not only the efficacy of legal norms within political society but the nature of legal obligation itself. Because public deliberation depends on this form of obligation, both to constrain it and to make its results binding, the affective aspects of this obligation are important forms of civil passion.

It is perhaps worth pausing at this juncture to acknowledge once again that there are very real dangers associated with the presence of passion in politics. These dangers are well known and have been exhaustively articulated by many theorists in the history of political thought in the West. It is precisely because the dangers are real and well known that the rationalist approach to judgment and deliberation has gained so much traction over the years. *Civil Passions* in no way minimizes the threat these dangers pose to social order and to impartial justice. The point of the book is not to bring more passions into political deliberation. Instead, the book begins by showing, partly by drawing on the neuroscience literature and partly by illuminating the affective moments in ostensibly rationalist theories of justification and deliberation, that practical deliberation inevitably incorporates affect. We cannot reach decisions about what to do in the absence of affective attachments and desires. Given that we cannot fully transcend the influence of sentiment, the challenge is to understand how the inevitable, affective dimensions of practical deliberation can be reconciled with the demands of impartiality. The bulk of the book answers that question. In this respect, the fact that passions can be disruptive in politics, while true, does not undercut the heart of the argument being offered here. Cruelty, bigotry, and destructive rage are very dangerous indeed. To counter them, however, we cannot turn to a form of reason that simply transcends affective modes of consciousness—because no such faculty is available to us, at least when it comes to practical deliberation and decision making. Instead of transcending affect, we need to civilize it. We need to identify principled criteria and public practices that can make affect serve impartiality to the greatest extent possible.

Moreover, while *Civil Passions* addresses current debates about democratic deliberation, its purpose is not to advocate for deliberation, or to argue that we need more deliberation than we currently have. In this sense, it differs from most contributions to the deliberative-democracy literature within political theory. I do accept the view, defended by deliberative democrats, that deliberation has an important place in any liberal democracy. In particular, public questions that raise issues of justice demand reflective and morally sound resolutions. Many political questions do not have this character and can be fairly settled through a simple competition of interests, provided that the competition meets certain procedural standards. Whether or not to allow gambling casinos to operate in the state, to increase public funding for the local zoo, or to impose term limits on elected officials are questions for which interest-group politics can typically provide adequate answers, provided it is fairly structured. By contrast, gay rights, abortion, affirmative action, and welfare reform are issues that involve basic justice. In all these cases, the central question turns on claims about what is due to persons and to citizens as a matter of equal respect or reciprocity. The wrong decision would amount to more than merely a political mistake; it would involve a moral violation with potentially grave damage to persons on the losing side, damage that could not be justified on moral grounds. Politics and morality clearly intersect quite a lot even in societies ordered by secular liberal governments. The implication of this fact is that citizens regularly have a moral obligation to deliberate reflectively and impartially about what should be done in their names. Matters of basic justice ought not be abandoned to the play of power or the unreflective aggregation of interests. Consequently, liberal democracy should make a place for deliberation, even if deliberation is not required in every instance of political decision making.

It is also important to see that deliberation is possible. Empirical studies, it is often said, show that elected officials almost never change their positions in response to principled arguments made by others—deliberation is an illusory ideal. Instead, log-rolling, bargaining, partisan loyalties, and the desire to maintain or increase personal power are the real determinants of these positions. It may be true that legislators do not often change their minds based on what other legislators say on the floor of Congress. But there is far more to public deliberation than what happens on the floor of Congress. Prevailing public opinions are influenced by deliberative interactions among citizens at large, which include a wide range of mechanisms for the communication of sentiments, such as print and other news media, participation in civil associations, political activism, and even the entertainment industry. *Civil Passions* takes an inclusive attitude toward the kinds of activities and institutions that promulgate deliberation in informal ways. To the extent that elected officials are responsive to changes in public opinion, their decisions are influenced, however indirectly, by public deliberation in this larger sense. Deliberation happens—not always impartially and not always in ways that translate directly into state decisions—but it happens. It happens among average citizens as well as elected officials, judges, bureaucrats, and political appointees. How else can we explain the many changes in American society over time that responded to moral claims pressed by individuals and groups who made their claims the subject of extensive, often impassioned, public debate? This book is concerned especially with the deliberation of average citizens as they reflect on the justice of proposed and existing laws, public policies, and institutions. The account developed here nevertheless has implications for theories of legislative deliberation, and for executive judgment and judicial decision making, although deliberation in each of these settings is constrained institutionally in ways that the deliberations of average citizens are not. I do not pursue these implications in any depth in this project, but they are addressed briefly in chapter 5, along with some of the additional institutional constraints that govern deliberation in the context of the three branches of the U.S. government.

Although deliberative democrats are right to hold that deliberation is important and possible, we should also be committed to the constraints on deliberative outcomes that are imposed by constitutional principles and fundamental individual rights.[22] Constitutional principles and individual rights must be subject to the scrutiny of moral judgment, of course. They are justified (when they are justified) in the same way that norms generally should be—namely, by appeal to impartial moral sentiment. A full justification of liberal constraints is beyond the scope of this study, although I believe they are in principle endorsable from within the impartial evaluative standpoint that moral sentiment makes possible. Above all, they demonstrate respect for persons, a principle that moral sentiment gives us grounds to affirm. The connection between moral sentiment and respect for persons is addressed at the end of chapter 3. It is true that specific principles and rights may properly be problematized in particular cases and made the subject of public deliberation. What exactly the constitutional right to equal treatment under law means to us, for example, and how we should understand this right in relation to affirmative action or gay marriage is certainly open to dispute. Yet as a general matter, and in the regular course of affairs, our constitutional principles and fundamental rights set valuable constraints on what democratic majorities may legitimately decide through deliberation. Deliberation in itself, even when it is impartial, is not enough to ensure public outcomes that are just. Constitutional principles and individual rights, like moral sentiment, give us access to additional standards, some internal and others external to the political order, and these standards ought to have a role in guiding our collective deliberation on matters of justice.

Deliberation is demanding, and for many people this fact may recommend against it. The truth is that citizenship imposes certain burdens on us. Liberal democracy makes these burdens light when compared with some other forms of government but it cannot do away with them entirely. The notion that liberty and equality—the great promises of liberal-democratic government—could be had for free is a dream. The realization of liberty and equality demands many things of us as citizens, but one of them surely is impartial deliberation. Unless public deliberation achieves impartiality, our decision making will be hostage to prejudice and the vagaries of power, with the result that those who have less (less status, less power, fewer resources) will get less (less freedom, less equality). Impartial deliberation is a key to making the promises of liberal democracy real for all of us. Yet liberal democracy also is necessary to the development of impartiality, or so I shall argue in the chapters to come.

There is a circle here, or at least a relationship of mutual dependence. If human beings were not fallible by nature, if we were not naturally limited in the extent of our sympathies and concerns, we would not need liberal-democratic institutions and practices to foster the extensive moral sentiment that impartial judgment requires. If the liberal-democratic principles of liberty and equality were self-justifying and self-actuating, and if the institutions of liberal democracy were self-guiding, we would not need impartial deliberation. As it is, we need both and they depend on each other.

While the demands of impartial deliberation are high, they are demands that we can satisfy, at least so long as we acknowledge the affective dimensions of deliberation. Again, to acknowledge these dimensions is not to bring more passions into politics. There are plenty of passions in politics already. Moral sentiment does involve the public communication of sentiments and a refined faculty of sympathy, and justice will require that some previously silenced sentiments find a new voice on the public stage. But the communication of sentiments is already happening all around us; deliberation is steeped in passions as it is. The challenge is to civilize the passions that we cannot avoid and that practical reason cannot fully transcend. Achieving impartiality requires effort and widespread practices of cultivation and self-cultivation, which foster an increasingly inclusive and more sensitive faculty of moral sentiment. But affective impartiality is achievable. Our mistake has been to regard impartiality as flowing from an ideal of reason that no one has ever known and that human beings are constitutionally incapable of realizing. The primary objective of *Civil Passions* is to correct this mistake, to advance our basic understanding of ourselves and the deliberative faculties of democratic citizenship. Passion and practical reason are not separate but deeply entwined. Impartial deliberation conceived in the old way is therefore a chimera. But the theory of moral sentiment gives us a new way to understand impartiality. This view is truer to who we really are even as it answers our aspiration for justice. The deep connection between norms and motives within moral sentiment links aspects of the self that rationalist approaches tend to divide. Moral sentiment makes the self-as-public-deliberator one with the self-as-political-agent and thus better empowers us to bring the conclusions of our deliberation to fruition in practice. It shows us that impartial deliberation feels as well as reasons, and that the path to justice is lighted by the glow of civil passions.

CHAPTER ONE

Justice and Passion in Rawls and Habermas

THIS CHAPTER EXAMINES the role of sentiments in the theories of justice and norm justification defended by Rawls and Habermas. My purpose is partly to bring out the relationship between the right and the good in a way that attends more carefully than previous work has done to the complexity of each theory in this respect.[1] Doing so helps to clarify the place of affect within the procedures of practical reasoning that constitute deliberation about justice because conceptions of the good naturally engage affective modes of consciousness. To value something as good is to hold it as an object of concern. The good differs from the right in this respect, as the latter makes no necessary claim on our affections. Rawls and Habermas both intend for the right to take priority over the good in our judgments about justice, but affective attachments to the good do have a place in both theories. In fact, affect enters into the right itself, through (for instance) the empathy involved in reasoning within the original position and the moral standpoint. In this respect, Rawls and Habermas turn out to be somewhat more nuanced as representatives of the rationalist paradigm of judgment than their critics often acknowledge. Yet the critics are not wrong to characterize them as rationalists. For even in accommodating affect they tend to subordinate it to forms of reason that aspire to be immune to the actual sentiments of real persons. The aspiration to transcend the influence of sentiment makes trouble for both theories, however, generating inconsistencies and deficits that remain unresolved.

The first section explores these issues in connection with Rawls, examining his concept of rationality, the sense of justice as a moral sentiment, and the notion of "congruence." The second section takes up Habermas's search for a "purer" proceduralism. Here I elaborate the tenuous divide between morality and ethical life, the place of affect in norm justification, and the difficulties raised by Habermas's effort to recontextualize the "abstractive" standpoint of justice. The accommodations and the deficits found in Rawls and Habermas point not only to the irrepressible place that conceptions of the good occupy within practical reasoning but also to the irreducible role of sentiment within moral judgment and public deliberation. Thus a careful analysis of the rationalist view suggests that even a nuanced rationalism has limits, for deliberation about justice cannot do without affect.

THE GOODNESS OF THE RIGHT: RAWLS

Rationality and the Good

Rawls characterizes his theory of justice as "deontological," by which he means that it "does not interpret the right as maximizing the good."[2] It differs from utilitarian theories in this respect. Justice-as-fairness does not set out to maximize the satisfaction of rational interests among the members of society; indeed, "there is no reason to think that just institutions will maximize the good" in this respect.[3] To be sure, justice-as-fairness does serve certain goods, and some of these goods are defined independently of (that is, prior to) what is right.[4] What it does not do is to pool all possible human goods together indiscriminately and then seek the greatest net balance of them all. Unlike classical utilitarian schemes, Rawls's theory gives certain goods (such as the "primary goods" and the good of autonomy) a privileged status.[5] In justice-as-fairness, the structure of the original position assures everybody a certain measure of these goods even if, in doing so, it fails to maximize the overall satisfaction of all persons relative to every conceivable human good. The justification for privileging these goods over others in this way does not derive from the ideal of justice that Rawls defends. Instead, it is grounded in a conception of the person characterized by "the two moral powers" (the sense of justice and the capacity to rationally pursue a life plan) and a higher-order interest in autonomy. Rawls presents this conception of the person in *Theory* as one of the "considered convictions" that form the fixed points of moral value in any liberal-democratic society.[6] This feature of the model reflects the fact that practical reasoning about justice always takes place within a horizon of concern that constrains its possible conclusions. Thus the fact that justice-as-fairness is a deontological view means not that it is free of appeal to any conceptions of the good but that it does not define justice in terms of a particular type of orientation to the good—namely, one that seeks to maximize the net balance of undifferentiated human satisfactions.

References to the good are not limited to the moral background that undergirds justice-as-fairness but also figure in the concept of practical reasoning at its heart. The rationality of the parties to the original position consists in instrumental reason aimed at satisfying particular ends.[7] Rationality so conceived always makes reference to some conception(s) of the good, whether construed narrowly as individual interests or more broadly as the personal convictions or values that orient one's plan of life.[8] In the original position it is the "primary goods" that stimulate practical reason, and they provide the concrete content needed to arrive at determinate decisions. If the parties did not desire these goods, the procedure could not yield the two principles of justice with the necessity of a "moral geometry," as Rawls demands.[9] It is true that his concept of practical reason combines rationality, which aims at the good, with what he later came to call "reasonableness," which is oriented to the right. The latter is modeled in the original position by the veil of ignorance, which in effect forces the parties to recognize the independent validity of the claims of others.[10] Whereas the structure of rationality incorporates affective concern, or desire, the contributions of reasonableness establish the impartiality of practical reason in matters of justice. Yet the central role of rationality within the decision procedure indicates that when we reason about justice we cannot do so without desiring the good. As Rawls puts it, "merely reasonable agents would have no ends of their own they wanted to advance by fair cooperation," and consequently no conclusions could be reached about justice.[11] The procedure suggests a way to think beyond the limits of one's private interests and personal convictions, but it does not simply replace the good with the right or require us to reason without reference to any ends.

This fact bears on the substance of justice, for it means that principles having no connection to our concerns are not ones that we could authorize as binding, since they could never be rational for us. Of course, the normative force of the two principles of justice does not come from the mere fact that they answer to the demands of rationality. That they serve human concerns, however defined, could not by itself justify the principles or make them obligatory, on Rawls's view. Arrangements that served human concerns without being authorized by those subject to them would lack legitimacy, however much good they might generate, and so they could never satisfy the standard of justice as fairness. Yet rational agents, who by definition seek to realize what is good for themselves, could not be expected to choose (under fair conditions) principles of justice that would be so much at odds with common human desires as to require self-abnegation for their fulfillment.[12] In this sense, the right and the good are co-original in justice-as-fairness. It could not be otherwise, given the nature of practical reason on Rawls's account, which holds sovereign authority in the procedures of norm justification.

The rationality of the parties in the original position thus models the fact that practical reasoning about justice, although ideally impartial, is affectively engaged rather than disinterested. As Rawls presents it, conceptions of the good necessarily stimulate affective modes of consciousness, notably desire. In fact, he defines the "good" as the satisfaction of rational desire.[13] To have a conception of the good therefore is to have an affective attachment to it or a desire to realize it; hence when we are rational we are also desiring.[14] This is a basic feature of human psychology, as Rawls conceives it, one that underlies both decisions and actions, and it figures prominently in the original position. Desire stimulates, even guides, practical reason, for it is the parties' desire for the primary goods (filtered through the veil of ignorance) that determines the outcome of the deliberation. The impersonal content of the primary goods together with the veil of ignorance neutralizes the potentially distorting effects that desire can have on our decisions. And yet the model preserves the form and function of desire within practical reason. It suggests that the impartial standpoint that shows us what justice requires rests not on the simple transcendence of sentiment but in properly orienting sentiment (via the standard of the reasonable) within practical reason. The original position is an abstraction but it is not devoid of affective concerns; these concerns figure centrally in the justification process.

The Sense of Justice as a Moral Sentiment

Despite the many Kantian features of his approach, Rawls once characterized *A Theory of Justice* as "a theory of the moral sentiments" on the grounds that it sets out "the principles governing our moral powers, or, more specifically, our sense of justice."[15] As we have seen, the sense of justice is one of the two capacities that constitute moral personhood and establish the basis of moral equality.[16] Together with the capacity to rationally pursue a plan of life, the sense of justice forms the background against which the abstractions associated with the original position take place. Rawls presupposes that the parties to the original position, like all liberal citizens and all moral persons in general, possess these powers. The sense of justice includes the willingness to abide by the two principles of justice that Rawls identifies, and to comply, as he will later say, with the requirements of public reason in one's life as a citizen. More fundamentally, however, the sense of justice refers to the general disposition to take up the moral standpoint represented by the original position when questions of justice arise. In fact, Rawls characterizes the sense of justice as a "conception-dependent *desire*."[17] Beyond motivating us to comply with established rules of right, then, the sense of justice moves us to seek out what these rules are, and to do so according to a particular procedure. At its heart is the desire to live with others on fair terms, which is something that Rawls thinks "exercises a natural attraction upon our affections."[18] In later work, he characterizes the sense of justice as a willingness or desire "to act in relation to others on terms that they also can publicly endorse."[19] This general disposition to fairness (as opposed to the desire to comply with a particular, established set of principles) comprises one part of what Rawls came to call "the reasonable."[20] When we assume the standpoint of the original position and imagine ourselves behind the veil of ignorance, we are exercising the sense of justice. As a conception-dependent desire, the sense of justice clearly has affective valence.[21] Without this general disposition, the decision procedure in the original position could not get off the ground.[22] Thus the affective attachment to the idea of being a just person precedes the reasoned deliberation about what justice requires, and the rationalist dimensions of Rawls's theory are unsustainable if they are removed from this context of affective concern. Taken as a whole, the account suggests that practical reason when applied to matters of justice must be embedded within an appropriate horizon of affective concern, much as it is embedded within a particular conceptual horizon of moral beliefs.

In addition to the sense of justice, other sentiments also play a role. Rawls notes, for instance, that the parties to the original position must be assumed to care about the well-being of the next generation.[23] This concern shapes the outcome of the deliberation; without it, the parties could not be relied upon to arrive at the two principles of justice that Rawls specifies. A general capacity for empathy likewise figures importantly. Empathy (together with imagination) is what makes possible the perspective-taking required of the parties.[24] They need empathy to hypothetically inhabit the standpoints of all the people they could turn out to be, to feel the rational desires of persons differently placed, and so to reason their way to the most advantageous arrangements for social cooperation. Deliberating about justice is an affective as well as a cognitive activity. It should come as no surprise, then, that late in *Theory* Rawls refers to the original position that models practical reason as "a certain form of thought *and feeling* that rational persons can adopt within the world."[25] It appears that sentiments such as empathy and the sense of justice are more than merely external supports for justice.[26] They seem to be connected in a fundamental way to the procedures of norm justification. Like our rational desire for the good, certain sentiments are integral to deliberation itself.

Congruence(s)

This interpretation draws support from Rawls's remarks about the congruence between the right and the good. He always insisted that the sense of justice must answer to our good and be "continuous with our natural sentiments."[27] Yet it cannot be merely one desire among others, for it must be "regulative" of one's "life plan" as a whole.[28] To establish stability, the sense of justice must answer to a special good, a good that we have reason to prefer to all others. For where personal convictions and private interests conflict with what justice requires, it is a crucial condition of social cooperation that justice generally prevail. To say that we have a reason to prefer this good to all others is not to say that we will always act on this reason; it is not to guarantee that the sense of justice will be effective in every case.[29] What Rawls means to show is that the high demands placed on us by the finality of justice are not irrational. He thinks it important to say why our principles of right "have the central role and significance in our life that they do. This account should lay out how these principles connect with human beings' needs, aims, and purposes."[30] For this reason, he argued in *Theory* that justice is congruent with the human good.[31]

The finality requirement in justice-as-fairness is met psychologically by the higher-order desire for autonomy, which makes it rational for us to be just even when doing so conflicts with many of our most pressing interests and most deeply felt convictions.[32] Only by "acting on the principles of right as having first priority" can we express "our freedom from contingency and happenstance."[33] Consequently, "in order to realize our nature" as autonomous beings, "we have no alternative but to plan to preserve our sense of justice as governing our other aims."[34] Since persons express "their nature as free and equal rational beings" by acting on the principles of justice, and doing so "belongs to their good," one can say that "the sense of justice aims at their well-being."[35] It bears repeating that the principles of justice are not justified solely by the fact that they serve human well-being. They are justified because they can be seen to have been willed by those subject to them. But the principles could not be so willed if they were thought to thwart human well-being. For this reason, Rawls attacks the idea, which he attributes to W. D. Ross, that "the highest moral motive is the desire to do what is right and just simply because it is right and just, no other description being appropriate." The problem with this idea, Rawls says, is that on such an interpretation "the sense of right lacks any apparent reason; it resembles a preference for tea rather than coffee. Although such a preference might exist, to make it regulative of the basic structure of society is utterly capricious."[36] The fact that the two principles of justice serve rather than thwart human well-being thus figures in their justification, albeit indirectly. Only in view of this fact is the desire to act justly something more than "a form of blind obedience to arbitrary principles unrelated to rational aims."[37] For it to be *right* the sense of justice must fairly serve the human good, at least in terms of the general interests in the primary goods and the good of autonomy.

In recent years, Rawls came to doubt the viability of the conception of the person on which the congruence argument originally rested. He began to see it as too controversial to stabilize justice in a pluralist society. In fact, the modifications to his theory evident in *Political Liberalism* reflect this worry.[38] They arose "from trying to resolve a serious problem internal to justice as fairness, namely from the fact that the account of stability in part 3 of *Theory* is not consistent with the view as a whole."[39] The pluralism of a modern democratic society makes it "unrealistic" to expect that all citizens will endorse the idea of a well-ordered society as it appears in *Theory*, because this idea is grounded in a comprehensive philosophical doctrine.[40] Central to that doctrine was Rawls's quasi-Kantian conception of the person, according to which autonomy is the overriding good and is realized through action in accordance with the two principles of justice. Because the congruence argument as originally formulated rests on a comprehensive doctrine, it cannot be relied upon to generate stability among all citizens under conditions of reasonable pluralism.[41]

Political Liberalism therefore offers a different argument for congruence based on the idea of an overlapping consensus. Although the "freestanding" status of the political conception of justice means that "it is neither presented as, nor is derived from," any of the comprehensive doctrines affirmed by citizens that form the background culture of civil society, Rawls nevertheless holds that this conception also should "have a justification by reference to one or more comprehensive doctrines."[42] The reason is that citizens will only actually affirm it "from within their own reasonable doctrines,"[43] which means that for them it must be justified with reference to their deepest personal convictions, the things they care about most. This congruence is the key to stability, as Rawls sees it. He insists that

> all those who affirm the political conception start from within their own comprehensive view and draw on the religious, philosophical, and moral grounds it provides. The fact that people affirm the same political conception on those grounds does not make their affirming it any less religious, philosophical, or moral, as the case may be, since the grounds sincerely held determine the nature of their affirmation.[44]

The overlapping consensus establishes congruence between the right contained in the political conception of justice and the notions of the good found in citizens' comprehensive doctrines. It thus connects the justification of norms to the concerns of citizens.

In this sense, the idea of an overlapping consensus is an effort to retain the rationality (read: desirability) of justice in the presence of reasonable pluralism. Like the congruence argument in *Theory*, this modified version also suggests the interpenetration of rationality and reasonableness, of stability and validity, of affect and cognition. By connecting the political conception of justice to notions of the good contained in citizens' comprehensive doctrines, the overlapping consensus explains why it is rational for them to affirm justice and to act on it. Only the fact that they *do* affirm it can establish its validity and make the obligations it generates normatively binding. But it is because justice is rational for them that they *can* affirm it. Habermas has challenged Rawls on this point, saying that this approach misconstrues the basis of validity by embedding the right within the good.[45] In reply, Rawls holds tenaciously to the position that "there is no public justification for political society without a reasonable overlapping consensus."[46] We must be able to "make the case that there are adequate reasons for diverse reasonable people jointly to affirm justice as fairness as their working political conception," and this is necessary to "establish the conditions for their legitimately exercising coercive political power over one another."[47] The implication is that the overlapping consensus contributes to the justification of the political conception of justice in addition to stabilizing it.[48] Rawls's insistence on this point is further evidence of the way in which affective concerns enter into the justification of norms. Norms of justice must be rational for us, hence desirable as well as obligatory, and desirable in ways that are connected to the concerns that orient our self-understandings and guide our plans of life. In this sense, then, affect interacts with intellect in the deliberative, or justificatory, process. This is one way of understanding what Rawls meant when he said that his theory of justice was at heart a theory of moral sentiment. Despite the many echoes of Kant that one finds in Rawls, there is an unmistakably Humean dimension to his account of the impartial deliberation that grounds justice as fairness.

Yet the Humean side of justice as fairness is not one that Rawls was keen to display. Indeed, he seems to have been deeply ambivalent about it. The discussion of congruence in *A Theory of Justice* comes only in Part 3, after all, and has seemed to many readers to be something of an afterthought, a concession to the demands of stability that is fully independent of the normative dimensions of the theory. Rawls worried, among other things, that the connection between desire and the justification of norms implicit in *A Theory of Justice* and *Political Liberalism* could be seen to bring the theory too close to some form of utilitarianism. Thus in *Justice as Fairness: A Restatement*, Rawls means to "correct" his earlier claim that justice as fairness is "part of the theory of rational choice." That was a "mistake," he says, which would imply "that justice as fairness is at bottom Hobbesian (as Hobbes is often interpreted) rather than Kantian."[49] Rationality is not "the sole normative concept" underlying the principles of justice but is always accompanied—even fully dominated, he now maintains—by the standard of reasonableness.[50] To be sure, Rawls had always insisted on the priority of the right over the good. Thus although the overlapping consensus does accord some justificatory weight to the conceptions of the good contained in reasonable comprehensive doctrines (that is, the congruence between these conceptions of the good and the principles of justice helps to justify these principles in the eyes of citizens), ultimately the justification of the principles can stand independently of this support. The principles of justice are to be honored "for their own sake,"[51] not merely because they are desirable in light of one's comprehensive doctrine, and in cases of conflict these principles override all other values that may be contained in one's comprehensive doctrine.[52] It begins to look as if the role of desire may be limited to the domain of stability after all.

Furthermore, in the principle- and conception-dependent desires with which Rawls associates the sense of justice, it is the principles and conceptions that do the normative work rather than the desires themselves. These desires are necessary components of the moral psychology of just citizens, but as Rawls puts it, "the force, or weight, of principle-dependent desires is given entirely by the principle to which the desire is attached, and not by the psychological strength of the desire itself. This strength . . . may enter into explanations of how people in fact behave but it can never enter into how they should behave, or should have behaved, morally speaking."[53] In these passages, Rawls seems to step back from the suggestion, implicit elsewhere in his work, that sentiments have a normative (not merely stabilizing) role to play in deliberation about justice. Nowhere is this retreat more evident than when he explicitly links his standard of reasonableness to Kant's notion of pure practical reason. The distinction between the rational and the reasonable

> parallels Kant's distinction between the hypothetical imperative and the categorical imperative. Kant's categorical imperative subjects an agent's rational and sincere maxim (drawn up in the light of the agent's empirical practical reason) to the reasonable constraints contained in that procedure, and thus constrains the agent's conduct by the requirements of pure practical reason. Similarly, the reasonable conditions imposed on the parties in the original position constrain them in reaching a rational agreement on principles of justice as they try to advance the good of those they represent. In each case the reasonable has priority over the rational *and subordinates it absolutely.*[54]

The absolute subordination of the rational to the reasonable—the subjection of reason infused with sentiment to reason that is somehow "pure," or purified of sentiment, like pure practical reason in Kant—confirms the *anti*-Humean aspirations of Rawls's theory. He wants the justification of norms to be fully independent of merely "psychological" considerations, such as the passions and desires of actual persons. And, like Kant, he thinks that reason can accomplish this. From this perspective, the contributions of affect within norm justification appear to be much reduced. Ultimately, it now seems, Rawls's attention to attachments and desires is largely a practical accommodation to feasibility, dreamed up after the real (cognitive) work of justification has been accomplished.

Yet the assertion that the reasonable subordinates the rational "absolutely" is at odds with the view, repeatedly pressed elsewhere, that "the right and the good are complementary."[55] Just institutions, Rawls says, "would serve no purpose—would have no point"—unless they sustained the conceptions of the good affirmed by citizens. In other words, "the just draws the limit, the good shows the point."[56] As Rawls argued in connection with Ross, principles or standards that have no point in this sense never could be normative for us; lacking a purpose that citizens can affirm (that is, desire), such standards would be arbitrary or capricious and lacking in any obligatory force. Thus the normative weight of the principles of justice is at least partly given by the point they serve, or their rationality. And this fact is at odds with the strict subordination of the rational to the reasonable in establishing normativity. In a similar way, the fact that the parties to the original position must weigh "the strains of commitment" in arriving at the principles of justice suggests that rationality is balanced with reasonableness, not subordinate to it, in the deliberation that justifies norms. The parties "must ask themselves whether those they represent can reasonably be expected to honor the principles agreed to in the manner required by the idea of an agreement."[57] And the class of things that we can reasonably agree to is drawn from the class of things that we can rationally choose, meaning the things we commonly desire.[58] No agreement will even count as reasonable, then, unless it is already rational. This hardly sounds like absolute subordination. True, Rawls treats the strains of commitment requirement as a matter of mere stability,[59] but it seems to have important implications for the nature of norm justification itself.

Moreover, the suggestion that the reasonable is in some sense like pure practical reason in Kant is confusing in light of the "psychology of the reasonable" that Rawls gives us.[60] This psychology is offered as an explanation for why we can expect citizens in a well-ordered society to have a disposition for reasonableness, or the willingness "to do their part in [just social] arrangements provided they have sufficient assurance that others will also do theirs."[61] Among the factors that explain this willingness are the circumstances of justice—namely, moderate scarcity and the fact that fair social cooperation generates "numerous possibilities of gains."[62] In addition, citizens are assumed to recognize the fact of reasonable pluralism together with the fact that it can be overcome only by "the oppressive use of state power."[63] The disposition to reasonableness, then, rests on the desire for gain in the face of scarcity and for security against state coercion. In short, the psychology of the reasonable is a form of rationality (in Rawls's sense of the word), and hence very far from Kant's pure practical reason.

What all this suggests is that there is a deep tension at the heart of Rawls's project between his rationalist aspirations and his sentimentalist assumptions.[64] It is a conflict between the Kantian and the Humean dimensions of his thought. He clearly wanted the former to be predominant. Hence in the end the role of affect is largely limited to stabilizing justice. Because he is committed to a deontological ideal drawn from Kant, he wants to ground the principles of justice in a deliberative procedure and personal dispositions that transcend the influence of affective, or "merely psychological," concerns. Yet his account shows that this transcendence cannot be sustained. The truth is that sentiments run through Rawls's theory of justice from beginning to end, and they influence—in fact, they help determine—the practical deliberation that generates and justifies the principles of justice. As we have seen, norms of justice must be rational for us, and therefore desirable as well as obligatory, and desirable in ways that reflect the affective concerns that orient us. The reasonable itself is shot through with desire and with the sentiments conveyed by empathy. In this sense, the right and the good are interdependent at the deepest level, and both are infused with affect. Rawls may have wished otherwise, but the absolute priority of the right is a chimera and the claim of reason's transcendence a myth.[65]

In Search of a Purer Proceduralism: Habermas

Morality versus Ethical Life

Habermas has said that he admires Rawls's theory of justice, shares its intentions, and regards its essential results as correct, but he has also expressed reservations about certain features of the Rawlsian project. Most especially, he worries that Rawls has made "concessions to opposed philosophical positions that impair the cogency of his own project" by undercutting its universalism.[66] This objection goes to the relationship between the right and the good as conceived in both *A Theory of Justice* and *Political Liberalism*, and it bears on the role of sentiment within moral deliberation and norm justification. First, Rawls's rational-choice account of deliberation in the original position implies that normative principles, including the principles of justice, "can be represented solely in terms of interests or values that are satisfied by goods."[67] Consequently, Habermas complains, Rawls "adopts a concept of justice that is proper to an ethics of the good" rather than the right, and thereby assimilates "the deontological meaning of obligatory norms to the teleological meaning of preferred values."[68] Although Rawls "wishes to do justice to the deontological intuition" of the priority of the right,[69] his reliance on the rational-choice model makes it impossible for him to do so because it means that persons are always also oriented toward the good and never solely toward the right. As we have seen, there is some truth to this criticism. Rawls himself seems to have had similar concerns, as evidenced by the ambivalence in his depiction of the relationship between the right and the good and his effort in later work to distance his account of justice from rational-choice theory.

Habermas also contends that Rawls's conception of the person, with its account of the two moral powers, builds "normative contents into the very procedures of justification."[70] This conception itself stands in need of justification,[71] and the appeals Rawls makes in this regard to the moral values implicit in the public political culture and the conceptions of the good found in the overlapping consensus of reasonable comprehensive doctrines only exacerbate the problem. They, too, belong to an ethics of the good, which lacks the power to justify universal moral obligations such as the principles of justice. The value orientations associated with "ethical life" as opposed to universal "morality" always belong to particular communities and traditions. As such, the former are contestable and hence cannot provide a stable basis for the universal validity that the principles of justice must claim.[72] Thus Rawls makes a theoretical mistake in confusing the right with the good, and also a practical mistake in relying for stability on ethical values that, given the fact of pluralism, cannot provide dependable support for universal norms. To satisfy the universalist aspirations of justice, Rawls's theory would have to keep "the procedural conception of practical reason free of substantive connotations by developing it in a strictly procedural manner."[73] Habermas's own account of norm justification aims to do exactly this.[74]

Like Rawls, Habermas seeks to ground the validity of norms, including the principles of justice, in the practical reason of willing agents.[75]

His model of norm justification is intended to be more explicitly deliberative than that of Rawls, however. It holds that "just those action norms are valid to which all possibly affected persons could agree as participants in rational discourse."[76] Here rationality carries a different meaning from that found in Rawls, since it refers to the reasoned "attempt to reach an understanding over problematic validity claims."[77] Reason oriented toward reaching mutual understanding stands in sharp contrast to Rawlsian rationality, as it has no independent objective in view. It is not purposive in the way of rationality in Rawls, which involves reasoning about how best to realize a given set of ends. Or rather, its sole end is to achieve mutual understanding—not to satisfy, through mutual understanding, some other desire. Whereas Rawls's model of practical reason treats rationality as the constant companion of reasonableness—and desire as integral to judgment— Habermas's discourse theory "uncouples" them.[78] The exclusion of rationality in the Rawlsian sense of the word is intended to prevent intrusions of the good into the pure proceduralism that the discourse model means to embody. There is no congruence between the right and the good built into the model. Instead, Habermas insists that "to do justice to the presumptive impartiality of moral judgments and to the categorical validity claim of binding norms, we must uncouple the horizontal perspective, in which interpersonal relations are regulated, from the vertical perspective, of my or our own life-project, and treat moral questions separately."[79] Only when reason has been purified of all conceptions of the good—or emancipated "from all contingent determinations"—can it authorize the universal norms that justice entails.[80] Reason and desire must come apart.

Justice demands that the norms binding us as persons ultimately answer to a universalization test derived from the discourse principle. This test holds that "for a norm to be valid, the consequences and side effects that its general observance can be expected to have for the satisfaction of the particular interests of each person affected must be such that all affected can accept them freely."[81] The test requires participants to transcend not only the boundaries of instrumental reason but also the realm of ethical life.[82] Ethical questions always "refer to a shared ethos: what is at issue is how we understand ourselves as members of our community, how we should orient our lives, or what is best for us in the long run and all things considered."[83] It is ethical insights that "influence how we orient our lives," and they do so "through the interpretation of our self-understanding."[84] The moral point of view also presupposes a particular self-understanding, but one that "explodes" every ethical orientation.[85] It subjects all such orientations, and the concerns they include, to the assessment of a disengaged form of reason that takes nothing as given but is prepared to submit every claim and conviction to the universalization test.

One effect of "uncoupling" morality from questions of the good life and the affective attachments that go with them is what Habermas himself refers to as "a motivational deficit."[86] It is true that he sometimes speaks as if the moral standpoint is an accomplished fact, the necessary historical outcome of the discrediting of traditional beliefs and values that modern science and social pluralism have wrought.[87] At other times, he treats the moral standpoint as entailed by the use of language itself.[88] Yet he also maintains that it represents a radical break with the purposive and ethically infused moral psychology normally operative among human beings, and he refers to the claims of reason that draw us to the moral standpoint as being only "weakly motivating."[89] Indeed, he has said that this motivational deficit is what made it necessary for him to theorize the legitimate role of legal compulsion in democratic societies in *Between Facts and Norms*.[90] The weakly motivating character of morality follows from the fact that moral reasoning as Habermas conceives it abstracts from the affective attachments and desires that normally animate action.

Affect and Justification

Nevertheless, sentiments do inevitably enter into the moral standpoint. After all, the "generalized reciprocal perspective-taking" involved in the universalization test requires solidarity and empathy on the part of all participants, much as in Rawls's model of the original position.[91] In fact, "without empathetic sensitivity by each person to everyone else, no solution deserving universal consent will result from the deliberation" at all.[92] Thus a "mature capacity for moral judgment" rests on the "integration of cognitive operations and emotional dispositions and attitudes."[93] This integration is central to the practice of norm justification. Justification makes the subjective feelings and attitudes of participants toward the norms under deliberation relevant to the validity of these norms as well. As Habermas defines it, validity rests on "the performative attitude of participants" in discourse, which means that it requires a feeling of affirmation by all involved. For this reason, he holds that "the moral-practical justification of a mode of action aims at an aspect *different* from the feeling-neutral assessment of means-ends relations."[94] Means-end reasoning can be conducted in a "feeling-neutral" way because it is possible to ascertain whether a given means has satisfied its objective without reference to the feelings of those affected by it. From this perspective, for example, one might say that an educational policy is justified if it helps all students learn more and perform better. Whether or not it succeeds in this regard is a judgment that can be made on the basis of test scores, for instance. This judgment need not refer to the feeling or subjective affirmations of the students themselves. By contrast, the justification of norms as Habermas envisions it does make the feeling of affirmation on the part of participants morally relevant. It would be impossible to conduct norm justification in a "feeling-neutral" way because the feeling of affirmation on the part of participants (in a suitably structured discourse) is the essence of justification.

The importance of this feeling is one reason why Habermas insists that the justification process must be an actual dialogue, in contrast to Rawls's formulation of the original position as a hypothetical thought experiment.[95] Validity is always validity *for us*—not in the sense that the normative force of principles can only ever be local, but in the sense that the validity of a norm expresses the performative attitude of assent rather than resting on the norm's objective congruence with an independent standard.[96] Even if it could be proven that a particular claim were morally true or that it would bring about a desirable end-state, for Habermas (as for Rawls) these factors could not themselves justify it as normatively binding. At the "post-traditional" level of justification, "the only law that counts as legitimate is one that could be rationally accepted by all citizens in a discursive process of opinion- and will-formation."[97] Justice only exists in the presence of the feeling of validity because only here can it be said that persons are aware of themselves as subject solely to laws they have given themselves. From this perspective justice rests on a feeling, an affective affirmation of the norms that bind us.

The process of norm justification also includes references to the good, despite Habermas's effort to establish a model of pure proceduralism that would avoid such references. Although the moral standpoint "unleashes the higher-level intersubjectivity of the deliberating collectivity" and thereby aims for "a structure purified of all substantive elements," it achieves intersubjectivity only through a reversibility of participant perspectives that "integrates the perspectives of each participant's worldview and self-understanding."[98] Such perspectives derive from persons' ethical orientations or conceptions of the good, as Habermas has said elsewhere.[99] The importance of integrating them rather than simply abstracting from them, as Habermas believes Kant's moral theory required, is another reason for his emphasis on the dialogical form of justification over monological models. And the moral standpoint of justice incorporates not only ethical perspectives but also participants' interests. After all, the principle of universalizibility holds that a norm is valid if all affected can accept the consequences it can be anticipated to have "for the satisfaction of everyone's interests."[100] The universalization test ensures that norms answer to only general or common interests rather than to the personal interests of a few, but (as in Rawls's theory) justice in Habermas does serve interests, and just norms can rely upon "universal assent because they perceptibly embody an interest common to all affected."[101] In fact, Habermas says that rationally motivated assent will typically "be combined with empirical acquiescence, effected by weapons or goods, to form a belief in legitimacy whose component parts are difficult to isolate."[102] It is important to see that this remark addresses the process of norm justification and not only the practical application of just norms, since it indicates that how a norm relates to our conceptions of the good will affect our "belief in its legitimacy."

When we do turn to application, it is clear that the incorporation of goods and interests within the moral standpoint that justifies norms contributes to stabilizing these norms. This is not to say that we will support just norms only to the extent that we believe they serve all the personal interests we bring to the process of deliberation. Justice does not serve every interest but it does serve some general interests, and to the extent that the interests it serves are truly general, they will be ones that all affected persons can recognize as belonging to them. Thus Habermas admits that allegiance to just norms is an "alloy" motive in the sense that it combines rational insight into their validity with affective concern for the goods they are believed to serve. In view of these considerations, he acknowledges that there is "a remnant of the good at the core of the right."[103] Insofar as justice is "what is equally good for all," norm justification represents a procedure in which "the good" is "extended step by step to the 'right.' "[104] In this respect, his account of justice is not exactly the model of pure proceduralism that he intends it to be. Indeed, the theory is marked by a deep ambiguity on this point.

There is another way in which the model introduces elements of moral substance into the procedure of norm justification. The reasons that figure in assessing the validity of claims and the justification of norms "count only against the background of context-dependent standards of rationality."[105] The "rational assent" required to establish validity is infused with values from the "lifeworld," which forms the context of discourse and includes "cultural traditions, social orders, and personal identities."[106] In fact, the moral standpoint presupposes "the backing of a massive background consensus."[107] The interests that the universalization test requires us to consider in justification are similarly colored by value orientations. "Needs and wants," Habermas says, always "are interpreted in the light of cultural values."[108] Thus to the extent that the moral standpoint incorporates the interests of all affected, it introduces substantive content from ethical life into justice. What the moral standpoint reflects, it seems, is not the absence of any conceptions of the good but the convergence of various such conceptions. The question is how, not whether, a procedural theory of justice incorporates these elements.

Thus in spite of his aspiration to a purer proceduralism, Habermas's account of justice incorporates goods and value orientations into the justification procedure via the reasons and the interests that figure in the universalization test. These same interests help to support adherence to the norms that result. Still, adherence may well demand more than an appeal to these interests. Just norms may require us to forsake our more particular interests, our deepest ethical convictions, and key aspects of our personal identities, and when they do so the general interests served by justice may not be experienced as subjectively more compelling than these other factors. Moreover, although Habermas sometimes acknowledges the elements of affect implicit in the moral standpoint, his overwhelming tendency, as one commentator has said, is to rely "heavily on the cognitive rather than affective dimensions of the self."[109] To the extent that practical reason achieves impartiality, it does so by largely transcending the kinds of sentiments that normally animate action. As we have seen, Habermas himself indicates that the predominantly rationalist character of the moral standpoint has a disabling effect on its ability to attract persons first to adopt it and then to comply with its conclusions. The "abstractive" achievements of the moral standpoint mean, he says, that "moral knowledge becomes detached from moral motivation."[110] While Habermas does not deny that we may have what Kant called an "interest of reason" in adopting the moral standpoint, he is not willing to assert with Kant that this interest is more powerful than other inclinations. And although he characterizes the aspiration to reach mutual understanding as a desire, the process of reaching understanding rests on a form of reason that stands apart from the "merely contingent" profiles of desire that normally motivate us. Reason on its own, at least as Habermas conceives it, is therefore only a "weakly motivating" force.[111]

Dilemmas of Recontextualization

To mitigate the deficiency of reason as a motivating force in morality, Habermas recommends that a concern for the moral standpoint be incorporated into the personality structure of the individual and that it be embedded in the cultural values of society. Both recommendations face difficulties that derive from other elements of his presentation, however. To be sure, the notion of incorporating an attachment to justice into the personality structure of the individual is by no means incomprehensible, and Habermas has set down a theory of moral development (following Jean Piaget and Lawrence Kohlberg) to describe what he has in mind. What is required is "the complete internalization of a few highly abstract and universal principles"—specifically, the principles embodied in the procedure of norm justification.[112] Internalization means that these principles and the practices associated with them become constitutive concerns for the individual, a part of her self-understanding. Henceforth she sees herself as the kind of person who wishes to live up to these ideals; her self-respect, even her identity as a whole, will be contingent upon doing so. This account of personality structure describes familiar features of personal identity for many members of liberal societies today.[113] Yet the viability of the model rests squarely on the fusion of the right and the good that it entails. For Habermas treats conceptions of the self as part of ethical life, as a function of one's orientation to the good.[114] Hence a personal identification with principles of right can only mean, given the terms of his analysis, that these principles have been incorporated into one's conception of the good, including one's view of what is good for oneself. This introduces an element of purposive rationality into the moral standpoint, since one's own self-respect and integrity now depend upon living up to the principles of justice.

This purposive element raises a difficulty for Habermas because he maintains that action oriented toward mutual understanding and purposive action oriented toward success are "mutually exclusive types of action."[115] If my depiction of the fusion of the right and the good required for the internalization of the moral standpoint is accurate, then these types of action cannot be mutually exclusive but must coexist, at least when it comes to justice. The just person will act simultaneously from a desire to reach mutual understanding and from a (success-oriented) desire to achieve self-respect or personal integrity. Internalization requires bridging what Habermas refers to as the "razor-sharp cuts between evaluative statements and strictly normative ones, between the good and the just."[116] Insofar as he insists on preserving these divides and mutual exclusions, his theory will be unable to account for the fact of the moral standpoint as a function of personality structure. And he does insist on these divides, pressing the importance of "an *absolute* priority of the right over the good, which alone would be commensurate with the categorical validity of moral duties."[117] In fact, the account of internalization I have suggested violates the ideal of autonomy that Habermas sees as a necessary component of the moral standpoint. As long as affective concerns and elements of ethical life (including the self-conception of the agent) influence decisions, Habermas maintains that "contingent, subjective determinations are still operative and the will does not act *solely* on grounds of practical reason." In such cases, "not every trace of *compulsion* has been expunged," which means that "the will is not yet truly free."[118] The moral standpoint demands precisely this freedom, for "moral obligations acquire an unconditional or categorical validity only when they proceed from laws that emancipate the will . . . from all contingent determinations and in a sense assimilate it to practical reason itself."[119] These passages, which reveal Habermas's commitment to a strong opposition between the right and the good, and between reason and sentiment, indicate that the theory cannot consistently embrace the fusion of these elements, although its success depends on doing so.

Habermas also holds that in order to engage our allegiance the moral standpoint must be recontextualized, which means being embedded within new forms of ethical life that "meet it halfway."[120] As others have shown, however, a form of ethical life that is abstract enough to be compatible with the moral standpoint would seem to be subject to the same dilemmas that plague this standpoint to begin with.[121] Part of what gives ethical life motivating force is that it entails "unquestioningly accepted" beliefs and values,[122] whereas a characteristic feature of the moral standpoint is the relentless reflexivity of reason within it. To the extent that ethical life comes to embody this reflexivity it may be expected to lose its motivating force. Additionally, the particularity associated with ethical life—its inclusion of specific conceptions of the good—is what gives content to deliberation within the moral standpoint. If our interests and our reasons always must be interpreted against a background that includes particular conceptions of the good and specific value orientations, what sorts of interpretations will be available once this particularity has been generalized? Will we be able to make sense of the deliberative procedure at all? Finally, it is not clear that any form of ethical life, even one consistent with the moral standpoint, could resist its problematizing effects. The result of reason continuously putting itself on trial *could* be endless iterations of rational discourse aimed at reaching understanding, as Habermas assumes, but it could also be a loss of confidence in reason and the end of rational discourse as a normative ideal, as some strands of postmodernism in philosophy and critical theory suggest.[123]

In recent work Habermas has turned to the coercive power of the law as the necessary supplement to post-traditional morality in democratic societies.[124] This power partially ameliorates the motivational deficit and the problem of decontextualization. But while the law can force us to comply with just norms, it cannot force us into the moral standpoint that authorizes them. The two poles of legal compulsion and rational cognition (at least as Habermas conceives it) equally undercut individual agency, the one because it replaces agency with forced obedience and the other because it disrupts the motivational sources of action found in ethical life.[125] Yet in the justification of norms, nothing can replace the exercise of agency, which authorizes norms and thereby makes possible the subjective feeling of validity. To rectify the motivational deficit is possible, as we have seen, but the solution would require moving beyond the strict dichotomies that characterize Habermas's moral standpoint. The consequence of addressing the motivational deficit is to undercut the pure proceduralism that he envisions. Specifically, it points to the necessity of treating morality and ethical life, reason and sentiment, the right and the good, normativity and moral psychology as interdependent and equally integral to moral deliberation and norm justification.

So there are resources implicit in Habermas's theory for addressing the problem of demotivation, but marshalling them will tend to jeopardize its aspiration to a purer proceduralism and its ideal of pure practical reason. These are limitations that we can and should live with. We can be affectively attached to certain principles and practices associated with rationalist theories of justice, but we must believe that they are good, even good for us, in order to engage our action. Not only action, but practical deliberation itself, necessarily incorporates sentiments insofar as it transpires within a particular horizon of concern and answers to the things that matter most to us. Our standards of right could never be normative for us if they were wholly independent of these concerns. Neither human agency nor practical reason can be abstracted entirely from affective concerns. Any theory of justice that fails to account for this fact will face not only a motivational deficit but also a normative one, for it will disable the deliberative procedures of norm justification. Yet the more the right is embedded within the good—the more justice makes reference to ethical life—the more the disagreements about the good found in all modern societies will infect justice, thus rendering liberal-democratic justice controversial in precisely the way that Habermas seeks to avoid. No theory of justice can fully overcome this difficulty.

Still, the problem of controversy can be mitigated through the right combination of institutions and political practices, a theme that we shall take up in later chapters. For now, the crucial point is that the rationalist aspiration to model practical reason and the justification of norms in a way that transcends the influence of sentiment is untenable. Because it cannot be sustained, the aspiration leads to theoretical inconsistencies, and it generates both normative and motivational deficits. Even the relatively nuanced rationalism found in Rawls and Habermas suffers from these difficulties. They are willing to accept the idea that affective concerns help motivate right action but they are much more ambivalent about the notion that such concerns figure in the justification of action or the norms that guide it. They are reluctant to tie the content and authority of moral and political norms to the psychological states of individuals. Consequently, we will need to go beyond Rawls and Habermas for a positive vision of how sentiments might contribute to impartial judgment about justice. What would be involved in taking seriously the notion that sentiments have a crucial role to play in judgment and deliberation? What would happen if we let go of the Kantian myth of reason's transcendence? The worry, of course, is that we would lose all critical traction, that under such conditions our moral judgments could never be impartial, our political deliberation never fair. Then, too, it may be difficult to see where the normative authority of our moral and political obligations might come from, the obligations entailed by the principles of justice, if these principles were grounded in nothing more noble than sentiments. More to the point, is there no difference—indeed, a large and important divide—between duty and desire? In the next chapter, we explore several recent attempts to envision answers to these questions. Each one moves away from the rationalist paradigm of practical reason to rethink judgment and deliberation in ways that more unambiguously welcome affect.

CHAPTER TWO

Recent Alternatives to Rationalism

THE RATIONALISM that characterizes the moral standpoint in Rawls and Habermas has been challenged in recent years on a number of fronts. The critiques we pursue here all make affect central to their accounts of moral and political judgment. In this way, they depart from some earlier challenges to the rationalist model. For instance, the virtue theory that emerged in the 1980s in the work of Alasdair MacIntyre, among others, argued that the path to excellence in moral judgment runs not through abstract reasoning about universal obligations but rather through the cultivation of particular moral virtues.[1] Together the virtues constitute the practical skills needed for human flourishing, including the deliberative reflection that properly orients us to the good and the right desire that attracts us to it. Moral theories that privilege the rational recognition of universal obligation over the practical cultivation of particular virtues, according to MacIntyre, run counter not only to key features of human psychology but also to the historical condition of postmodernity.

Michael Sandel's communitarian critique of Rawls took a somewhat different tack. It challenged the idea that moral deliberation could abstract from the particular ways of life and conceptions of the good that shape our identities as members of specific communities. Sandel rejected the individualism of the rationalist model, arguing for a conception of the self as "encumbered" by its association with a particular collectivity and the duties this association entails.[2] Another influential line of attack came from the proponents of identity politics or "difference theory," most notably Iris Young. This position contested the impartiality of the rationalist approach to justice and the universalism of the norms it generates. Young argued that the abstract reason of Rawls's original position and Habermas's moral standpoint tended to replicate the particular perspectives of the privileged and the powerful, and to exclude the perspectives of others, especially members of marginalized groups. Consequently, the rationalist procedures of deliberation and norm justification were not truly impartial and the norms they justified could never be universally valid.[3]

In challenging the moral priority of universal obligations, the viability of individualism, and the true scope of "impartial" reason, these critics brought crucial considerations to the fore. Yet none of them explored in any depth the place of sentiment within deliberation. In this chapter we look at several groups of theorists whose critiques of rationalism explicitly elaborate the importance of affect. The first group argues for an affective ethics of care as opposed to the disinterested morality of abstract principle associated with rationalist models of justice. The second group includes those working on the role of emotions in moral and political judgment. The contributions here are both philosophical and empirical, with the latter issuing from neuropsychology as well as political science. Finally, we consider several contemporary accounts of moral judgment inspired by David Hume, which specify the ways that sentiments interact with intellect to generate judgment and to constrain it. As powerful and as important as these various accounts are, however, each is subject to certain difficulties, and in the course of this chapter we shall explore their limits as well as their contributions.

Affect in the Ethics of Care

Carol Gilligan's *In a Different Voice* initially introduced the argument for an ethics of care into debates about moral development and cognitive psychology. In an empirical study of the relationship between moral judgment and action, Gilligan observed that women "often define moral problems in a way that eludes the categories of moral theory and is at odds with the assumptions that shape psychological thinking about morality and about the self."[4] The standard model of maturity in moral development, like moral reasoning in the dominant paradigms of justice, centered on "the ability to judge dispassionately, to weigh evidence in an even-handed manner, balancing the claims of others and self" in relation to abstract rules of right.[5] Gilligan pointed out that the empirical research on moral judgment that grounded this standard model of maturity had been based on all-male samples. Her own interviews with persons at different stages of life, with male and female college students, and with women who were considering having an abortion brought to light "a different voice," one in which reasoning from abstract principles figured less importantly than feelings of care, where "the self as a moral agent perceives and responds to the perception of need" in others.[6] Her findings therefore called attention "to a major design problem" in the prevailing theories of moral development, such as that of Lawrence Kohlberg. She then went on to develop an alternative account of moral judgment in which the previously excluded care ethic figures prominently.

In the last twenty-five years Gilligan's research has been appropriated and extended by theorists (mainly feminist theorists) working in psychology, moral philosophy, and political theory. Whereas Gilligan's own work was modest in its normative claims on behalf of the care perspective (she adopts a largely descriptive tone, presenting the care ethic as a different but not necessarily superior voice), more recent contributions have argued for the positive value of care as an important corrective to the moral standpoint of justice. Care theorists have disagreed about whether the ethic of care is intrinsically feminine or gender-neutral, and about whether it is properly conceived as a competitor to the justice perspective or a complement to it. On at least two points, however, there is general agreement. First, the objects of concern within the care ethic are persons not principles. Secondly, the ethics of care does not generate universal, or even generalizable, moral judgments. These aspects of the care ethic raise certain difficulties for a theory of moral and political judgment, as we shall see presently. But before exploring the limits of the care ethic, let us consider its contributions.

First among these is the attention it gives to the issue of moral motivation. As Virginia Held puts it, "a shortcoming of most standard moral theory," including the accounts of moral judgment found in the dominant, rationalist models of justice, is that "it construes ethics too much in terms of knowledge."[7] The problem with this is that

> it leaves unaddressed the question, Even if I know what I ought to do, why should I do it? It assumes that knowledge will motivate action, but as soon as we recognize a capacity of the will to defy the dictates of reason or the counsels of knowledge, we are left with the gap between knowledge and action unfilled by theories that see ethics as a branch of objective knowledge.[8]

By contrast, in "recognizing the component of feeling and relatedness between self and particular others," the ethics of care addresses "motivation as an inherent part of the inquiry" into right and wrong.[9] Held cites the example of caring between parent and child to illustrate this point. The love one feels for one's child, she says, "already motivates much of what one does and much of what one concludes [in deliberating from the care perspective] one ought to do."[10] Because the care ethic engages an affective mode of consciousness, and because affective modes of consciousness are necessary to generate human action, the care ethic avoids the motivational deficit that plagues rationalist models of moral judgment and deliberation about justice.

The role of affect is not limited to motivating moral action, for the ethics of care also gives feeling a place in moral understanding itself.

The rationalist paradigm, as Held says, applauds "the cultivation of certain appropriate feelings" but values these feelings only "for their assistance in carrying out the requirements of morality, not in helping us to understand what these requirements are."[11] On the care model of moral judgment, by contrast, the feeling of care for particular others is itself a form of practical rationality.[12] It guides us in distinguishing right from wrong and in determining what course of action we ought to take. As Gilligan says, care is not only a feeling but also "a way of knowing."[13] By way of illustration, she compares two medical students, each describing their own decision not to report a fellow student who had violated the school's prohibition on drinking. One student described the decision in terms of justice considerations, reflecting on whether the school's policy was fair, among other things. The other student explained the decision not to turn in the drinker on the grounds that doing so would not be "a good way to respond to this problem, since it would dissolve the relationship between them and thus cut off an avenue for help."[14] Thus the ethic of care brings the affective feeling of concern for others into the practice of moral judgment itself.

Several difficulties with this approach limit its value as an account of moral and political judgment, however. The first is that the theory does not contain within itself adequate grounds for distinguishing good from bad forms of caring. Insofar as care is a feeling of concern that responds to the needs of others, it will tend to generate indiscriminate responses. We may care for bad people, and here care will blind us to the very distinctions that moral judgment should illuminate. Additionally, care may be shaped by false consciousness and thereby generate inappropriate feelings of concern (as in the loyalty a battered woman shows for her batterer). Of course, any form of evaluative judgment is bound to go wrong sometimes. Yet this potential for error is exacerbated in the case of the care ethic by the fact that the perspective of care contains no principled grounds for correcting itself. Finally, even appropriate care may inappropriately (or unjustly) privilege the interests of some over those of others in our judgments. The need to address these deficiencies is frequently acknowledged by care theorists. The most common solution is to appeal to abstract standards of justice as a corrective to care. Thus Held maintains that "caring relationships need a floor of justice,"[15] and Joan Tronto says that "to address and to correct the problems with care that we have noted requires a concept of justice."[16] Robin West likewise insists that the pursuit of care needs to be constrained by principles of justice in order to avoid the dangers of "racism, nationalism, tribalism, or speciesism."[17] Yet the appeal to justice as a corrective for care leaves the justice perspective itself largely untouched. Because this perspective is called upon to mitigate the dangers of care, it is treated by care theorists in the traditional way, as disengaged, abstract, and affectless. Yet to treat it this way is insufficiently ambitious. The important ways that affect (including care for persons and principles) might figure *within* impartial deliberation about justice are undertheorized by the ethics of care.

The inability of the care ethic to support generalizable judgments and general rules of right also constitutes a serious problem. Care theorists are right to worry about models of moral and political judgment that equate good judgments with a form of adherence to abstract rules that is insensitive to context. Nevertheless, general standards are important because without them we could not hope to coordinate social action or to get along with others, especially the many others in political life for whom we have no special feelings of care. A theory of moral judgment that makes no place for general principles or cannot yield general rules is seriously handicapped. And by treating care as antithetical to the generalizable judgments that characterize the justice perspective, the ethics of care once again neglects the important ways that affect might contribute to establishing general rules of right within deliberation about justice. So there are good reasons to go beyond the ethics of care in the quest for a viable model of affective deliberation. And the theorists of care are not the only ones who have brought affect into moral judgment in recent years. The interdisciplinary literature on emotion that has emerged over the last generation also has challenged prevailing models of evaluative judgment, and has brought to light features of practical reason that have been too long neglected.

Emotional Judgment

Empirical Findings

Antonio R. Damasio's work on the role of emotion within practical reasoning has proved enormously influential across a range of disciplines. Drawing on research in neuroscience and neuropsychology, Damasio argues that feeling is "an integral component of the machinery of reason," particularly the practical reason that figures in decision making in the personal and social domains.[18] He acknowledges that intense emotions can sometimes thwart sound judgment, but insists that the intellect can only generate decisions about how to act with the help of emotional cues.[19] In studying patients with injuries or diseases that had debilitated parts of the brain controlling emotion, Damasio found that these patients were often unable to reach determinate conclusions about what to do.[20] As the result of a brain tumor, for example, one man lost his ability for emotional feeling. His "disaffectation" meant that "topics that once had evoked a strong emotion no longer caused any reaction, positive or negative."[21] This change had devastating consequences for him at work:

> Elliot would read and fully understand the significance of the material, and he certainly knew how to sort out the documents according to the similarity or disparity of their content. The problem was that he was likely, all of a sudden, to turn from the sorting task he had initiated to reading one of those papers, carefully and intelligently, and to spend an entire day doing so. Or he might spend a whole afternoon deliberating on which principle of categorization should be applied: Should it be date, size of document, pertinence to the case, or another?[22]

By destroying his ability to feel emotion, the damage to Elliot's brain "prevented him from assigning different values to different options, and made his decision-making landscape hopelessly flat."[23] Similar difficulties affected his relationships with family and friends. His cognitive functioning was intact but the emotional deficit left him unable to make sound judgments. He became unemployable, threw away his savings on crazy schemes, alienated his friends, and was twice divorced. Elliot emerged as "a man with a normal intellect who was unable to decide properly, especially when the decision involved personal or social matters."[24] The damaged brain structures that undermined his full capacity for affect "happened to be those necessary for reasoning to culminate in decision-making."[25]

According to Damasio, affective responses function within decision making as "somatic markers" that (1) reduce the number of viable options under consideration and hence focus deliberation; and (2) keep alive the emotional force of the desires or goals toward which the deliberation ultimately aims. When we are deciding what to do, several things happen very quickly, so quickly and so habitually that we rarely take notice of them: "Imagine that *before* you apply any kind of cost/benefit analysis to the premises, and before you reason toward the solution of the problem, something quite important happens: When the bad outcome connected with a given response comes into mind, however fleetingly, you experience an unpleasant gut feeling."[26] Thoughts of the positive outcomes connected to other responses generate pleasant feelings. These affective reactions of pleasure and pain, desire and aversion, function as incentives and alarms that rapidly reduce the number of viable alternatives from which we choose, thereby increasing the accuracy and efficiency of the decision process.[27] They reflect learning through prior experience, and it is reasonable to think that they are often infused with social values, although Damasio does not elaborate the latter point. In the moment of decision, somatic markers operate as the prereflective limiting conditions of deliberation, but in other moments they may themselves be subjected to reflection.[28] We have the ability to deliberate about the value of the emotional responses that we feel. Some of them may be beyond our control, but others can be modified if they generate self-destructive behavior or prove to be counterproductive to our settled purposes.

In addition to making deliberation more efficient by limiting the number of viable options, affect keeps the end or purpose of the deliberation, and the desire to achieve this end, alive in our minds. An airline pilot charged with landing his aircraft in bad weather must not allow emotionalism to obstruct clear thinking. Yet his judgment still relies on affective modes of consciousness because "he must have feelings to hold in place the larger goals of his behavior in that particular situation," feelings tied to his responsibility for the lives of his passengers and crew as well as his own desire to live and to protect his family from the calamity his death would entail.[29] Part of what made Elliot such a poor decision maker, after all, was his inability to really care about anything. Affective systems in the brain animate deliberation, and Elliot's disaffectation robbed him of the grounds for rational choosing. As Damasio puts it, the brain systems concerned with emotion and feeling constitute the energy source not only for external action or movement but also for "internal action" or decisions.[30] It may not always feel that way, for "a good number of our daily decisions apparently proceed without feelings."[31] All this means is that the affective attitudes that guide and constrain deliberation are not always the focus of our direct attention. Without attention, they will tend not to register in our consciousness.[32] But their effects can be profound even when they operate unconsciously. Indeed, Damasio insists that this is the normal condition of decision making. Models of deliberation that postulate a form of practical reason devoid of sentiment therefore are misguided. The experiences of Damasio's research subjects suggest that "the cool strategy advocated by Kant, among others, has far more to do with the way patients with prefrontal damage go about deciding than with how normals usually operate."[33]

It is important to acknowledge that there are limits to the conclusions that can be drawn from this research. The precise brain impairments represented in the studies differ from case to case, making generalizations somewhat tenuous and findings difficult to replicate. Moreover, until recently most studies depended on self-reporting and observation of patients' outward behavior. Only in the last fifteen years has functional magnetic resonance imaging (fMRI) made it possible to (in effect) look inside the brain as subjects carry out particular tasks, and so to correlate behavior with actual evidence of brain function. And what this research establishes is indeed correlation not causation. It can show that damage to emotion centers in the brain correlates with impairment to the deliberative process, for instance, but it does not prove that the former has caused the latter. More and better data is rapidly emerging with the advance of technology and increasing interest in the scientific community, but researchers are only beginning to grasp the complexity of brain functioning within the deliberative process.

Nevertheless, Damasio's work is suggestive when it comes to understanding the various capacities and brain systems involved in practical reason and decision making. Although neuroscience itself has not elaborated the implications of these findings for politics, several recent studies in empirical political science have drawn on them to explore the emotional nuances of political judgment.[34] Noteworthy among them is the collaborative work of George Marcus, W. Russell Neuman, and Michael Mackuen. Marcus et al. take issue with what they characterize as the dominant view of political judgment within political science today, which sets reason at odds with emotion and regards politics as being in need of protection (via reason) from the passions of citizens. They identify two primary ways in which affective attitudes deriving from the limbic system in the brain contribute to deliberation and decision making. First, emotion indirectly guides "strategic choices about behavior" by shaping our dispositions. Dispositions rely on "emotional assessment to control the execution of habits: we sustain those habits about which we feel enthusiastic and we abandon those that cause us despair."[35] It is habitual responses that govern the majority of political decisions for most people. When citizens make decisions in politics (as, for instance, in voting), their judgments are generally "casual, even thoughtless," drawing on patterns of thought and behavior that have emotional salience for them and that have become ingrained habits.[36] So emotional responses shape the habits that guide most political deliberation.

Emotions also can shake up our habitual patterns of judgment, however. This is the second way that emotions affect political decision making. What Marcus et al. call the brain's "surveillance system," involving emotional responses to external stimuli, "acts to scan the environment for novelty and sudden intrusion of threat."[37] Here emotion signals the findings of our continuing analyses of the environment, raising the flag of anxiety when we perceive novelty or threats, for instance, and focusing our attention on relevant objects. We engage in active political deliberation when the surveillance system triggers certain emotions, especially anxiety.[38] Whereas most of the time we respond to political matters habitually and we "unthinkingly" rely "on past thought, calculation, and evaluation,"[39] the emotional trigger of anxiety disrupts these habits. Active, thoughtful deliberation needs the stimulation of emotion to get it going, and Marcus et al. insist that empirical studies of voting behavior support this conclusion. Consequently, people who remain "dispassionate" about politics are less likely to make rational judgments because they lack the emotional impetus needed to motivate "more deeply reasoned decisions."[40]

Whether or not election data support their view is beyond the scope of this study. For our purposes it is enough to point out a conceptual deficiency in their approach. Despite the careful attention they give to emotion, their own model of good political deliberation ironically tends to neglect it. For the role of emotion here is either to undermine good deliberation, insofar as emotions control the dispositional habits that make us respond to political questions unreflectively, or to jump-start good deliberation through emotional signals such as anxiety. Thus Marcus et al. tell us that "emotion enables conscious consideration to be invoked for circumstances that merit the use of reason,"[41] and that anxiety "initiates the state of mind we call rational."[42] But how does emotion contribute to good deliberation itself, once deliberation is underway? How does it figure in practical rationality? These questions are not pursued, although there are indications that good deliberation on the model of Marcus et al. marginalizes emotion in favor of a standard rational-choice account. The latter holds to a view of reason that, although oriented to the satisfaction of specific concerns, is otherwise impervious to the influence of sentiment. The book's conclusion contends that "the Affective Intelligence perspective is fundamentally complementary to and commensurate with rational choice approaches."[43] In other words, affective intelligence is not offered as an alternative to the rational-choice model of deliberation. On the contrary, it is a theory about the "conditions under which engagement of rational choice is more or less likely," and it leaves untouched not only the specific viability of the rational-choice view but the nature of good deliberation more generally.[44] It also tends to reproduce, however unintentionally, the old dichotomy between reason and sentiment rather than reconceive the nature of practical reason in a way that incorporates sentiment within it. To ascertain what actually happens within sound deliberation and to discover the contributions of sentiment within this process, we will need to go deeper into the nature of deliberation than Marcus et al. have done.[45] The recent philosophical literature on emotion offers some valuable resources.

Emotions in the Philosophy of Judgment

Over the past twenty years a lively conversation about the emotions has emerged within moral philosophy and philosophical psychology. Philosophers have characterized the emotions in new ways so as to challenge the traditional dichotomization of reason and the passions. Thus many have defended "cognitivist" accounts of emotion according to which emotions include beliefs and involve cognitive capacities. They have also tried to specify more precisely the proper role of emotion in moral life, including its place in moral character, judgment, and action. This is a rich and varied literature, far too wide-ranging to cover it all in any depth here. One theorist whose philosophical contributions on the emotions stand out, both for their quality and for their quantity, is Martha Nussbaum. At the same time, certain dilemmas raised by her approach illuminate fundamental challenges that any account of affective deliberation will need to address. For these reasons, I focus on Nussbaum in the discussion that follows, occasionally drawing on other accounts where relevant.

Nussbaum defends a cognitivist view of emotion, which distinguishes emotions from other affective attitudes (moods and appetites, for instance) on the grounds that emotions include beliefs.[46] Being angry, she says, "is not like experiencing a bodily appetite." For whereas hunger and thirst are "relatively impervious to changes in belief," anger "seems to require and to rest upon a belief that one has been wronged or damaged in some significant way by the person toward whom the anger is directed."[47] Like other beliefs, emotions can be true or false.[48] They may be mistaken on matters of fact, for example, rendering their propositional content incorrect.[49] If I am angry at Joe for missing our appointment but have misremembered the date, then my anger is in this sense false, based upon the mistaken belief that Joe stood me up. Emotions can be false in another way as well. In addition to propositional content, emotions have evaluative content. My anger at Joe combines the proposition that he missed our appointment with the evaluation that missing appointments is a bad thing, that it constitutes an offense or a moral violation of some sort. The anger will be false if either of these beliefs is wrong; so if missing appointments is not really a bad thing, then I am wrong to be angry at Joe. As Nussbaum puts it, my anger says that "it is right to be upset about that: it makes a truth-claim about its own evaluations. It asserts the real value of the object, it says that getting upset is a response to something really important, not just a whim."[50] The cognitivism of Nussbaum's view distinguishes it from the accounts of emotion found in the ethics of care literature, as well as those of Damasio and Marcus et al., since none of these others insists on the truth-value of emotions.

By virtue of their cognitive content, according to Nussbaum, emotions do more than supply motivational support for the conclusions of moral judgment.[51] Emotions, she says, are "not just a psychological adjunct" to ethical thought but are "a part of ethical thought itself." This is a crucial point. Emotions are more than merely "the fuel that powers the psychological mechanism of a reasoning creature, they are parts, highly complex parts, of this creature's reasoning itself."[52] Specifically, emotions figure in judgment as "modes of vision, or recognition."[53] A person of practical insight "will cultivate her emotional openness and responsiveness in approaching a new situation. Frequently, it will be her passional response, rather than detached thinking, that will guide her to the appropriate recognitions. 'Here is a case where a friend needs my help': this will often be 'seen' first by the feelings that are constituent parts of friendship, rather than by pure intellect."[54] Likewise, as we have seen, feelings of anger can alert us to moral violations. Emotional disengagement therefore represents a threat to sound moral judgment. In fact, Nussbaum "warns us of the ways in which theorizing can impede vision"[55] by disengaging us from our emotional life. To the extent that theorizing dominates one's consciousness, it may preclude the emotional sensitivity that enables one to respond to the true claims of morality. For this reason, "the intellect is not only not all-sufficient, it is a dangerous master" in ethical matters.[56]

Another feature of Nussbaum's view that links it to other recent work on the emotions is her insistence on the value of particularism in moral judgment, as against the reign of general rules and the rationalist vision of a generalized moral standpoint.[57] General rules can play a role in moral judgment, but they should not be construed as "normative for perception, the ultimate authorities against which the correctness of particular choices is assessed." Instead, they are "rules of thumb, highly useful for a variety of purposes, but valid only to the extent to which they correctly describe good concrete judgments."[58] The good judge looks not to general rules but rather investigates and scrutinizes "the nature of each item and each situation, to respond to what is there before her with full sensitivity and imaginative vigor." She does not "fall short of what is there to be seen and felt because of evasiveness, scientific abstractness, or a love of simplification."[59] Her "intent focusing on the concrete" is "an end in itself."[60] Nor does she aspire to a generalized standpoint that would leave behind her own concrete identity. In judging, "all of her personality is actively involved."[61] She brings to the situation her personal history of "conceptions and commitments, and a host of past obligations and affiliations (some general, some particular), all of which contribute to and help to constitute her evolving vision of a good life. The organized internalization of these commitments constitutes her character."[62] So moral judgment is not a matter of applying general rules to particular cases and it does not involve the adoption of a generalized standpoint. Indeed, "we can give no general account of deliberative priorities, and also no general account of the techniques and procedures of good deliberation, that would suffice to discriminate good from defective choice."[63] Judgment consists in our personal responses to particular situations and the emotion-guided "perception" of the relevant moral features of these situations.[64]

Although the "priority of the particular" rules out a general account of deliberative priorities and techniques, still the theory does not end in relativism. Following Aristotle, Nussbaum holds that what moral perception "aims to see is (in some sense) the way things are."[65] Good judgment involves the "correct perception" of the moral meaning of a situation, or "true ethical perception."[66] The emotions are "modes of vision or recognition" that allow us to see the ethical "nature of the practical situation . . . for what it is."[67] The function of judgment is thus to convey to us the intrinsic moral value that inheres in the world, and good judgment can be distinguished from bad judgment on the basis of whether or not it accurately perceives this independent moral order. Human nature is the key to this order. Nussbaum treats human nature as normative, defining it teleologically as "what a human life needs in order to be complete."[68] We can identify true emotions and sound moral judgments on the basis of the fact that they are consistent with the components of a complete human life, assuming that there is a fixed set of these components and that we can discern them accurately. The evaluative content of emotions, then, should answer to the standard of human perfection. Anger at injustice is valid because it is true that injustice tends to obstruct human flourishing. Thus the "absence of formula" in moral judgment "does not mean that we have laissez-faire, or that any choice one makes is all right. There are many ways of wrecking a ship in a storm, and very few ways of sailing it well."[69] The complete human life is to be defined in fairly narrow terms, then, and this standard can help us distinguish true from false emotions and good from bad moral judgments.

Nussbaum's effort to show that emotion-based moral judgment can rise above the narrowest forms of subjectivism and relativism, even achieve objectivity, is valuable. It moves the debates about emotion's role in judgment forward in a fruitful way. The appeal to human nature as a normative standard is also promising. As we shall see in the next chapter, the Humean view similarly finds cognitive content in sentiments, and it seeks to ground the objectivity of moral judgment partly in a notion of human nature. The Humean view, however, resists reliance on the contestable doctrine that true moral entities inhere in the world independently of the human activity of valuing things, and it avoids controversial conceptions of the "complete" human life. It seeks objectivity in more empirically verifiable, less lofty quarters. Moral judgment, on this view, does involve perception but not perception of intrinsic moral value. Whatever common moral value exists is generated by human concerns. The Humean approach to judgment is also partly an expressivist one, then, and this sets it apart from Nussbaum's account.[70] And because it does not look to "real" moral entities to ground the objectivity of judgment, this approach puts much greater stock in a general account of the techniques and procedures of judgment, as exemplified by its account of the generalized standpoint of moral sentiment. These features of the Humean view are elaborated at length in chapter 3.

One difficulty posed by Nussbaum's account of emotion, especially in later work, is that her cognitivism runs so deep that it sometimes seems to minimize the influence of affect nearly to the point of extinguishing it altogether. To acknowledge the role that beliefs play within emotions is one thing; to reduce emotions to mere beliefs, as she more than occasionally does, is another thing entirely. It is true that in one place she describes emotions as "composites of belief and feeling,"[71] and as a general matter she is clearly intent on challenging the vision of disengaged intellect that characterizes rationalist models of judgment and deliberation. Yet the concept of emotion that she employs too often loses touch with the affective mode of consciousness that distinguishes emotions from cognitions such as thoughts and beliefs. Indeed, she more often defines emotion as thought than as a combination of thought and feeling. "Belief is sufficient for emotion," she says at one point;[72] and elsewhere she insists that "feeling" properly understood "does not contrast with our cognitive words 'perception' and 'judgment,' it is merely a terminological variant of them."[73] Although she acknowledges that emotions typically are experienced in connection with affect or feeling, the latter plays no part in the definition of emotions themselves. Emotions are not fundamentally feelings but rather "cognitive states."[74] We should recognize that "some feelings . . . will often accompany them," but emotions per se can be defined "in terms of these evaluative recognitions alone."[75] Indeed, the whole concept of "affect" turns out to be superfluous to emotion as Nussbaum understands it.[76] Emotions consist of two *thoughts* and nothing more: "thought of an object combined with thought of the object's salience or importance."[77] What we normally think of as feelings of grief, for instance, ultimately reduce to thoughts about the loss of something valued.[78] So Nussbaum defends the value of emotions for moral judgment but only by largely excising affect from them. Thus affect itself turns out to have surprisingly little bearing on judgment. Emotions influence judgment but emotions are not themselves affective states, and the affects that may accompany emotions have no substantive value for moral judgment. In this respect her view bears a striking affinity to standard rationalist accounts. She is surely right to say that emotions (like Blackburn's "concerns") frequently contain cognitive content, but it is a strange phenomenology that equates emotions with thoughts alone and strips them of the affective valence that is the distinguishing feature of how we so often actually experience them.

Along these lines, one might wonder what it means to speak of an object's "salience" or "importance" in the absence of affect, as Nussbaum does when defining emotion. When we talk about something's salience or importance for us we typically mean to indicate how much we care about it, the feeling that it matters to us. This feeling can be redescribed in terms of a thought, but to call it by a new name does not change the facts of our experience. The philosophical distinction between different "directions of fit," articulated first by G.E.M. Anscombe, is relevant here.[79] The concept has been widely used to distinguish "cognitive" from "conative" states of mind. Some psychological states have a "mind-to-world" direction of fit in the sense that

> it is incumbent on them to fit the world. Their role is to provide an accurate representation or picture of the way the world is. By way of its representational content, a given belief (or other *cognitive* state) represents the world in a given way. . . . Given its direction of fit, a belief succeeds if in fact it fits the world. In short, it succeeds if it is *true*. A false belief fails by failing to fit the world. Remedy requires change of belief, not a change in the world. . . . Other psychological states have the *world-to-mind* direction of fit. From the perspective of the subjects in such states, it is incumbent on the world to fit them. Their role is to provide a representation, not of how the world is, but of how the subject requires it to be. By way of its representational content a desire (or other *conative* state) requires the world to be in a certain way.[80]

Whereas cognitive states are able to be evaluated as true or false, conative states are not.[81] This difference reflects the divergent nature of the two states. They are different ways of experiencing the world, they represent different psychological functions, and they have different conditions for success.

When Nussbaum talks about emotions as involving thoughts that have salience and importance for us, she effectively acknowledges the conative dimension of emotion. For something to be important or salient for me, for it to matter to me that something be one way rather than another, is for me to be in a psychological state that has a "world-to-mind" direction of fit. The attitude of caring about something, whatever it might be, involves the desire that the world be a certain way. The conative states that distinguish emotions from mere thoughts and beliefs are states of affective engagement.[82] To be sure, my emotional feeling of anger at an instance of injustice includes the beliefs that an injustice has been committed and that injustice is wrong. There is a mind-to-world direction of fit here that is able to be evaluated in terms of truth or falsity. But an anger response entails more than just these cognitive states. It also reflects my thwarted desire that justice should prevail, which is a conative state with a world-to-mind direction of fit and an affective valence. The reason for my anger, in other words, is that justice *matters* to me. And to say that justice matters to me is to say that I want the world to be a certain way—namely, just.[83] The point is that there is more to emotion than cognition, an irreducible element that Nussbaum's account leaves out.

Insofar as conative states cannot be evaluated in terms of truth—the faithful representation of independently existing features of the world simply does not capture the purpose or orientation of these states—there will be an element of emotion that eludes characterization as true or false. This fact may explain why Nussbaum is so keen to exclude affect from the emotions that figure in moral judgment. In order to sustain her conviction that good judgment is the true perception of moral value that inheres in the world, it is important that judgments take the form of cognitions with propositional content that can be evaluated in terms of truth. Given that judgment involves emotions, if emotions should be found to contain noncognitive contents, then it would no longer be possible to describe moral judgment strictly in terms of the correct perception of true moral value. So Nussbaum's exclusion of affect should not be surprising in light of her conviction that moral judgment is the correct perception of independently existing moral truths. She wants to protect emotion-guided moral judgment from charges of emotivism and subjectivism, and she wants to protect moral life from the loss of common standards. These aspects of her view reflect a respectable concern, which is the fear of relativism. There are other alternatives to relativism, however. The Humean approach intends to preserve more fully the affective valence of sentiments and concerns within judgment while acknowledging that they also have cognitive components. In the next section, we explore several contemporary accounts of moral judgment inspired by Hume. They do not all fully succeed in incorporating affect while avoiding relativism but they open up new terrain in the study of moral judgment and practical deliberation.

HUMEAN PERSPECTIVES

One Hume-inspired account of practical deliberation has come from Bernard Williams. Challenging what he takes to be the rationalist ideal of impartiality, he shows that practical deliberation is ineluctably grounded in certain kinds of sentiments. He elaborates his view by way of a distinction between internal and external reasons for action. When we examine statements of the form "*A* has a reason to *Φ*," Williams says, there seem to be "two different sorts of interpretation" available to us.[84] On the first (internalist) interpretation, the sentence implies that "*A* has some motive which will be served or furthered by his *Φ*-ing, and if this turns out not to be so the sentence is false."[85] The second (externalist) interpretation holds that "there is no such condition, and the reason-sentence will not be falsified by the absence of an appropriate motive."[86] Williams defends the internalist view, saying that "the only real claims about reasons for action will be internal claims."[87]

Like Hume, Williams holds that the reasons for action that figure in deliberation—including moral deliberation—must be relative to an agent's "subjective motivational set," which he refers to as the agent's *S*.[88] Deliberative reasons must draw on elements in *S* if they are to explain the agent's decisions and actions. The point of internalism is "the idea of a man's ground projects providing the motive force which propels him into the future, and gives him a reason for living" and for deciding in particular ways.[89] It is important to see that the internalist view need not posit psychological egoism on the part of agents. The elements in *S* "do not have to be selfish, in the sense that they are just concerned with things for the agent." They may even be altruistic, as, for example, the desires to "work[] for reform, or justice, or general improvement."[90] Although he uses the language of desire, Williams intends this term to have wide application. One's motivational set "can contain such things as dispositions of evaluation, patterns of emotional reaction, personal loyalties, and various projects."[91] The relevant concerns need not be selfish but they must be one's own, or embody the affective dispositions and desires that uniquely constitute the character of *this* agent. We must, as Williams elsewhere insists, deliberate from who we are, and who we are is in large measure defined by our affective concerns.[92] Thus practical deliberation "involves an *I* that must be more intimately the *I* of my desires" than the rationalist account of judgment allows.[93] One problem with abstracting from personal desires, or concerns, as the impartial standpoint posited by Kant and neo-Kantian accounts of moral deliberation requires, is that "it is rather hard to explain why the reflective self, if it is conceived as uncommitted to all particular desires, should have a concern that any of them be satisfied. . . . It is unclear, then, why the reflective self should try to provide for the satisfaction of those desires."[94] This is not simply a motivational problem, or a difficulty of motivating adherence to the results of deliberation. It involves the deliberative process itself. An agent with no particular desires has no reason to choose one course of action over another and therefore has no basis for deliberation at all. As Rawls himself has said, practical deliberation always needs a point, and the point is given by the agent's concerns.

Despite its grounding in an agent's existing concerns, the deliberative process can reform one's reasons for action. In the first place, we should not "think of *S* as statically given. The processes of deliberation can have all sorts of effect on *S*."[95] Where elements of *S* are based on false beliefs, for example, deliberation that reveals the error will lead to a change in *S*. Moreover, an agent may be ignorant of some fact "such that if he did know it he would, in virtue of some element in *S*, be disposed to *Φ*."[96] It is also possible for an agent to be ignorant of some element in *S* itself, as when subconscious desires or fears influence judgment.[97] Where deliberation brings such an element to light, the agent may find that, in light of other elements in *S*, the relevant desire has lost much of its force, or perhaps gained new force. The method of reflective equilibrium has a part in the deliberative process. But in all these instances of deliberation, practical reasoning is animated and constrained by the affective concerns that orient one's identity and motivate one's action.

The externalist disputes this, of course, and on the basis of what may seem to be plausible considerations. Just because I do not wish to join the army, the externalist wonders, does this really mean that there is no reason to do so? Does it mean, in particular, that there can be no morally relevant reasons, no normatively binding reasons, for joining the army? What about my country's need of defense, or my family's? Williams insists that external-reason statements cannot be explanations of action, or grounds for deliberation, at least when taken on their own. Nothing, he says, "can explain an agent's (intentional) actions except something that motivates him so to act."[98] But external reasons by definition do not refer to motives that the agent already has. Consequently, in order for an external-reason statement to explain action, "some psychological link" between the reason and the agent's existing motivational set is needed.[99] It must be possible to reason from the existing internal reasons of the agent to this new external one. But this demand poses a paradox: It requires that "the new motivation be in some way rationally arrived at, granted the earlier motivations." At the same time, it must not be derivable from the earlier motivations because, in that case, "an internal reason statement would have been true in the first place."[100] In short, the viability of external reasons would require that they be both derived from and not derived from the agent's internal reasons, and these conditions could not simultaneously hold true.

Williams concludes that internalism in some form is the only alternative. Yet internalism need not entail that the only reasons for action are to be found in the immediate desires of which an agent is consciously aware. As we have seen, deliberation can yield new reasons for action under the right circumstances; it can lead a person "to see that he has reason to do something which he did not see he had reason to do at all."[101] If new claims can be shown to engage or intersect with our existing concerns, they can become reasons for action, even if they clash with some of our existing desires. I may loathe jogging and desire only to avoid it, but the fact that jogging promotes health (when combined with my general desire for physical well-being) will generate a reason for me to value it and to do it. I may have no desire to join the army, but the fact that I care about my country and my family gives me reasons to do so anyway. Thus claims that clash with some of our immediate conscious desires may nevertheless constitute reasons for us, provided that they connect up with other elements in our motivational sets. Claims that can make no such connection will lack the status of reasons for action and for decision.

An interesting feature of Williams's approach is that he grounds his theory of deliberation in an account of the conditions of moral agency. What moves us to act are motives, and motives entail desires and other affective concerns. Consequently, for practical reasoning to result in action or in decisions to act, it, too, must incorporate affective modes of consciousness. His account allows for the correction and the expansion of motivating desires insofar as one can stand back from one's desires and reflect on them, but Williams resists the idea that practical deliberation can be disconnected from these desires altogether.[102] What he means to oppose is the rationalist view that there are some obligations that generate reasons for any rational agent to act, whatever her actual motivational profile may be. In opposing this view, however, Williams also sees himself as rejecting the possibility of impartiality.[103] And a consequence of eschewing impartiality, he says, is that "we may not be able to find anything that will meet a demand for justification made by someone standing outside" the perspective of the individual agent.[104] In contrast to Nussbaum, Williams's account of moral deliberation is affective all the way down, and he accepts the relativism that this feature seems to entail. But is relativism really a necessary consequence of this view? Williams concedes the point too easily. The rejection of rationalism need not entail a rejection of impartiality. A theory of moral judgment that takes affect seriously might still find grounds for common standards and for impartial decision making. Williams arrives at skeptical conclusions after rejecting Kantianism and utilitarianism, but there are other ways to understand impartiality, including the Humean account of moral sentiment that we take up in the next chapter. Impartiality matters if we care about achieving social coordination and honoring the duty of respect for persons. As Williams himself has said, it is important to find "a basis" for "respect for freedom and social justice and a critique of oppressive and deceitful institutions."[105] A basis for such respect that makes a legitimate claim to impartiality is not out of reach for affective deliberation. A theory of affective deliberation should aim for impartiality, and we should not suppose in advance that the effort will be fruitless.

One reason for Williams's skeptical conclusion may be the individualism that underlies his moral psychology. This is not to say that he is inattentive to the social context of moral life. Particularly in his work on shame (but not only there) Williams is sensitive to the ways in which social interactions and interdependence shape our moral experience. Yet in analyzing the nature and limits of moral judgment, he treats the moral agent as a relatively isolated unit. This individualism makes important resources unavailable to him, such as the social fabric of moral sentiment and the generalized standpoint of moral judgment that one finds in Hume, which help to sustain a measure of impartiality within judgment. What is needed is a careful look at the intersubjective constitution of the individual motivational profiles that animate and orient moral judgment. In addition, an account of affective deliberation needs a deliberative perspective that somehow moves beyond the personal desires of the individual agent. As Blackburn puts it, "if we have in ethics nothing but the clash of desires, attitudes, and emotions, then there is something misleading about the way ethical demands present themselves to us. For they present themselves as having their own independent force, as binding and inescapable."[106] This problem is largely neglected by Williams, but it has been explored in great depth by Michael Smith, another philosopher of moral judgment whose approach is explicitly intended to be Humean in key respects.

The distinctive character of moral demands gives rise to what Smith calls "the moral problem." On one hand, in moral practice "the participants are concerned to get the answers to moral questions *right*."[107] This fact refers to the objectivity of moral judgment; it implies that moral questions have correct answers and that the function of moral judgment is impartially to discover objective moral facts. On the other hand, moral judgments are practical. They seem to be "opinions about the reasons we have for behaving in certain ways," and "having such opinions is a matter of finding ourselves with a corresponding motivation to act."[108] As a consequence:

> Moral judgments have two features that pull in quite opposite directions from each other. The objectivity of moral judgment suggests that there are moral facts . . . and that our moral judgments express our beliefs about what these facts are. This enables us to make good sense of moral argument, and the like, but it leaves entirely mysterious how or why having a moral view is supposed to have special links with what we are motivated to do. And the practicality of moral judgment suggests just the opposite, that our moral judgments express our desires. While this enables us to make good sense of the link between having a moral view and being motivated, it leaves it entirely mysterious what a moral argument is supposed to be an argument about; the sense in which morality is supposed to be objective.[109]

Smith means to solve the moral problem. He begins by drawing a distinction between the "motivating" reasons that explain an agent's action and the "normative" reasons that justify the action. His solution consists in combining a Humean account of motivating reasons with an anti-Humean (essentially Kantian) account of normative reasons. The two types of reason have at least one thing in common, which is that "citing either would allow us to render an agent's action intelligible."[110] Yet they differ quite dramatically in other respects. For whereas motivating reasons are best construed as desires, normative reasons are properly described as truths or true beliefs.[111] Smith insists that this distinction is necessary to make sense of the fact that one can desire to act without valuing the action, or value something without desiring it.[112] In other words, "our motivating reasons may come apart from the normative reason claims that we accept."[113] Thus a drug addict may desire heroin even while thinking that heroin is ruining his life. Or one can believe that giving to charity is a good thing but lack the desire to do so. An account that simply equates normative reasons with personal desires cannot explain these relatively familiar phenomena,

Smith says. It cannot explain the two divergent features of moral judgment as being both practical and objective.

What is needed is a definition of value (that is, of normative reasons) that builds in something more objective than personal desire but that remains connected to the practical force of desire. Smith goes on to argue that normative reasons consist in "what we would desire to do if we were fully rational."[114] He specifies five criteria for full rationality:

> (1) the agent must have no false beliefs; (2) the agent must have all relevant true beliefs; (3) the agent must deliberate correctly; (4) the agent must not be suffering from compulsions, addictions, emotional disturbances, and the like; and (5) the agent's profile of desires must be internally consistent with one another, or systematically justifiable.[115]

Moral judgment consists in reflecting on the normative reasons for an action, and this means asking ourselves if we would desire the action under the conditions of full rationality.

One's actual desires have no place here. The truth of normative reason claims hinges on "a convergence in the desires of fully rational agents," but "reason itself determines the content of our fully rational desires, not the arbitrary fact that we have the actual desires that we have."[116] Smith contrasts his view with that of Williams on this point. On Williams's account, an agent's normative reasons for action are "relative to her actual desires."[117] In this sense, Williams ignores or denies the basic distinction between motivating and normative reasons that Smith is pressing here. In order to sustain the distinction, however, Smith must violate certain principles that are central to his own view. For example, his account of normative reasons requires that some desires are "produced by the agent's beliefs about the reasons she has, beliefs she acquires through rational deliberation."[118] Yet elsewhere he has insisted that beliefs and desires have fundamentally different "directions of fit."[119] Beliefs on their own cannot change what we want or wish for—beliefs by themselves cannot change the desires we have—because their function is not to change the world but only to understand or express it. In other words, beliefs about my hypothetical rational desires will not on their own constitute motivating reasons for me to adopt these desires. And if I do not adopt them, even in a hypothetical way, then the practicality of morality will not be preserved. Blackburn raises a similar objection, saying that "it is one thing to allow that something would be recommended" from Smith's fully rational standpoint "and another to value it."[120] In this respect, Smith's "solution" to the moral problem is no solution at all because it fails to establish the requisite balance between moral judgment's claim to objectivity and its claim to practicality. His solution achieves objectivity only by undermining practicality.

So we should question Smith's assertion that "reason itself" can generate desires. Given their different directions of fit, it is doubtful that the intellect on its own has a direct causal effect on desire. The intellect does allow us to reflect on the value of the particular desires that we have, and when it operates according to the criteria Smith sets down, then some of the desires that we begin with may well drop out, while new desires may enter in. But we can only ever reflect on the value of a particular desire in light of other desires that we have. The intellect enables us to determine whether or not the desires we have are marred by false beliefs, ignorance, or compulsion, and it informs us when our desires conflict with one another. But intellect by itself can neither generate new desires from whole cloth nor eradicate existing desires. It sometimes feels as if the intellect does have this power. Recall the earlier discussion of how reflection on one's misplaced anger may contribute to dissolving it. Without an intervening desire to relate to others in a way that is free of the emotional baggage of old resentments and past history, however, the effects of intellectual understanding on one's feelings would be null. Intellect can affect our affective modes of consciousness but only when it partners with affective modes of consciousness. Properly understood, practical reasoning is an exercise of this partnership. The claim that "reason itself determines the content of our fully rational desires" is therefore misleading.

If Williams gives a powerful account of the practicality of moral deliberation that comes at the expense of moral objectivity, Smith errs on the other side. In order to sustain some measure of objectivity in deliberation and avoid relativism, he develops what amounts to a rationalist account of moral motivation, despite having begun with an explicitly affective view of it. Not unlike Nussbaum, he lets the specter of relativism drive him to a rationalism that he originally seemed intent on avoiding. The final approach we shall consider in this chapter does a reasonably good job of striking a balance between the poles represented by Williams and Smith. Simon Blackburn offers an account of moral judgment that, unlike Smith's, remains true to its Humean roots and to an affective model of judgment, but that is nevertheless friendlier to impartiality than the view defended by Williams.

Recall that Williams rejected the aspiration to impartiality because he associated it with rationalism, not seeing that it might be possible to combine impartiality with affectively engaged deliberation. Whereas Williams "can be interpreted as mounting an escape bid from the *requirement* that one's behavior bear . . . impartial scrutiny," Blackburn finds that he himself feels "uncomfortable when I have to contemplate hypothetical conversations in which I could only present myself as unconcerned about common ground, and in which my final recourse would have to be some version of 'because it is mine.' "[121] So a central purpose of his theory is to show how moral judgments can achieve a measure of objectivity and impartiality without abandoning the affective basis that makes moral deliberation practical. In seeking to establish the objectivity of deliberation, his theory bears a certain affinity to Nussbaum's approach. Yet he rejects the belief in the inherent moral value of the external world that underlies her account.

Blackburn denies that "the order of the universe is an ethical order," and insists that "even if it were, we would have no access to what the order is."[122] Hence moral judgment cannot be construed as the true perception of intrinsic moral value. Instead, the "essential phenomenon" of ethics is "people valuing things."[123] Moreover, even "if we supposed that belief, denial, and so on were simply discussions of the way the world is, we would still face the open question" of "what importance to give it, what to do, and all the rest."[124] For any given fact, he insists, "there is a question of what to do about it."[125] This question can only be answered by reference to what *matters* to us, or what Blackburn refers to as our "fundamental concerns."[126] His view is a form of expressivism, as it holds that moral judgments express human valuation of the world rather than reporting or describing independent value inhering in the world. And for Blackburn the concerns that shape moral judgment engage affective as well as cognitive modes of consciousness. Moral judgment is a process of turning input, consisting of our empirical perceptions about the world, into output, or evaluative decisions about how we should act: "So we can see our cognitive relations with the world, our capacity to represent it as being one way or another, as tied in partnership with the mechanisms of emotion and of affect that turn the input into output. Our emotional dispositions and our representations act together to issue in action, with neither apparently able to achieve its results without the other."[127] In the absence of affective engagement—namely, the concerns that make certain things rather than others matter to us—"the will is rudderless" with regard to both action and judgment.[128]

Moreover, the concerns that guide moral judgment are not fundamentally different from the concerns that guide us in other domains. It is true that we commonly believe moral claims to have a special status that carries unique force. In the best cases, this sense of the special force of moral considerations can move us to make the effort to do good things that we might otherwise avoid doing. But human societies also pay a heavy price for the common belief in the special status of morality. "Moral certainties, and the causes and crusades mounted in their name, are dangerous things," and people "seldom treat each other as badly as they do when they feel they have a right or preferably a duty to behave as they do."[129] The conviction that moral considerations are wholly different from—and in some sense sovereign over—the basic concerns that animate us in other areas of life opens the door to the kinds of moralism, including fanaticism, that tend to disrupt society and interfere with individual well-being. Still, the phenomenology of moral commitments does set them apart from "mere desires and preferences."[130] They simply feel different, and a theory of moral judgment needs to account for this difference, at least as a phenomenological matter.

To this end, Blackburn invokes the notion of an ascending staircase to analogize both the distinct feeling of moral obligation and the continuum between moral and nonmoral considerations. He begins from the thought that what distinguishes moral considerations is that they "are other people's business."[131] A moral transgression is something that "is of legitimate concern to others" because it involves a violation not merely of some particular interest but of a general norm in which all have a stake.[132] We should think about such concerns in terms of "a staircase of practical and emotional ascent:"

> At the bottom are simple preferences, likes, and dislikes. . . . We can then ascend to reactions to such reactions. Suppose you become angry at someone's behavior. I may be angry at you for being angry, and I may express this by saying it is none of your business. Perhaps it was a private matter. At any rate, it is not a moral issue. Suppose, on the other hand, I share your anger or feel "at one" with you for so reacting. It may not stop there, but I may also feel strongly disposed to encourage others to share the same anger. By then I am clearly treating the matter as one of public concern, something like a moral issue. I have come to regard the sentiment as legitimate. Going up another step, the sentiment may even become *compulsory* in my eyes. . . . This should all be seen as an ascending staircase, a spiral of emotional identifications and demands.[133]

The key point of the staircase analogy is that "there is no one place on the staircase that identifies a precise point, before which we are not in the sphere of the ethical, and after which we are."[134] Moral claims are indeed different from others, but they are different in the degree to which they bear on social coordination, not different in the kinds of concerns upon which they rest. Ethics has the importance it does not because it serves a closed set of uniquely "moral" concerns—God's commands, say, or universal obligations derived from pure practical reason—but "because of its place in co-ordinating our social lives. It makes things go better."[135] And it makes things go better relative to the standard set by the common human concerns that orient us in other domains, not in view of some different and distinctively "moral" scale. Along similar lines, Erving Goffman has argued that morality arises when ordinary social anticipations are transformed into "normative expectations, into righteously presented demands" or "moral claims."[136] From this perspective, morality involves (a) *demands* on us (b) by *others* (c) that are *justified*. It involves demands in the sense that morality means to regulate the future action of individuals by means of settled expectations. These expectations are imposed (directly and indirectly, consciously and unconsciously) by the others with whom one shares a common interest in social coordination. These expectations are justified to the extent that they effectively regulate actions in which all have a stake, and do so in ways that serve common human concerns.

So moral judgment transpires on the terrain of our common concerns and is guided by them. As in Williams, our judgments always reflect the background of affective dispositions and desires that constitute our "motivational sets" and animate our actions. But in contrast to Williams, Blackburn holds that this feature of judgment need not stand in the way of impartiality. There "does exist a voice of humanity," he insists, and this can underwrite "the drive to impartiality inherent in universal prescriptivism."[137] Indeed, it can establish the "objectivity" of moral virtue. Blackburn appeals to human nature here, and to what he calls "Hume's reminder of the basic building blocks of human living."[138] Despite the diversity that we see across societies, we should also remember "the constancies." We are all "social animals, with certain biological needs," for instance; consequently, "we have to coordinate our efforts; we have to establish systems of property and promise-keeping and sometimes even government."[139] These universal concerns establish the objective moral value of the decisions and actions that answer to them. Likewise, cruelty is morally objectionable "because it exhibits the intention to cause pain," and pain is something that human beings by nature are concerned to avoid.[140] Moral judgment will be impartial, on this view, to the extent that it embodies concerns that are common among human beings in general rather than merely conventional for a particular society or idiosyncratic to an individual person. Notice, however, that the objectivity of moral judgment in this sense does not rest on the perception of intrinsic moral value in the world. There are no inherent moral values in the external world because moral value is a function of human concerns. In this respect, Blackburn's view differs from that of Nussbaum, despite the fact that both make appeal to human nature. Moreover, Blackburn's standard of human nature refers to common human desires and aversions rather than to an ideal of human perfection, or the "complete" human life, as in Nussbaum. In these respects, the sources of normativity are meant to be more empirically verifiable and less controversial. For Blackburn, too, all our profiles of concern are in some degree "contingent" because there is no necessity in their being as they are.[141] Although he does not spell this out explicitly, his thinking in this regard seems to be as follows: Human nature is relatively constant over time but it is an empirical phenomenon and in principle open to change. However improbable it may be that human beings should come at some future date to universally desire pain rather than seek to avoid it, it would not be logically impossible for them to do so. In this sense, the human aversion to pain, however common, remains contingent. If it were to change, cruelty would not be so objectionable. Insofar as we can now identify some general human concerns, however, we can say that there are general, objective moral values. These values even may sustain categorical imperatives in the sense that there will be some things we are morally obligated to do, or refrain from doing, whatever our immediate desires may be. Thus "avoiding cruelty or fraud or injustice can be a fixed, non-negotiable prompt of concern" for us even in the face of additional, countervailing personal desires.[142] A Humean, Blackburn says, "can issue the injunction to avoid cruelty—whether you want to do so or not."[143] This account thus suggests the possibility of affective but impartial judgment.

The path to affective impartiality runs through what Blackburn (following Hume) refers to as "our sentimental natures,"[144] and this represents another way in which affect figures in moral judgment. Impartiality, or the ability to adopt a common point of view, involves abstracting from one's own self-interest but not by means of disengaged intellect. Instead, we achieve impartiality by sympathetically experiencing the sentiments of others. Nothing other than human sentiments could provide the ultimate basis of impartial moral judgment because, on Blackburn's view, moral value is a function of human concerns, not something that inheres intrinsically in the world. Insofar as "we naturally sympathize with the pleasures and pains of others," we tend to "praise and encourage actions that promote pleasures and avoid pains, and dislike and discourage actions that do the reverse."[145] Human beings are so constituted as to be affected by the sentiments of others; sympathy engenders a natural resonance between us. This tendency can be fostered or hindered by socialization,[146] and it is enhanced by the natural desire for esteem.[147] The latter motivates us to consult the sentiments of others in our decisions and actions; we wish to be valued by them and this requires that we orient ourselves to their values, to the sentiments that shape their concerns. In doing so, we come to adopt a perspective that transcends the limited standpoint of individual interest and idiosyncratic desire. This perspective facilitates forms of judgment that rise to the level of the ethical in that they make assessments on the basis of public concerns rather than private likes and dislikes. On this basis, one can distinguish personally disliking a man from impartially determining that he has done wrong. Yet the difference lies not in a distinction between reason and passion; it is rather a question of whose sentiments are included in the process of assessment.

The common point of view is not unique to the domain of ethics. Life is full of instances in which our own success depends on the ability to make assessments that leave aside our personal likes and dislikes, as well as our interests:

> If my enemy does something, such as fortify a city, and does it well, on the one hand I can curse it as an obstacle to my own ambitions or my own security, but on the other hand I can also admire it as well-adapted to its purpose, strong, well-formed, and so on. These are impersonal standards for good fortifications: they describe what anybody who fortifies a city is likely to want. Is it strange that we should be able to perform this feat of abstracting from our own interests in this way? Presumably not, for we need to tell *in general* what are the good features of a well-fortified city.[148]

So there is nothing uniquely ethical or moral about the capacity to adopt a generalized standpoint, and there should be nothing mysterious about it. The familiar desires to be valued by others and to accomplish our settled purposes drive us to seek impartiality, and our tendency to sympathize with the sentiments of others enables us to achieve it. Blackburn acknowledges that the generalized standpoint of sympathy "is not a move to the interests of *everybody* considered impartially."[149] In incorporating the sentiments of others it focuses on those who are most directly affected by the quality or action under consideration, and among these persons we tend to be most attentive to those we know best and care about most. In other words, "we assess people by considering their impact on a fairly immediate circle: friends, family, business associates, for example."[150] To be sure, the need to realize our settled purposes will sometimes require us to consider the interests of others beyond this narrow circle. We find ourselves confronted with "continual contradictions" or conflict in our relations with others when we fail to consider their sentiments. This fact puts pressure on sympathy to extend itself over a wider range, and encourages our judgments to become more fully generalized. Yet even here the standpoint of moral judgment is based on what people feel (on our actual and imagined perceptions of their sentiments), and this fact appears to make judgment vulnerable to the dangers of mere conventionalism. To address this difficulty Blackburn's standard of human nature steps in, providing an additional basis for objectivity. Judgments that run afoul of universal human concerns will be unsound, whether or not they incorporate the actual sentiments of particular others. There are objective grounds to disapprove of cruelty even if no one in a particular community believes that cruelty to, say, religious minorities is wrong.

This brief synopsis of Blackburn's view suggests that it may be possible for judgment to be both affectively engaged and impartial, or objective. It suggests that a Humean approach may hold promise for rethinking the rationalist understanding of moral judgment and public deliberation. Like the other theorists of affect examined in this chapter, Blackburn insists that practical deliberation cannot proceed on the basis of pure intellect. Unlike most of them, however, he is committed to the ideal of impartiality and the possibility of generalized norms. Yet Blackburn's model is limited in its own way, too. His appeal to human nature as a mechanism for checking conventionalism is insufficiently attentive to the difficulties of knowing what human nature consists in and to the controversies surrounding this question. Human nature as a guide for judgment always must be interpreted, and our interpretations are apt to be influenced by the same conventional opinions that the standard of human nature is intended to correct. These opinions, in turn, are likely to reflect prevailing social exclusions and power inequities. In short, Blackburn's account neglects the ways in which moral judgment is inevitably a political phenomenon, or sensitive to the political context in which it occurs. Nor does he explore the implications this model of judgment might have for political deliberation.[151] The remainder of this book addresses these issues.

Extensive as the existing literature on affective judgment is, it has not generated an adequate model of affective impartiality for moral judgment and public deliberation in the context of liberal-democratic politics. Since much of this literature comes from moral philosophers, who are primarily addressing debates in metaethics, its limits for public deliberation ought not be held against it. In drawing attention to these limits, my purpose is not to criticize these contributors for failing to answer questions they never set out to address. My aim is instead to indicate where we ought to go from here, and how this previous work might usefully be extended to the study of political life. We need a theory of judgment that goes beyond emotions to include concerns as well, that goes beyond concern for particular others to include the concern for justice, that reflects the full integration of cognitive and affective states within practical reasoning, and that attends to the social and political contexts within which judgment and deliberation occur.

For inspiration, we turn next to Hume. His account of moral sentiment offers valuable resources for thinking beyond the limits of contemporary approaches, resources that have been largely neglected by recent theories of moral judgment and democratic deliberation. Hume's model is not perfect but it represents an important alternative path to the impartial deliberation for which our contemporary theories of justice rightly aim.

CHAPTER THREE

Moral Sentiment and the Politics of Judgment in Hume

HUME TREATED moral judgment as a reflective passion, a form of sentiment in which thought and feeling are integrated at the deepest level, yet structured in highly specified ways. Although he regarded sentiments as key to judgment, he did give the intellect an important role. He also took pains to establish the objectivity and impartiality of judgment. In fact, Humean judgment achieves its impartiality through the mechanism of a generalized perspective, and in this respect it bears a striking affinity to contemporary rationalist accounts of moral judgment and public deliberation. Yet Hume shows us why it is important to achieve impartiality in judgment without sacrificing affect, and how it is possible to do so. The generalized perspective of judgment, as he conceives it, grows out of, rather than abstracts from, the usual sources of human agency as they are found in our common attachments and desires. Indeed, Humean judgment gains both motivational efficacy and normative authority from its footing in these affective concerns. It is a naturalistic account, but one that recognizes the social and cultural dimensions of human nature and that makes a place for moral agency.

Drawing mainly on his *Treatise of Human Nature* and *An Enquiry Concerning the Principles of Morals*, this chapter elaborates the operations of judgment as moral sentiment, showing how Hume's concept of judgment avoids narrow subjectivism and achieves a significant measure of impartiality without sacrificing affective engagement. At the same time, I offer a critical analysis of the ways in which the structure of the political order permeates the passions on which affective judgment rests. Insofar as moral sentiment is socially constituted, and hence affected by existing laws and political practices, it will tend to reflect prevailing social inequalities and exclusions, thus perpetuating rather than correcting prejudice. The natural limits of sympathy on Hume's account exacerbate this danger. For all its value in showing how affective and cognitive modes of consciousness interact within moral judgment and deliberation, then, Hume's theory is incomplete on its own terms. The irrepressible political dimensions of moral sentiment mean that Hume's account needs to be supplemented by a commitment to democratic equality, liberal rights, and contestatory public debate, a commitment that takes us beyond Hume's own philosophy. To achieve its great promise of affectively engaged but impartial judgment, the Humean approach needs liberal-democratic politics.

IMPARTIALITY AND THE FEELING OF JUDGMENT

Hume's account of the affective sources of moral judgment follows from the conviction—shared by men such as Shaftesbury and Hutcheson, his predecessors in the moral sentiment school—that reason on its own cannot motivate action.[1] The faculty of reason, as he uses the term, is limited to discerning relations between things, either "the abstract relations of our ideas" (demonstrative reason) or "those relations of objects, of which experience only gives us information," including "matters of fact" (probabilistic, practical reason).[2] Probabilistic reason alerts us to relations of identity or resemblance and relations of causality; it identifies the means needed to achieve our ends; and it gives us access to matters of fact. Although reason as the "inferences and conclusions of the understanding" can "discover truths," Hume says, "where the truths which they discover are indifferent, and beget no desire or aversion, they can have no influence on conduct and behavior."[3]

Since he is convinced that morality does influence behavior, he concludes that moral judgments must not derive from reason alone (T 457).[4] Insofar as they direct our actions, moral judgments must incorporate desires and aversions, or affective concerns. These concerns motivate and guide moral judgment by giving us things to care about. As Hume puts it, "where the objects [of reasoning] themselves do not affect us, their connexion can never give them any influence" on our actions (T 414). So the distinctions between good and bad, right and wrong, virtue and vice that constitute moral judgments and guide moral actions are motivated at least in part by affective concerns in the form of desires and aversions. Such concerns provide the grounds of judgment: We judge favorably things that generate pleasure (properly conceived) and we disapprove of things that generate pain. Furthermore, the approval and disapproval that we feel on contemplating particular actions and types of character are themselves sentiments. For "when you pronounce any action or character to be vicious," Hume says, "you mean nothing, but that from the constitution of your nature you have a feeling or sentiment of blame from the contemplation of it" (T 469). To judge someone virtuous "is nothing but to *feel* a satisfaction of a particular kind from the contemplation of a character," he insists; "the very *feeling* constitutes our praise or admiration" (T 471; emphasis in original). And our praise or admiration forms the judgment.

Critics of moral sentiment theory often worry that grounding moral judgment in affective modes of consciousness means subjecting judgment to the arbitrariness commonly associated with passions and emotions. This was certainly Kant's view,[5] and similar concerns lie behind contemporary rejections of Humeanism as "subjectivist" and "emotivist."[6] Hume was very much aware of this danger, and he set out to show how moral judgments might achieve a significant measure of reflective impartiality and yet remain sources of personal engagement. This impartiality is established in several ways: first, through the social fabric of moral sentiment; secondly, through the generalized perspective of moral sentiment; and third, through the mechanism of human nature that underlies moral sentiment.

The Social Fabric of Moral Sentiment

The social fabric of moral sentiment as Hume conceives it means that our judgments always reflect more than merely private responses to the world. What could be more obvious than the fact that feelings of approval and disapproval—our habits of evaluation—are in large part socially constituted? But Hume's point goes beyond the simple assertion that individuals tend to adopt the norms of their society or social group. Indeed, he denies that there ever could be such a thing as a truly individual evaluator at all. Judgment is a social phenomenon because moral feeling has an intersubjective basis. The faculty of sympathy is the key. Sympathy communicates the sentiments of others to us so that we feel their pleasures and pains, and our judgments are built upon this communication (T 316-17). Communication is facilitated by the fact that the same range of passions affects us all, although the objects of the passions may differ. Nothing that one person can feel will be totally unfamiliar to another, for no one can "be actuated by any affection, of which all others are not, in some degree, susceptible" (T 575f).

It is important to see that "sympathy" in Hume, in contrast to contemporary usage of the term, is not primarily a disposition or a virtue but rather a faculty of the mind with an informational function, much like imagination or memory. Like them, it operates automatically within consciousness not simply as the result of individual will or character.[7] It should therefore be distinguished from "benevolence" or "pity," passions that move us to act out of concern for another. Sympathy as an informational faculty is not a passion at all, and it entails no desire, hence it is not itself a source of action. And it need not involve a care for the well-being of the person whose sentiments it conveys. As Hume says, "my sympathy with another may give me the sentiment of pain and disapprobation, when any object is presented, that has a tendency to give him uneasiness; tho' I may not be willing to sacrifice any thing of my own interest, or cross any of my passions, for his satisfaction" (T 586). In this sense, the account of judgment Hume offers, although grounded in sympathy, by no means assumes or entails that persons will behave benevolently.

It is true that Hume's use of the term fluctuates somewhat. He occasionally does use it to convey a disposition that resembles benevolence, as when he says that sympathy "makes me concern'd for the present sorrows of a stranger" (T 385). This fluctuation has puzzled many readers.[8] The fact is that Hume makes reference to what he calls "different kinds of sympathy" throughout the text (T 387), although he is insufficiently careful in distinguishing them from one another and holding to the distinctions consistently. The primary sense of sympathy (call it "S1") is the faculty of mind with the informational function. Sympathy in this sense enables us to resonate with the affective experiences of others, to be moved by the sentiments that others express. Sympathy in this sense is not itself a passion, hence not itself an affective state, but it communicates passions to us and stimulates similar passions in us. This communication of passions forms the basis of moral sentiment, as it gives rise to feelings of approval and disapproval. As a vehicle for the communication of sentiments, sympathy in this form necessarily entails (or is always accompanied by) affective modes of consciousness, even though it is not itself an affective state. Moreover, to the extent that sympathy generates feelings of approval and disapproval it is likewise inextricably bound up with the affective states that constitute moral sentiments. The second sense of sympathy in Hume (call it "S2") *is* itself an affective state, or a form of passion. Sympathy in this sense involves caring for another person; it is the benevolence or pity that "makes me concern'd for the present sorrows of a stranger."

Although the two forms of sympathy are distinct, there is a way in which they naturally come together. S1 can cause us to react to the suffering (or pleasure) of another person in ways that may mimic the feeling of concern for that person. When S1 conveys to me the pain you experience as a victim of racial discrimination, the unpleasantness I vicariously experience generates in me a feeling of disapproval for the practice of discrimination. This moral sentiment does not depend on my feeling a form of S2 toward you, but it may resemble that type of benevolence from the outside. In other words, it may appear as if I disapprove of discrimination because I care about you personally (or because you personally matter to me), but such is not necessarily the case in the operation of S1. At the same time, however, Hume makes it clear that S1 may be facilitated by S2, or by concern for the relevant others whose sentiments S1 conveys. We tend to be moved more powerfully by the sentiments of those we know and care about. Moreover, how deeply we enter into the sentiments of others may mark the difference between sympathy as a faculty of communication and sympathy as a feeling of concern (T 389). S1 can be "extensive" (T 386) or narrow, depending in part on the strength of the original sentiment communicated, on the proximity of the persons involved, and on other contingencies such as the interests and dispositions of the sympathizer. S2 can be either strong or weak (depending on the intensity of the feeling of concern).[9] We shall have more to say about these factors presently. For now it is enough to note that the more powerfully I experience the pains and pleasures of another the more likely I am to care about him or her, all else being equal. Yet even where the effects of sympathy are too weak to motivate concern for the well-being of another, the sentiments conveyed still provide the grounds of judgment (T 586).

The key point is that in assessing the phenomena that confront us in the world, human beings are continuously responding to the responses of others, and sympathy gives us access to these responses. "As in strings equally wound up," Hume says, "the motion of one communicates itself to the rest; so all the affections readily pass from one person to another, and beget correspondent movements in every human creature" (T 576). Sympathy reverberates within and between persons in complex ways to generate moral sentiments of approval and disapproval: "Thus the pleasure, which a rich man receives from his possessions, being thrown upon the beholder, causes a pleasure and esteem; which sentiments again, being perceiv'd and sympathiz'd with, encrease the pleasure of the possessor; and being once more reflected, become a new foundation for pleasure and esteem in the beholder" (T 365). Money is a primary pleasure for the rich man because of the security it brings and the goods it makes available. When I contemplate my rich neighbor, sympathy makes present to me his pleasure in this regard, which causes me to approve (or, as Hume says, "esteem") his condition, or to value wealth—being rich seems to be a good thing. My esteem then becomes a new source of pleasure to my neighbor, who enjoys his riches even more knowing how much they are generally valued. Pride adds a secondary pleasure to the primary one, increasing it and making it more complex. It also gives me further cause for valuing wealth, as sympathy conveys to me the additional enjoyment that pride generates for him.[10] Through such layered reverberations of sentiment, sympathy gives rise to judgments of value, which are thus intersubjective at the deepest level.[11]

The intersubjective character of judgment should not be taken to preclude the possibility of individuals who can, so to speak, think for themselves. Moral judgment is not a matter of blind conformity to social norms. Where the mores of a society reflect "bigotry and superstition" they "confound the sentiments of morality," and a good judge will look beyond them.[12] Hume insists that the prevalence of prejudice and false opinion in an age is not sufficient to justify its moral mistakes, such as slavery among the ancients. Yet the way to avoid, or resist, the mistakes of one's social group is to be in conversation with a wider range of persons, not to turn inward and disengage from social commerce. The relevant "conversation" may be metaphorical—facilitated through reading literature and history, for example—but it is necessary. We are by nature interdependent and communicative social beings, and so it is not surprising that our standards of value are intersubjectively arrived at. Leaving aside those with serious personality disorders, no one generates all their own values from whole cloth. The modern individualism that one finds in Kant and Nietzsche, and that has had a recent renaissance in the work of theorists such as George Kateb, was foreign to Hume.[13] Yet there *is* a place for individual judgment in Hume's account. My judgment and decisions may reflect the intersubjective background that constitutes moral sentiment but when I am asked to judge or decide in any particular case, it is *I* who must do so. Particular acts of moral judgment and practical deliberation are carried out by individuals, and individuals bear responsibility for the decisions they make.

Nevertheless, the social character of moral sentiment partially mitigates the danger of narrow subjectivism raised by treating moral judgment as a feeling, for our judgments (like our feelings) are never solely our own. This intersubjectivity also makes moral judgment a political phenomenon. If our feelings of approval and disapproval arise partly in response to the reactions of others, the nature of our social relations will have a significant impact on these feelings. Imbalances of power that are a function of the political order exaggerate the perceived distance and differences between persons and may disrupt the operation of sympathy (in both senses of the word). In this respect, the political order inevitably inscribes moral sentiment and the judgments to which it gives rise with the prevailing relations of power. So although the social fabric of moral sentiment means that moral judgments are more than merely idiosyncratic likes and dislikes, it cannot by itself adequately insulate judgment from the pressures of social life and the effects of collective prejudice. On its own, it cannot make our judgments sufficiently impartial. Impartiality requires not merely intersubjectivity but a properly generalized perspective.

The Generalized Perspective of Moral Sentiment

Although moral judgment is grounded in feelings, only certain kinds of feelings count. It is only "when a character is considered in general, without reference to our particular interest, that it causes such a feeling or sentiment, as denominates it morally good or evil" (T 472). Through sympathy and the exercise of imagination we experience the pleasure or pain that a given character trait generates for the person who possesses it or those affected by it. Only sentiments arising from such a perspective, which is detached from private interests, can establish virtues and vices or generate obligations. The shift to the generalized standpoint changes the meaning and moral significance of the sentiments that result. Whereas my personal aversion to pain tells me that cruelty would be bad for me and that I should fear it, the generalized standpoint tells me that cruelty is in general bad for everybody, and that there are therefore grounds to disapprove of it.[14] The difference between fear and disapproval in this context is the difference between a personal perspective of prudential concern and a common perspective oriented toward social coordination. The former tells me that I should avoid being treated cruelly; the latter tells me that I should avoid *being* cruel. The generalized perspective marks the difference between moral sentiments and other kinds of feelings by introducing impartiality into judgment. Just as we habitually (even automatically) correct for the impressions of our physical senses, so we adjust our moral judgments to prevent them from being distorted by circumstances and self-love (T 581, 583; E 63n1, 64, 65n1). Despite appearances, I know that the houses I observe from my seat on an airplane at 29,000 feet are not actually the size of ants. Similarly, although I want my candidate to win and his opponent to lose, I can recognize (perhaps even admire) the brilliance of his opponent's well-run campaign. We compensate for distortions in judgment (whether perceptual or interest-based) all the time; the impartiality of moral judgment is not unique in this regard. On the basis of this impartiality Hume can distinguish, as one commentator puts it, between what people *do* approve and what they *should* approve.[15]

This distinction, which implies that people sometimes fail to approve what they should, suggests that the generalized perspective may not come to us as automatically as do corrections of the physical senses. Hume offers it as an ideal rather than as a fact. Yet one of the appealing things about Hume's moral theory is that his ideals always have a footing in the facts about who we are as human beings. In this case, the generalized perspective builds on and extends the automatic but minimalist operation of sympathy, which is a natural feature of our moral psychology but which is not naturally as extensive or as free from self-love as impartial judgment requires.[16] For one thing, sympathy does not naturally extend equally to all affected parties but tends to privilege one's nearest and dearest. It also may be distorted by self-interest and obstructed by perceived differences among persons, or by the faculty of comparison, which reverses sensations and accounts for envy and malice (T 376-77). The generalized perspective therefore must be learned and cultivated. It needs the support of common social virtues, including compassion and self-restraint. Education and socialization are important. We shall have more to say about the cultivation of moral sentiment in later chapters.

The pressures attendant on living together with others also help to foster the development of corrected judgment:

> When we form our judgments of persons, merely from the tendency of their characters to our own benefit, or to that of our friends, we find so many contradictions to our sentiments in society and conversation, and such an uncertainty from the incessant changes of our situation, that we seek some other standard of merit and demerit, which may not admit of so great variation. (T 583)

Judgments based on self-love and limited sympathy turn out to be poor guides for action because they regularly conflict with the judgments of others, and we cannot operate successfully on this basis in a world characterized by interdependence. We need common moral standards because we depend on others to meet our basic needs and satisfy our fundamental purposes. The only way to achieve the needed social coordination is for persons to reliably interact on the basis of common rules and shared standards. Moreover, in the absence of a perspective that delivers critical distance, our own sentiments would regularly conflict with one another over time as we encounter new situations.[17] Too much fluctuation in the evaluative standards that guide practical deliberation renders deliberation unstable. We need our standards of approval and disapproval to be fairly consistent over time in order for them to serve as useful guides to action, and hence we have grounds to strive for a generalized perspective. Moreover, to exclude the sentiments of certain persons without adequate grounds would be to demonstrate a lack of the moral quality that Hume called "humanity."[18] So although this perspective is not automatic, it does have a basis in the natural operations of sympathy, in the virtue of humanity, and in the desire to have stable guides for action. Consequently, "experience soon teaches us this method of correcting our sentiments" (T 582). And in cultivating the generalized perspective we foster impartiality in our judgments.

The sentiments that give rise to moral judgment within the generalized perspective respond to the perceived usefulness and agreeableness of the object under consideration (T 590-91). The pleasing sensation of approval arises when we perceive some action or character to be either useful or agreeable to the person who has it or those affected by it (T 591). When I make a judgment about the courage of Martin Luther King, for instance, the faculty of sympathy allows me to register the pleasures and pains of King himself and those affected by his courage in light of its usefulness and agreeableness. Their (imagined) feelings are made lively in my mind in the form of impressions, and it is on this basis that I experience the sentiment of approval or disapproval.[19] In appealing to usefulness and agreeableness, Hume emphasizes that we evaluate actions and characters based on their general rather than their particular effects. For example, a benevolent person is esteemed as virtuous because benevolence is normally useful to society, even though in a particular case some accident may "prevent its operation, and incapacitate him from being serviceable to his friends and country" (T 584). This is another aspect of the generalized perspective. The imagination generalizes the effects of benevolence, thereby allowing us to pass "easily from the cause to the effect, without considering that there are still some circumstances wanting to render the cause a compleat one" (T 585). Because we respond to the general effects of certain actions and characters, we need not be personally familiar with those involved in order to form a judgment in any particular case. Hence we "blame equally a bad action, which we read of in history, with one perform'd in our neighborhood t'other day" (T 584). Without ever having known Pol Pot or the victims of his abuses we have cause to disapprove of him, and if we adopt Hume's generalized perspective, we will do so.

Perceptions of usefulness and agreeableness have a cognitive dimension because they involve reasoning about matters of fact and relations of cause and effect. Hume even remarks in the *Enquiry* that "it is requisite to employ much reasoning, in order to feel the proper sentiment" in moral matters (E 5-6, 125-26). One is likely to feel very differently about a man who has just shot her neighbor when reason alerts her to the fact that the man acted in self-defense. Moreover, part of what accounts for the difference in feeling here is the thought that wanton violence could not be generally useful. Without being able to reason, we could not feel in the appropriate ways. Then, too, human pleasures and pains themselves often involve reflection. The pain of discrimination, for instance, could only be experienced by a being with complex cognitive capacities. In this respect, judgment clearly combines affective modes of consciousness with cognitive ones. The sentiment-based account is not purely affective, then, and it is not unreflective. But the key to moral judgment in Hume is reflective *feeling*. In achieving impartiality, judgment never abandons the affective mode of consciousness. Consequently, moral judgment operates by means of "engagement and captivation," as one interpreter puts it, rather than dispassionate calculation.[20]

Because the generalized perspective incorporates the sentiments of those who are affected by a given character or action as well as the sentiments of the person whose action or character it is, the possibility of divergent inputs always exists. This is another way in which moral judgment is intrinsically political. Rather than looking to an external standard of right or to the commands of a higher authority, Humean judgment represents the sentiments of those affected. In a pluralistic polity that accepts diversity of interest and opinion, moral judgment inevitably will be marked by a measure of internal conflict. It will be inscribed with the same degree and type of contestation found in the polity as a whole. The nature of the political order thus affects the character of moral judgment. What happens, then, when the sentiments of the relevant parties, as communicated by sympathy, conflict? Are we to take all such sentiments at face value, giving equal weight to each? In evaluating the courage of Martin Luther King, for instance, we are faced with such a conflict. Although useful and agreeable to most African Americans at the time, white segregationists had a different experience of it. In communicating to us the sentiments of those affected by King's courage, sympathy will convey feelings of both pleasure and pain, sentiments of both gratitude and resentment. Should we approve or disapprove of it? How are we to reach an evaluation in the face of opposing inputs?

Hume himself offers little direct guidance in this regard. Adam Smith's modifications to the theory of moral sentiment were intended in part to address this difficulty. Smith pointed out that in assessing an action or character we need to consider not only the sentiments of those affected but also the propriety of these sentiments. Is your anger (and the pain it embodies) suitable or proportional "to the cause or object which excites it?"[21] If not, this sentiment ought not figure in the moral judgment of an impartial spectator. The standard of propriety has implications for the quandary that arises for the generalized perspective in the face of opposing inputs. In light of this standard, some of the sentiments of affected parties will carry normative weight but others will be ruled out of consideration. Smith was right to emphasize the importance of adopting a critical perspective on the sentiments that constitute moral judgment. Without this, moral judgment is bound to be incoherent (because internally inconsistent) and normatively suspect (where it incorporates sentiments that are themselves indecent or unjust).

Even though Hume himself never articulated a systematic standard for assessing the propriety or normative value of the sentiments that figure in moral judgment, he did recognize the importance of critical reflection in this regard. He makes it clear that the sentiments that fig-ure as inputs in the generalized perspective are in principle subject to moral evaluation. Hume had little patience with sentiments that were colored by prejudice, ignorance, or superstition. The sentiments "are perverted" in a person who "never sufficiently enlarges his compre-hension, or forgets his interest as a friend or enemy."[22] Prejudice, he says, "is destructive of sound judgment" and generates sentiments "which may be pronounced erroneous."[23] Hence "the taste of all indi-viduals is not upon an equal footing" in moral matters as much as in aesthetic ones.[24] He mentions in this regard "the want of humanity and of decency" found in characters drawn by ancient poets such as Homer. Their objectionable character discredits the normative force of their feelings. Consequently, "we are not interested in the fortunes and sentiments of such rough heroes." Indeed, he says, "we cannot prevail on ourselves to enter into [such a poet's] sentiments, or bear an af-fection to characters, which we plainly discover to be blameable."[25] So the normative force accorded to particular feelings within the gen-eralized perspective depends in some measure on the character that stands behind them, specifically on whether this character is itself en-dorsable by an impartial observer in light of the sentiments of those affected by it. It also depends on whether the sentiments in question answer to the virtue of "humanity" and whether they are attentive to the relevant facts. Just as the feelings of a bigot should carry no weight with us, so the sentiments of a man who is mistaken about the causes, character, or consequences of an action should not affect our assess-ment of the action.

Thus in some cases there will be grounds for weighting opposing inputs differently. If we consider, from within a suitably general stand-point, the beliefs and character traits that motivate the segregationist's negative response to the courage of Martin Luther King, can we en-dorse them? Do the dispositions that stand behind the African-Ameri-can response to King stimulate sentiments of praise or blame? If we find that we can approve of one set of sentiments but not of the other (as seems likely in this case), then we have grounds to weigh them differently. This differential weighting can help resolve the conflict of sentiments within the generalized standpoint and facilitate a determi-nate evaluation in the matter at hand. In this sense, moral evaluation is often an iterative process. Any one act of evaluation may call for (and build on) other evaluations, and it should be responsive to the ideal that Hume called "humanity."

There are nevertheless bound to be some cases in which a conflict of inputs cannot be resolved by iterations of evaluation and differential weighting. Sometimes the sentiments of those affected by a given character trait or action will conflict without there being grounds for us to disapprove of any of them. Here we face irreducible moral conflict, which makes a singular, determinate evaluation impossible. This indeterminacy may be thought regrettable but it should not be seen as constituting a flaw in the Humean approach to judgment. Instead it reflects a real and ineradicable feature of moral life, which is that human goods are irreducibly plural.[26] The things that matter to us do not always (or perhaps ever) fit together into a single harmonious whole. Therefore the soundest moral judgment sometimes is a mixed one. In a similar manner, when a given quality is agreeable but not useful (or vice versa) it will be difficult to arrive at a determinate evaluation. Courage is a quality that Hume thinks we tend to find immediately agreeable (E 90) but it may be put to ill purpose, as in the case of brave military conquests that bring misery to many people. In this case the generalized standpoint should represent feelings of both pleasure and pain. Yet what could be more familiar than the experience of finding that, on reflection, our moral evaluation of some phenomenon is mixed? The suicide bomber is a figure who inspires a certain uneasy fascination in many of us today because our revulsion for his act is mixed with the fact that we cannot help but be impressed by his courage. We can deplore the act, and we should do so, but our disapproval does not say all that may legitimately be said on the matter. There is a moral remainder here, which consists in our common response (however uncomfortable it makes us in this case) to the agreeableness of courage. Hence it is not surprising to hear someone remark that it is sad, and a waste, that the suicide bomber (or the despot, or the conqueror, or the traitor) used his admirable courage to such barbarous purpose. This judgment reflects a suitably dual evaluation. A model of moral judgment that would generate a single, perfectly determinate evaluation in such cases could never be true to the complexity of human experience and the plurality of human goods. It is a virtue, not a vice, of Humean judgment that it makes room for this complexity.

The faculty of sympathy allows us to generate abstract principles of right and wrong that transcend the narrowness of self-interest and personal prejudice, which is the key to impartiality, but it does not lead to a perfectly universal point of view. The generalized perspective of moral judgment never reaches to the level of perfect universalism because sympathy is limited in its effects. Much as we feel our immediate interests more powerfully than those that are remote, so we are most strongly moved by the sympathetic communication of sentiment among those who are closest to us, both in terms of physical proximity and in terms of perceived likeness (T 318). Sympathy makes the happiness and misery of others "affect us," but only "when brought near to us, and represented in lively colours" (T 481). Hume gives us reason to extend sympathy as far as possible, but he recognizes that this extension does not come naturally to us. As we have seen, the limits of sympathy in this regard make Humean judgment vulnerable to distortions arising from the biases of one's society and social group. Inequalities exacerbate this dynamic because sympathy is less likely to register the sentiments of the powerless in the judgments of the more privileged. Here again moral sentiment will reflect the relations of power fostered by the prevailing social and political order. Hume's relatively unambiguous account of esteem for the wealthy offers an example. Our more democratic polity gives a stronger voice to the poor than did Hume's own society. It further extends (at least by comparison with eighteenth-century Britain) the reach of sympathetic communication to include their sentiments, and thereby makes for judgments of the rich that are far more mixed than what Hume reports.

These considerations suggest that for moral judgment to be sufficiently impartial, an egalitarian political order will be called for. Indeed, the fullest realization of impartiality will require a social context structured by liberal rights, vigorous public deliberation, and active democratic contestation, as I will argue presently. Hume himself was insufficiently attentive to the political nature of judgment in this regard. He saw that sympathy was limited in its reach but he did not explore the ways in which the natural limits of sympathy interact with social inequalities and exclusions established by the political order to mar the impartiality of moral sentiment. True, he disapproved of extreme inequality on the grounds that "a too great disproportion among citizens weakens any state" and is not "suitable to human nature."[27] Yet he never connects the political structures that foster and protect inequality to the structure of moral judgment. Still, he was committed in his way to showing how our judgments could attain the greatest measure of impartiality. To mitigate the limits of sympathy and enhance the impartiality of judgment he looked to human nature.

The Role of Human Nature

Hume's writings are full of references to human nature as shaping our responses to the world and thereby providing some common ground of moral feeling (hence judgment) even across societies (T 183, 287, 318,

469, 547n1, 619; E 47). He does admit that human nature is "change-able," or diverse, in many of its particular manifestations. Yet he insists that some needs and purposes are common to human beings, and these help shape our responses to the world. Consequently, human nature dissuades us from approving of certain things. Both domestic and civil slavery, for instance, "trample upon human nature" and this gives us cause to disapprove of them.[28] One who is judging from the general-ized perspective and informed about human nature will do so. The fact that some persons have defended slavery in the past, or that others participate in this practice in parts of the world today, shows that such persons either have failed to adopt the generalized perspective or have been insensitive to human nature (in Hume's sense of the term) or both, resulting in flawed judgment.[29] Other things, such as security, prosperity, and mutual attachment, are valued everywhere because they answer to basic human needs.[30] Likewise, Hume once said that a man who is insensitive to friendship "does not know himself. He has forgotten the movements of his heart."[31]

To say that human nature supplies a normative standard for moral judgment is not to say that human nature is wholly good. Not all things that are naturally human are morally good. Selfishness, envy, and even cruelty seem to be naturally occurring features of the human condition but Hume nowhere suggests that we should admire them. Those who appeal to human nature as a standard thus often distin-guish between human nature as a description of features that are com-mon to human beings and human nature as an ideal of human perfec-tion. For the most part, Hume resists the teleological understanding of human nature, conceiving it instead as a set of empirically verifiable, common concerns. His approach is closer to the thin theory of human nature found in liberals such as Locke than to the perfectionism of Ar-istotle. Yet it does provide grounds for discriminating between the as-pects of human nature that carry moral weight and those that do not. The purpose of morality, on the Humean view, is to coordinate individ-ual and group behavior in ways that generally make human lives go better. There are some desires and aversions that are widely shared among human beings, and hence constitute common concerns, but that tend to promote suffering or obstruct social coordination. The desire to dominate, for example, or the aversion to "otherness," or simple selfishness, are all familiar to most of us, but when widely enacted they thwart rather than support the purposes of morality. They also mani-fest a "want of humanity," or insensitivity to the concerns of others. Therefore they offer little in the way of positive guidance for moral judgment. Human nature as a moral standard in Hume refers to those common concerns the satisfaction of which is generally compatible with the satisfaction of other such concerns, with social coordination, and with the virtue of humanity. Human nature so conceived further mitigates the danger of subjectivism in moral judgment by establishing some common grounds of evaluation.[32]

To be sure, the guidance human nature offers is minimal. There will be numerous moral questions—as well as matters of social and political policy—on which it will not yield determinate decisions (T 533).[33] On the basis of human nature some policies will turn out to lack normative authority, but the range of policies legitimately claiming authority will be quite broad, and here custom, legal convention, and the inclinations of the individual will rightly have a role. So long as they do not contravene the (minimalist) logic of human nature, Hume sees no reason to object to this diversity.[34] In fact, we should expect diversity, given the intersubjective quality of moral sentiment, which entails that variations in the cultural conditions that structure social interactions will find expression in our judgments.

The appeal to human nature may seem to sit uneasily with Hume's skepticism. There is some merit to this concern. If human nature is conceived in terms of an invisible set of final ends or a standard of human perfection, then the quest to know it is indeed at odds with Hume's skepticism and with his empiricist method more generally. According to this method, it is "experience only, which gives authority to human testimony."[35] Yet when human nature is seen as a collection of common, empirically verifiable needs, responses, and desires, it turns out to be compatible with Hume's larger philosophical project.[36] In fact, the study of human nature properly conceived is the heart of this project. In discussing his own philosophical purposes in the *Treatise*, book 1, Hume says that he aims to "contribute a little to the advancement of knowledge" by steering philosophers to "those subjects, where alone they can expect assurance and conviction" (T 273). First among these subjects is "human nature," he says, including the needs and purposes that experience reveals to be common among human beings, for "human nature is the only science of man" (T 273). Like other judgments derived from experience and observation, which are always in some degree probable only,[37] our notions of human nature are fallible and subject to revision. We can expect more assurance and conviction on this subject than on the metaphysical questions traditionally pursued by philosophers, but we should nevertheless resist dogmatic assertions of certainty. When pursued in a suitably modest spirit, the empirical study of human nature—its tendencies and commonalities— turns out to be consistent with rather than contrary to Hume's skepticism. Indeed, Hume continues, "the conduct of a man, who studies philosophy in this careless manner, is more truly sceptical than that of one, who feeling in himself an inclination to it, is yet so over-whelm'd with doubts and scruples, as totally to reject it" (T 273). To reject the concept of human nature out of hand, to turn away from the guidance it may suggest, would be its own kind of dogmatism. Hume gives human nature a central place in his epistemology and moral philosophy, although he leaves its content open to revision based on what empirical observation reveals.[38]

In addition to human nature, Hume suggests that good judgment is guided by features of the external world. To be sure, he denies that moral sentiments simply respond to moral value inhering in things themselves. Once again, he differs markedly from Aristotle in this respect. Aristotle also envisioned an affective dimension to moral evaluation, holding that the virtuous person's love of the good is a mark of his excellent judgment. But in Aristotle moral feeling is a response to the inherent moral order of the natural world itself. The feeling of moral approval arises (or arises appropriately) when real goodness is on display. The moral feelings of the virtuous person are an index of qualities existing independently in the world. Hume's view is different. The feeling of approval is not a report about the intrinsic moral status of phenomena in the external world. Instead of reporting value, moral sentiment expresses it, although it expresses this value in an impersonal way.[39] Hume regarded his sentiment-based approach to judgment as a great advance over existing moral philosophy, as it allowed him to explain the "origin" of any action's "rectitude or depravity" without recourse to "incomprehensible relations and qualities, which never did exist in nature, nor even in our imagination, by any clear and distinct conception" (T 476). It put the sources of moral and political right on the naturalistic terrain of human needs and purposes—rather than tying them to external standards—and opened them to the light of scientific understanding.

Kant famously objected to the naturalism of Hume's theory on the grounds that it was incompatible with our prephilosophical experience of morality. As one recent writer puts it, "we ascribe to morality a very special kind of authority over our motives," one that it seems "could not possibly have a purely naturalistic source."[40] Kant's challenge in this regard is important: any viable account of the sources of moral and political right (or normativity) needs to be able to accommodate the phenomenology of the moral "ought," the feeling that there are some things we must (or must not) do, a feeling that has a distinctive character and a special urgency when compared with the feeling of what we happen to desire. Although Hume himself does not address this issue directly, the Humean approach can indeed accommodate the phenomenology of "ought" without sacrificing its naturalistic basis.

We can account for the special status of moral claims partly on the grounds that they reflect human needs that are especially fundamental and purposes that are especially common. They do not differ in kind from other interests in the way that reason's "interest" in moral duty, on Kant's view, is different in kind from empirical inclinations.[41] Yet our awareness of the fact that moral claims mark out especially fundamental human concerns gives these claims a distinctive character and a feeling of special urgency. The difference between concerns that generate moral judgments and obligations and those that do not is a difference in the degree to which these concerns reflect fundamental, shared needs and purposes, rather than a difference in the kind of concerns that they are.

In part, too, the distinctive phenomenology of the moral "ought" follows from the fact that moral sentiment rests on a generalized perspective, one that considers multiple sentiments and responds to general rules (for example, we praise benevolence on the basis of its general tendency to be useful). These generalizing features make moral sentiment feel quite different from personal desire, which is intrinsically particular. Moreover, because moral claims reflect concerns that are shared, the failure to respect them puts the interests of others in jeopardy, which usually triggers objections from them. This feature distinguishes moral failures from the failure to satisfy one's personal desires, which typically leaves others unmoved. The moral "ought" is arrived at intersubjectively, and it responds to the fact that we are interdependent beings. Consequently, others have a stake in our moral actions, which imbues moral obligation with a feeling that further distinguishes it from personal desire, as obligations are socially enforced in ways that personal desires are not. This fact is internalized at the earliest of ages and reinforced consistently throughout one's lifetime. Together these considerations help explain the distinctive phenomenology of moral claims and obligations. They make it possible to meet the Kantian objection without abandoning Hume's naturalism.

This naturalism figures in moral judgment partly because the claims of human nature constrain the generalized perspective by setting limits on which sentiments properly figure in our judgments. In addition, Hume indicates that sound moral judgment attunes itself to a certain resonance between objects in the world and human nature, or the organs of human perception and sentiment, as described in the essay "Of the Standard of Taste." This essay addresses "the sentiments of men" as they bear on both aesthetics and morality. Although neither beauty nor moral virtue actually inhere in objects or persons themselves, nevertheless "there are certain qualities in objects, which are fitted by nature to produce those particular feelings"—namely, the feelings of admiration and approbation.[42] Human responses place the value on things but these responses are not arbitrary, or not always so. For example, we tend to respond positively to works of art and to persons that exhibit "inner consistency and uniformity of the whole."[43] Hume also insists that every work of art has "a certain end or purpose," and that "it is to be deemed more or less perfect, as it is more or less fitted to attain this end."[44] Here again, reason (as Hume defines it) "is requisite to the operations" of judgment, as it enables the causal thinking necessary to evaluate the perfection of an object in this respect. The central point for present purposes, however, is that our sentiments of approbation (whether moral or aesthetic) need not be random or idiosyncratic. These sentiments respond to real features of the external world and they reflect common tendencies in human nature, although in so responding they express our valuation of the world rather than registering value that inheres in it. Judgment is a kind of attunement to, and appreciation for, qualities and patterns of behavior that resonate with the structure of the human mind (in the case of beauty) or support common human needs and purposes (in the case of morals).

Proper attunement and appreciation in this regard depend upon "soundness" in judgment. "In each creature," Hume says, "there is a sound and a defective state; and the former alone can be supposed to afford us a true standard of taste and sentiment."[45] We would not ask a deaf man to judge the quality of an opera, for instance, and a delirious man "has no manner of authority with us" in epistemic matters.[46] Likewise, we typically care more about "the approbation of a wise man than . . . that of a fool" (T 321). The generalized perspective of moral sentiment figures importantly here, as the principal consideration in establishing the soundness of judgment is that one must "preserve his mind from all *prejudice*."[47] Impartiality is the key. This means that one should abstract from one's own interests and private perspective in assessing the action or character under consideration. Indeed, Hume says, "I must depart from [my own] situation; and considering myself as a man in general, forget, if possible, my individual being and my peculiar circumstances."[48] But in abstracting from self-interest we do not abandon the passions for a form of reason that has been emptied of affective content. Without feeling—specifically, the feelings of pleasure and pain that yield the reflective passions of approbation and disapprobation—we could not arrive at any judgments at all. The perspective of the historian furnishes an example of what Hume has in mind. He contrasts the historian with "the man of business," who considers the characters of others "as they have relation to his interest," with the result that "his judgment [is] warped on every occasion."[49] The philosopher's judgment is also flawed because he "contemplates characters and manners in his closet," where "the general abstract view of the objects leaves the mind so cold and unmoved, that the sentiments of nature have no room to play, and he scarce feels the difference between vice and virtue."[50] The historian, however, "keeps in a just medium betwixt these extremes, and places the objects in their true point of view. The writers of history, as well as the readers, are sufficiently interested in the characters and events, to have a lively sentiment of blame or praise; and, at the same time, have no particular interest or concern to pervert their judgment."[51] The whole purpose of Hume's generalized perspective, then, is to achieve a form of reflective feeling, not to silence feeling for the purpose of "rationally" ascertaining the rules of right.

So affect figures in judgment in two ways: in the general horizons of concern that motivate and guide judgment by giving us things to care about (the conditions of judgment); and in the particular sentiments communicated by sympathy within the generalized perspective (the inputs of judgment). It is important to see that moral sentiment is reflective. Reason, as Hume defines it, contributes by enabling us to perceive relations of cause and effect as well as those of identity or resemblance. It also allows us to ascertain relevant matters of fact, and it identifies the most effective means to our ends. And the sentiments that sympathy conveys (including pleasures and pains) are themselves reflective in most cases. Judgment arises as our affective, but not unreasoned, responses to the world are filtered through the generalized perspective and informed by the facts. Our judgments reflect the social fabric of moral feeling as well as responses that have a footing in human nature. Together, these features establish a reflective, impersonal standpoint, and hence a significant measure of impartiality, in the moral sentiments and the judgments they generate.

FROM THE PHENOMENOLOGY OF JUDGMENT
TO THE JUSTIFICATION OF NORMS

The discussion thus far has treated Hume's analysis of judgment from the phenomenological perspective, or the perspective of how we experience it. The main function of book 3 of the *Treatise*, as well as that of the second *Enquiry*, is to explain the origins and the structure of our common experience as it bears on moral life, including judgment. Hume has been criticized for what some readers see as the *merely* phenomenological character of this account. These critics believe that he failed to provide a normative theory of judgment, or a process by which we could assess the validity of the judgments we happen to have. Some even accuse him of psychologizing morality. Yet Hume does go beyond psychology and phenomenology in his treatment of moral judgment. Although the bulk of his analysis is indeed concerned with explaining the experiential facts of judgment, he introduces a normative perspective in the concluding passages of both the *Treatise* and the *Enquiry*.[52] These passages even suggest a general method of norm justification for the evaluation of prevailing standards of right.

After having explained "the moral approbation attending merit or virtue" in the first part of the *Enquiry's* conclusion, Hume turns in part 2 to consider what he calls "our interested *obligation*" to virtue (E 118; emphasis in original). The earlier analysis of judgment had revealed the process by which we come to value what we call "virtues" and to be motivated to act in accordance with them. What this earlier analysis did not tell us is why we *ought* to value virtue, or why virtue is obligatory for us. How can we be sure that the qualities we consider to be virtues are worthy of our approbation? To establish the basis of this obligation—to justify the norms that virtue entails—Hume asks us at the end of the *Enquiry* to look to "the true interest of each individual" (E 119).[53] Are the virtues useful or agreeable to the person who has them and those who are affected? Do they support rather than thwart common human needs and purposes? Do our standards of right have a basis in fundamental human concerns? If we can answer in the affirmative, then our virtues and the standards they entail will be justified.[54] Likewise, in the conclusion to the *Treatise* Hume tells us that moral sentiment acquires "new force, when reflecting on itself, it approves of those principles, from whence it is deriv'd, and finds nothing but what is great and good in its rise and origin" (T 619). This reflection "helps us to form a just notion of the *happiness*, as well as of the *dignity* of virtue" (T 620; emphasis in original). In so considering, we employ the same generalized, sentiment-based perspective involved in moral approbation, but here judgment operates at a higher order of complexity. For now judgment is asked to evaluate itself: what do we feel when we contemplate the prospect of a life lived according to our existing moral judgments?

The notion of human nature plays an important role in norm justification. As we have seen, human nature refers to the empirically verifiable concerns and responses to the world that observation tells us are common among human beings. People commonly abhor being enslaved, for instance, and commonly feel the power of the religious impulse; they typically find tyranny and cruelty disagreeable; they see promise-keeping as generally useful and mutual attachments as sources of pleasure. Human beings are psychologically and physiologically constituted so as to largely share such responses, so that the intersubjective dimension of judgment intersects with its basis in human nature. Hume's idea is that moral approbation and disapprobation, as well as the higher-order judgments involved in norm justification, track these common responses. He regards these responses as "intrinsically normative," as one commentator says, in the sense that aside from human needs and purposes, "there is no normative point of view from which morality can be challenged."[55] In this respect, Hume's empirical science of human nature is very much intended to yield normative conclusions, to generate an "ought" from an "is."

True, his modesty regarding the fallibility of empirical knowledge should be understood to carry over to moral judgment. If our judgments of right and wrong rest in part on fallible assessments of human nature, then a measure of moral restraint is always called for. Even so, it is fair to say that Hume understated how difficult it can be to see and feel human nature operating in us, and to distinguish it from the social customs and legal conventions with which it always interacts. In part, this difficulty reflects the fact that power imbalances and social exclusions may distort our perception of human nature. What we feel to be "common" depends on whose experience we take into account. But even leaving aside the effects of inequality, the difficulties of knowing oneself and distinguishing the natural from the socially constructed in one's responses are impossible to deny, especially in light of the fact that moral sentiments are always also intersubjective.

This is another place where liberal-democratic politics can help to fill out the Humean account—as we are about to see—by incorporating democratic contestation into higher-order judgment and allowing our sense of human nature itself to be challenged and revised in light of wider experience. Indeed, the interpretative complexities associated with human nature as a standard make such contestation necessary to sound judgment. Yet the difficulties of clearly identifying human nature do not reduce Hume's account of norm justification to de facto conventionalism. Moral sentiment may be intersubjective at the deepest level, and our notions of human nature may be shaped by social life, but Hume suggests that with respect to some basic human concerns the responses of different persons regularly coincide. On the basis of such concerns, one can say that a political system that established slavery, or obstructed mutual attachments, or systematically thwarted the religious impulse, or made promise-keeping untenable, would be morally objectionable. By violating these common concerns it would fail the test of Humean justification. Thus when people disapprove of tyrants or slaveholders or liars, we can say with Hume that

"from the constitution of [their] nature [they] have a feeling or sentiment of blame from the contemplation of it" (T 469).

Hume's account of norm justification also introduces an element of
reflexive agency that may otherwise seem to be missing from his moral
philosophy. That is, Humean judgment often appears to be merely re-
active, emphasizing retrospective evaluation of other persons' character traits rather than deliberation about one's own future action.[56] One
commentator even has argued that "the priority the Humean gives to
spectatorial-based judgment evaluating character and action effectively displaces the deliberative process engaged in by agents."[57] It is
certainly true that Hume himself did not work out all the implications
that his sentiment-based approach to evaluative judgment might have
for future-oriented practical deliberation, especially in the political
context.[58] Yet in describing how we come to affirm the "interested obligation" to virtue, Hume attributes to the judging subject an active, deliberative role. The impartial observer applies the generalized standpoint to herself. Judgment still takes the form of a sentiment of
approval or disapproval, and this sentiment is in effect a reaction to
the prospect of a life lived according to our first-order judgments. But
the perspective of this second-order judgment is unmistakably that of
a moral agent, one who is asking herself whether or not she should go
on living by the standards that have guided her in the past. To be sure,
in Hume's example we see the agent endorsing her sentiments rather
than reforming them. Hume was somewhat skeptical about the individual's ability to radically transform her character, and he had no desire to encourage the internalized war on vice that he associated with
the "monkish virtues" (E 108). Still, in the very act of asking whether
she can approve of her character, Hume's moral agent treats herself
as responsible for determining her future actions and authorizing the
judgments that will guide them. In this respect Hume's concept of
norm justification points in the direction of practical deliberation.

Deliberation and Hume's Internalism

Deliberation differs from evaluation in being action-guiding. Its function is to reach determinate conclusions about what to do. Deliberation
can be either moral or prudential. If moral, deliberation is guided by
moral sentiment; if prudential, it is guided by interest, or by desires
and concerns not tutored by the generalized perspective or measured
against the claims of human nature. In what follows, our main concern
is with moral deliberation. Hume clearly thought that moral evaluation had a deliberative purpose. He insisted upon grounding moral

evaluation in reflective sentiment precisely because he was convinced that these evaluations played a role in guiding action. It is "impossible that the distinction betwixt moral good and evil, can be made by reason," he says, "since that distinction has an influence upon our actions, of which reason alone is incapable" (T 462). Moral evaluations "have an influence on the actions and affections"; they "excite passions, and produce or prevent actions" (T 457). In deciding what we ought to do in moral matters, our decisions incorporate the evaluations of moral sentiment as these emerge from the generalized perspective and are tested against what empirical experience tells us about human nature. In other words, moral deliberation for Hume consists in bringing the evaluations of moral sentiment to bear on one's choice of action in a particular context. The sentiment of approbation I feel when contemplating the virtue of courage gives me grounds, when faced with a choice, to seek the courageous path rather than the cowardly one. Indeed, it provides a normative basis for the obligation to do so. Yet one might wonder how moral evaluations, even those grounded in sentiment, can affect action at all, given that Hume's theory of volition stipulates that action arises only in response to the experience or the prospect of pleasure and pain (T 414, 399; and see 367).[59]

Moral evaluations have motivational power when brought to bear on the deliberative process because they respond to (and constitute) reflective pleasures and pains. Remember that the sentiments of praise and blame arise when we contemplate a particular motive or character trait from within the moral perspective and perceive the pleasures and pains that arise for the person who has it and those who are affected by its general consequences. My evaluation of another's courage reveals the pleasures that courage generates in this regard, and my natural propensity for pleasure causes this evaluation to "affect" me, as Hume says, when I deliberate about what I myself should do. Courage is not always pleasant for the one who has it, of course—or at least it is not always simply pleasant. Yet Hume believed that human beings on the whole are so constituted as to find courage in itself immediately agreeable, even when its effects are questionable (E 90).[60] And while acts of courage can have negative consequences, it is also true as a general matter that almost nothing of importance to human society could be accomplished without courage. The evaluation of courage in light of the pleasure and pain it tends to generate thus gives me grounds to care about being courageous as a general matter, and this concern puts pressure on my actions. Moreover, the sentiments of praise and blame are themselves, respectively, forms of pleasure and pain (T 590). Thus when I consider engaging in conduct of which I disapprove, I face the unpleasant prospect of self-disapprobation. The aversion to this pain can motivate me to act differently.[61] In this sense, the moral sentiments of praise and blame are underwritten by what Hume calls "calm desires," in particular "the general appetite to good and aversion to evil" (T 417).[62] And because desires are among the "direct passions" that generate volition (T 399) it should not be surprising that the moral sentiments, or our moral evaluations, have the power to motivate action.[63]

In other words, evaluative judgment involves conative as well as cognitive states of mind. It is cognitive in that the judging agent has a mind-to-world orientation. She is trying to determine if a particular course of action, when considered impartially, would be good or right, rather than merely expressing some personal desire. In assuming the impartial standpoint, one's aim is to accurately perceive the empirical data the world offers (which includes the sentiments of those affected), not to shape the world to one's own ends. Yet moral judgment is also conative insofar as what makes something right or good is in part that it generates pleasure when considered from within the generalized perspective. The sentiment of approval that results from this perspective is a function of human beings' naturally conative attitudes toward pleasure and pain. In other words, the "general appetite to good and aversion to evil" that underlies moral approval has a world-to-mind direction of fit. Within the generalized perspective, the impartial judge registers the pleasures and pains of those affected by the object under consideration and responds affectively to them. To approve of courage is to cognitively register the impersonally arrived at, but nevertheless conative, wish that courage should be manifest in the world and to resonate with (or share in) this wish. Moral judgment in this respect also has a world-to-mind direction of fit. Likewise, the empirical data we register in attending to the claims of human nature themselves have a conative structure, for the standard of human nature that Hume suggests consists in common human concerns, or desires and aversions that we tend to share. Thus the empirical data that we "cognize" in the cognitive aspect of moral judgment are either intrinsically conative (as in the claims of human nature) or they naturally generate conative responses, which then constitute the evaluation, or the feelings that generate moral sentiment within the generalized perspective. As one interpreter puts it, because the feelings of approbation and disapprobation "simply *are* conative states of mind, or passions," it turns out that "the conditions under which one judges that an action or a character trait is or is not justified are identical to the conditions under which one has a motive towards or away from that action or trait."[64] For this reason, moral judgment-as-evaluation can function as the basis of the deliberation that guides moral action.

To say that moral sentiments have the power to guide action is not to guarantee that they will do so in any particular case, of course. Other desires and concerns may intervene, and Hume emphasized that human beings are often moved more powerfully by their immediate interests than by their most important ones (T 428, 418). Additionally, where moral judgments are mixed (as in the case of courage, which is both pleasant, because immediately agreeable, and often painful, because costly) their motivational force may point in contrary directions. As a result, objectives that we acknowledge to be valuable may sometimes have "but a feeble influence either on the will or the affections" (T 427). The affective dimensions of moral sentiment do not make right action automatic, then. Yet the fact that our evaluative judgments are themselves affectively engaged, grounded in the same sentiments that normally generate action, means that deliberation guided by these judgments is constitutively connected to common human motivations. In this way, the Humean approach to deliberation differs from the Kantian, rationalist model, which posits a deep divide between the psychological factors that regularly motivate action (passions and desires) and the normative basis of moral evaluation (a form of reason that abstracts from passions and desires). The connection between norms and motives in Hume insulates his account of moral judgment from the motivational deficit that plagues the rationalist approach. This seems to have been one of his objectives insofar as he saw his theory as not only "more correct in its precepts" than the rationalist alternatives of his day but also "more persuasive in its exhortations" (T 621).

Moreover, although reason, as Hume defines it, does have a role in practical deliberation, reason itself is not the source of the normative authority of our decisions, as it is on rationalist views. Deliberation begins with an evaluation, such as the thought that cruelty is vicious. This evaluation arises from moral sentiment. The reflective feeling of blame that I experience when I contemplate cruelty tells me that I ought to avoid being cruel. Recall that to register the generalized sentiment of aversion from within the moral standpoint is to feel disapproval. Disapproval just is the feeling of aversion when directed to a human agent and informed by the sentiments of those affected. This feeling would not be possible without reason—aversions often are responses to the projected consequences of particular actions and characters, which we could not identify without reason—but it cannot be reduced to intellect alone. Moral sentiments, as we have seen, are always also conative in nature, never strictly cognitive. Beginning from the evaluation that cruelty is bad, Elizabeth Radcliffe has reconstructed the role of reason within Humean deliberation in the following way:

(1) Cruelty is vicious, or I ought to avoid being cruel [derived from a feeling of moral displeasure];

(2) Not talking about my success in front of my friend is necessary to avoiding cruelty in this case [derived from reason];

(3) Talking about my success in front of my friend is vicious, or I ought not talk about my success in front of my friend [derived from feeling and reason].[65]

Reason helps us make sense of the relevant facts in the case at hand, and here it points out the causal connection between cruelty and talking about one's success. One could not reach determinate conclusions about what to do in this instance without reason. In this sense, the deliberative process necessarily includes reasoning. Yet the moral authority of the conclusion is not a function of reason standing apart from sentiment. This authority derives rather from the normative force of the moral sentiment in premise (1), which is a function of feeling as much as reason, and which ultimately comes from the basic human desire to avoid pain. As Radcliffe says, although both sentiment and reason contribute to the conclusion, Hume "would not allow that action in accord with the conclusion is right because it's *rational*."[66] Hence we can deliberate from evaluation to action even though reason, as defined by Hume, is not authoritative either in establishing the evaluations or in commanding the actions. What makes the action right is its consistency with the moral sentiment disapproving of cruelty.

Many readers interpret Hume's view to mean that there is no basis for reflecting critically on our actions, or on the grounds of action in general. Some recent commentators have decided that because Hume's view denies normative authority to reason per se it precludes the possibility of practical reasoning altogether, even of the merely prudential type, thus undermining deliberate action entirely.[67] His notorious remarks at *Treatise* 2.3.3 are frequently cited in this regard:

'Tis not contrary to reason to prefer the destruction of the whole world to the scratching of my finger. 'Tis not contrary to reason for me to chuse my total ruin, to prevent the least uneasiness of an *Indian* or person wholly unknown to me. 'Tis as little contrary to reason to prefer even my own acknowledg'd lesser good to my greater, and have a more ardent affection for the former than the latter. (T 416)

This passage in no way denies us the possibility of a critical perspective, however. There are many things one can say against preferring the destruction of the world to the scratching of one's finger: it is cruel, shortsighted, selfish, and lacking in the virtue that Hume called "humanity," for instance.[68] These considerations are grounded in moral sentiment and in a prudential concern for one's own long-term interest. So although reason as Hume conceives it may not by itself provide a powerful or significant basis for criticizing action, fundamental human concerns do provide this basis. Reason is authoritative not in itself but because of where it leads when it is operating effectively, which is to the realization of the things that matter most to us.[69] We need reason to determine the extent to which a particular action will tend to support or to thwart these concerns. Hume does have an account of deliberation, and hence an account of practical reasoning, although his overly narrow definition of the term "reason" tends to obscure it from view. Indeed, his de facto account of practical reasoning is a valuable one because it presses us to think more expansively about the grounds and process of deliberation. Deliberation, as Hume conceives it, is not devoid of intellect, but it involves more than merely intellect. The process of practical reasoning is a holistic one, in which cognition and affect are deeply entwined.

The conviction that the intellect is morally authoritative not in itself but only in conjunction with the things that matter to us is a mark of Hume's particular brand of "internalism." Internalism is often described as the view that norms of right constitute in themselves motives for action.[70] Defined in this way, internalism contrasts with moral views that separate the content of a norm from the source of its attendant motive. The latter approach is illustrated by certain versions of Christianity, in which adherence to the moral norms commanded by God is motivated not by an attractiveness in the commands themselves but by the external threat of divine punishment.[71] On this definition both Hume and Kant are internalists because both see the motivating force of normative standards (or moral obligations) as being internal to the standards themselves rather than dependent on external causes. There is another way to understand Hume's internalism, however, which distinguishes him sharply from Kant. For Hume, the concerns that generate our allegiance to moral norms (and that generate the norms themselves) are internal to the common dispositions that structure the psychology of persons as empirical beings. This aspect of Hume's internalism is echoed in the view espoused by Bernard Williams, discussed in chapter 2 of this volume. In contrast to Hume and Williams, Kant's account of moral duty and its motive represents a radical departure from this psychology, as the interest of reason that generates respect for the moral law is external to the usual concerns of human beings as members of the phenomenal world and in no way depends on these concerns.[72] Hume's internalism is closely connected to his conviction that reason alone cannot motivate action; Kant's internalism, by contrast, depends on reason's power to do so.

Some have rejected Hume's internalism as patently egoistic and hence incapable of sustaining the other-regarding concerns that morality necessarily entails. Others have seen it as imposing unacceptable limitations on the structure of moral judgment. The worry is that on this view a person never could be brought to see the value of something that she did not already value. This would seem to make moral debate meaningless. And by precluding meaningful debate, the objection goes, this view would rule out social criticism and reform, rendering moral and political life static. These worries miss the mark of Hume's internalism, however. The egoism charge can be dispelled by attending to the varied elements in what Williams calls a person's "motivational set,"[73] or horizon of concern. Hume explicitly denounced "the selfish philosophy" then associated with Hobbes and Mandeville (E, appendix 2). He did not reject the notion of self-interest but he was convinced that we are regularly moved by concerns other than self-interest. Our concerns may include love for particular others, loyalty to a group or a cause or a principle, even the desire to see justice done.[74] The common thread here is, as Blackburn says, a disposition to care, a mode of consciousness in which our desires or affections are engaged. Hume's internalism means that in the absence of such concerns, moral injunctions will lack not only motivational efficacy but also normative force, as standards of right that lack a footing in fundamental human concerns never could be normative for us.

It is important to remember, as we saw in connection with Williams, that this form of internalism can accommodate moral criticism and the possibility of reform. We are capable of reflecting on the concerns that shape our judgments, and these concerns may change in the light of new considerations. Reason, as Hume defines it, has an important role here. It can point out cases in which our concerns are premised upon false beliefs about matters of fact or incorrect perceptions of causal relations (T 416, 459). If I oppose gay marriage because I think it leads to the erosion of traditional marriage, then evidence to the contrary gives me reason to change my view. The effects of reason in this regard are framed by the larger collection of desires and commitments that constitutes my horizon of concern, however. Evidence about the causal effects of gay marriage on traditional marriage will influence my judgment only if I care about traditional marriage. This concern, too, is subject to revision based on new considerations introduced by reason, provided that these new considerations are related in some way to other concerns that I already have. Thus we can reflect on our ends and not only on the means to these ends, although such reflection always transpires on the terrain of our existing concerns and beliefs. In some cases one's existing concerns may be less than fully conscious. Media coverage of black civil rights demonstrators being abused by Southern police officers galvanized the American majority in the late 1950s and early 1960s, in many cases because the anger people felt on seeing this abuse made them aware for the first time of the strength of their commitment to, or concern for, social justice.[75] Through this type of critical engagement, Humean internalism allows for an agent, as Williams puts it, to "come to see that he has reason to do something which he did not see he had reason to do at all."[76]

Even though Hume was somewhat skeptical about the individual's ability to transform her character radically, he very clearly believed that the education of sentiments was possible:

> Let a man propose to himself the model of a character, which he approves: Let him be well acquainted with those particulars, in which his own character deviates from this model: Let him keep a constant watch over himself, and bend his mind, by a continual effort, from the vices, towards the virtues; and I doubt not but, in time, he will find, in his temper, an alteration for the better.[77]

Hume insists, however, that the cultivation of character must proceed by engaging the passions and desires that help constitute it. To diminish "or augment any person's value for an object, to excite or moderate his passions, there are no direct arguments or reasons, which can be employed with any force or influence."[78]

Rawls has objected to this aspect of Hume's internalism. He denies that the ideals that seize our attention and capture our concern can only do so by enlivening passions that already exist within us.[79] It sometimes happens, he says, that "we are introduced to an ideal, a certain way to lead our life, and then and there . . . we are, as it were, seized by that ideal, which from then on deeply affects us."[80] In such cases the force of the idea as a "rational principle" comes from what Rawls elsewhere calls "the authority of reason."[81] Reason itself, as a faculty that transcends existing passions, can seize us so as to determine our deliberations and motivate our actions. It is true, as Rawls points out, that Hume never definitively disproved this possibility. On the other hand, none of the rationalists (including Kant himself) have provided a persuasive, positive proof of reason's power in this regard. In fact, the "conversion" experiences to which Rawls refers in this passage are better understood as involving a combination of reason and existing passions than as a form of reason that transcends the passions. In describing such experiences, what people usually say is that the new ideal seized them because it answered to something that was of ultimate concern to them, or that in light of this ideal certain sentiments that they had now suddenly made sense as never before. We can reform our sentiments, but not as an act of pure intellect. Reform of this kind arises only in connection with other concerns and affective aims that we already have. How could it be otherwise? We can only ever deliberate—about our own character or anything else—in light of the things that matter to us. The fact that there are things that do matter to us is a function of our reflective passions, our affective nature interacting with our intellect. This interaction infuses deliberation at the deepest level and it is constitutive of practical reasoning. Conceived in this holistic (and internalist) way, practical deliberation does not need to partner with passion to generate conclusions because it necessarily incorporates passion.

Hume's internalism helps explain why he teaches us about the distinctions between better and worse sentiments mainly in his literary and historical writings rather than through the philosophical venue of the *Treatise*. One teaches the higher desires by showing their attractions and thereby engaging our affections. Thus Hume's *History* portrays Alfred the Great, whose character he describes as "perfect," as an attractive figure not only to others but also to Alfred himself. As one interpreter puts it, the ultimate test of Alfred's merit and virtue is that "we must want to *be* Alfred as much as we would want to be in any other relation to him."[82] The narratives and moral exemplars that populate Hume's literary and historical writings educate the deliberative faculty by engaging our affections for higher and more noble desires—that is, desires that can be endorsed as useful or agreeable from within the generalized perspective and that answer to human nature. The main point for present purposes is that even though we always deliberate in light of our existing concerns, moral deliberation is not thereby held hostage to unreflective appetites or merely private desires. Our concerns can be revised in light of procedures and standards that are neither idiosyncratic nor random. Indeed, we can deliberate not only about what we ought to do but also about who we ought to *be*, and on the basis of this kind of deliberation we are capable of making changes in ourselves.

Practical deliberation about what to do interacts on a continuing basis with judgment as evaluation. In deliberating about what we ought to do we may find ourselves questioning the evaluations that guide us, or seeking out additional evaluations to illuminate a particular quandary. Imagine a man who finds himself witness to certain illegal corporate practices in his workplace. He approves of courage, let us say, and he sees that in this situation courage calls for him to expose the wrongdoing. Still, he wonders what will become of his family if he blows the whistle, for he is their sole source of support. What to do? To reach a determinate conclusion that results in action will require revisiting the activity of judgment-as-evaluation. Is his obligation to his family more or less important than the obligation to act with courage or to expose illegal activities? The return to evaluative judgment may not resolve the conflict of values involved here, of course. The point is that we regularly fall back on judgment-as-evaluation when we are engaged in action-guiding deliberation. What could be more natural in difficult cases than to wonder if the values to which we are committed are worthy of our allegiance? This question is often provoked by the activity of practical deliberation and the pressing need to act on the values we purport to hold. Consequently, action-guiding deliberation and judgment-as-evaluation are closely bound together. Practical deliberation builds on the results of evaluative judgment but periodically returns us to the activity of evaluation.

Because they are so deeply connected, the difficulties that attend Hume's model of moral judgment-as-evaluation carry over to his account of practical deliberation. Insofar as our decisions about what we ought to do are guided by moral sentiments, obstructions of impartiality within moral sentiment will yield biased and unsound deliberation. The intersubjective character of moral sentiment makes judgment sensitive to the configurations of power established by the prevailing political order. In addition, the natural narrowness of sympathy means that the generalized perspective of moral sentiment will tend to replicate existing exclusions and biases within society.[83] And our perceptions of human nature, which are meant to mitigate these difficulties and to supplement the sympathetic communication of sentiments, may reinforce rather than challenge the limits of prevailing sentiment. Insofar as the normative force of moral sentiment comes from its impartiality, however, a compromised impartiality will undercut the validity of the moral sense itself and discredit our moral distinctions and choices.

These difficulties thwart the aspiration to impartiality that is evident in Hume's writings. Impartiality matters. The value of impartiality follows from the importance of morality itself as offering an impersonal standpoint for the adjudication of conflict and guidance for future action on the basis of shared norms. So if there is a basic human interest in morality, as Hume insists that there is, then there must also be a basic interest in the fullest cultivation of moral sentiment and the impartiality it makes possible. The generalized perspective should therefore be sensitive to the sentiments of *all* those affected because only in this way can we reliably coordinate social action and avoid the internal contradictions of judgment over time that render practical deliberation unstable. Thus there are prudential reasons to think, as one commentator puts it, that "we can never fully exclude any of our fellows from the sphere of our moral concern."[84] And impartiality, as a manifestation of the virtue of humanity, is something that answers to human nature and elicits the reflective endorsement of an impartial observer reflecting on her own character. This disposition is useful and agreeable to the person who possesses it and to those affected by it. One who deliberates with impartiality can bear her own survey.

These arguments for the value of impartiality point indirectly to an ideal of equal respect, defined as a recognition of the common humanity of persons as ends in themselves. Although this ideal is most often associated with Kant and neo-Kantian moral theories, there are Humean grounds for affirming it. To be sure, Hume himself never argued for it in so many words or made it the direct object of analysis, as Kant did. Nevertheless, the ideal of equal respect can be justified on the basis of Humean insights and by means of moral sentiment. It makes sense to regard respect for persons as an obligation that derives from our humanity. There is, in effect, a deontological justification for this value, although it is not Kant's justification. Relevant here is the fact that norms arise out of the reflective sentiments of human beings. What this means is that we are, as human beings, the sources of the norms that govern us. In this sense, human beings are autonomous, or morally self-governing. The autonomy of the Humean subject differs from Kantian autonomy, of course. It rests on sympathy and reflective sentiment rather than on pure practical reason. Yet similar implications flow from the fact of autonomy, however different its practice and sources. In particular, the fact of autonomy in the Humean sense implies that we owe others recognition of their equal status as participants with us in the process of norm generation, which establishes a legitimate claim that we regard their basic moral standing as equivalent to our own. In particular, it establishes a general moral right to be included in the sphere of moral concern, to have one's sentiments count within the generalized perspective of impartial judgment. Moral sentiment can affirm this duty by means of sympathetic identification with the pain that autonomous beings feel when they are treated as mere means, or denied consideration as participants in the collective generation of values. Not many things generalize to all of humanity, but surely the desire to have one's concerns count with others is one of them. Sympathy for the pain of being simply disregarded, or morally discarded, generates a moral sentiment of disapproval. In sympathizing with the painful condition of nonrecognition, we find grounds to approve of the ideal of equal respect among those who share in the capacity for reflective autonomy. Respect for persons so conceived is one way of understanding what Hume referred to as the "virtue of humanity."

The emphasis on suffering in the preceding discussion might be thought to make the justification of equal respect too broad. If sympathy entails treating the suffering of others as morally significant and hence means treating others as moral equals, it may seem to require equal treatment for all beings capable of suffering, including nonhuman animals. I do believe that the moral sentiment view suggests a justification for certain obligations to animals. If this line of thought were developed it would likely show that much of what human beings do to other animals today is deeply wrong. To develop this view would take us far from the purposes of *Civil Passions*, however, and I shall not pursue it here. Whatever our obligations to animals may be, there are grounds for thinking that they will not be exactly the same as our obligations to other human beings. The distinctive capacity of human beings to be norm-generating creatures, together with the distinctive need we have for social coordination with other persons, give us a special relationship (and a special moral orientation) to the members of our species. Thus the human capacity for reflective autonomy gives rise to a distinctively human claim to equal respect and to a distinctively human form of suffering when this respect is withheld. Furthermore, because the justification for equal respect rests on our common capacity to be norm-generating, the way to honor this duty is to practice deliberative equality, or to incorporate all relevant sentiments into the deliberative standpoint. This practice makes persons equal participants in the process of generating the norms that bind them, and thereby treats them as ends in themselves. It demonstrates the virtue of humanity.

The right to equal respect (and the duty of deliberative equality) therefore can be justified by means of moral sentiment and with reference to the human capacity for reflective autonomy. Implicit in the practice of moral sentiment and the virtue of humanity are grounds for valuing this ideal. In turn, the ideal of equal respect helps fill in the account of what makes sentiments endorsable within the generalized standpoint, providing additional criteria for the proper inclusion of sentiments. So there are Humean reasons to affirm the value of impartiality and equal respect. And these principles, which support the most inclusive form of moral sentiment, are also supported by it. Nevertheless, although impartiality and equal respect can be justified on broadly Humean grounds, the defense of these values goes beyond anything Hume himself explicitly articulated; moral sentiment theory needs to go beyond Hume in this respect. It also requires more attention to the political context of judgment and deliberation than what Hume offered. While it would be foolish to demand perfection of anything human, including moral sentiment, we can do better in this regard than what Hume's own model accomplished. Since judgment and deliberation cannot do without the passions, the best hope for impartiality lies not in trying to transcend the passions but in reforming the political context that helps shape them. To avoid the distortions that follow from sympathy in its untutored form and extend the limits of the human imagination, we need political conditions of freedom and equality. As Tocqueville said in reflecting on the differences between old-regime Europe and modern democracy, sympathy flows more freely among citizens who are equal. The result is that citizens of democratic societies know one another's sentiments more clearly than do those who live under the conditions of relative inequality that marked Hume's own political society.[85] Formal liberty and equality are not enough, however. Sound moral judgment and deliberation also require active public dialogue and debate, which expand our horizons of concern and our sympathies by exposing us to the sentiments of those outside the familiar terrain of our families and social groups. A more truly impartial but still affectively engaged deliberation thus requires liberal-democratic politics, although Hume himself did not look in this direction. If we are serious about the Humean approach, we will need to go beyond Hume. The politics of judgment point to the need for liberal and democratically engaged forms of public discussion and political action.

CHAPTER FOUR

Affective Judgment in Democratic Politics

To ACHIEVE THE PROMISE of impartiality, both the generalized stand-point and the standard of human nature within Humean judgment need to be regularly contested and informed by voices that challenge the status quo. Hume's own account of judgment is incomplete on its own terms and in need of support from an explicitly articulated ideal of equal respect as well as a regime of liberal rights and contestatory democratic politics. Hume was no advocate of active democratic politics, of course. The notion of an engaged citizenry was associated in his mind with political turbulence,[1] including the excesses of the English civil war,[2] as well as the instability of ancient republics.[3] Although he championed enlightenment—he hoped that his new moral science would dispel superstition and humanize moral and political life—the last thing he wanted was more people passionately involved in debates about public affairs. He feared religious and partisan enthusiasm in politics and believed that the violent passions they engendered should be subdued. To be fair, constitutional liberal democracy was still in its infancy, and Hume could not bank on the transformations it would bring. In the centuries since he wrote, the development of liberal-democratic political institutions has mitigated the dangers of extremism and instability. By tempering the power of the democratic sovereign through mechanisms such as the rule of law, the separation of powers, and individual rights (among other things), liberal democracy has constructed a safer arena for the democratic activism that so worried Hume. Moreover, Hume was insufficiently attentive to the distorting effects of power on moral sentiments and judgment. To the extent that liberal-democratic institutions and activism can mediate these distortions, they are precisely what his theory of moral judgment needs. And while Hume himself did not make this connection, we have seen that there are indeed Humean grounds for affirming the value of equal respect, from which a justification for liberal democracy naturally flows.

This chapter explores the moral sentiment model of individual judgment in the context of contemporary liberal-democratic politics. On the one hand, it focuses on the ways in which liberal democracy can support the extension of sympathy and thereby enhance the impartiality of evaluative judgment and practical deliberation. This includes institutional mechanisms such as equal voting rights and representative government, as well as informal practices of public contestation and debate. On the other hand, the chapter looks at how moral sentiment can contribute to the deliberative judgments of individual citizens on important public issues that raise questions of justice. It is important to see that public deliberation on such issues properly incorporates practices of individual as well as collective judgment. Although political theorists often treat public deliberation as if it were exclusively collectivist in form, the truth is that for liberal-democratic citizens the individual perspective of moral judgment and the collective perspective required for legitimate public decisions are interactive, at least when it comes to matters that involve justice. In deliberating about issues such as abortion, gay rights, or welfare reform, for instance, we move back and forth between the question of what we, as citizens of this particular polity, can reasonably be expected to agree upon and the question of what is morally right. Democratic legitimacy demands some measure of agreement among citizens in reaching decisions that are coercively enforced by the state, and this requires deliberation together with others in terms of commonly held, explicitly public values. Yet public values sometimes go wrong, running afoul of justice or threatening other important human goods. Moreover, the agreement required for political legitimacy, which tends to privilege the status quo, can obstruct the implementation of new and better visions for the future. Individual moral judgment can be a powerful corrective to these dangers of collectivism, which makes it a valuable resource for liberal democracy. And although a distinctive feature of liberalism is that it largely leaves moral questions to individual judgment rather than requiring all such questions to answer to the collective will, many matters of social and political policy do raise claims of justice or basic liberties and therefore involve morality. For these reasons, a good deal of political deliberation does—and should—stimulate the exercise of individual moral judgment on the part of citizens.

Achieving a just political order thus depends on individual as well as collective judgment, and so it calls for the exercise of moral sentiment. For now we leave aside the role of moral sentiment within the formal procedures of public deliberation as "will-formation," which generate coercively enforced laws and policies. In liberal democracies, these procedures introduce additional criteria beyond individual impartiality for the justification of legitimate political decisions. Public deliberation in this formal sense will be the subject of chapter 5. Here we consider instead the more informal practices of deliberation as "opinion-formation" among citizens on issues of public importance, and the role of impartial individual judgment within it.[4] Moral sentiment properly conceived sets the criteria for sound judgment in this form. At the same time, the practices of public dialogue and debate among citizens have the potential to foster and enrich moral sentiment. The first part of the chapter shows that active political engagement among citizens, and participation in the many informal processes of public deliberation as opinion-formation, can enhance the scope and sensitivity of moral sentiment, thus supporting impartiality in judgment. In short, the communication of diverse sentiments is crucial to the cultivation of moral sentiment, and the politics of judgment in this sense calls for an inclusive, "deliberative system" approach to the communicative practices that shape public opinion on questions of moral significance. In the second part of the chapter we explore how judgment as moral sentiment contributes to public deliberation as opinion-formation, and examine the relationship between the moral sentiment model and key liberal principles, such as neutrality, toleration, and individual rights. Finally, we consider some of the ways that liberal democracies might foster the cultivation of moral sentiment.

Sympathy and Contestation in the Deliberative System

The natural faculty of sympathy upon which moral sentiment rests is limited, as we have seen. Because sympathy can extend only as far as does our awareness of others' sentiments, the sentiments of marginalized persons—those whose identity or status sets them outside the majority's frame of reference—may tend not to register within the generalized standpoint of average citizens. Empirical studies confirm this, showing that those with more power tend to be relatively ignorant about the life experiences and sentiments of the less powerful.[5] The limits of the imagination in this regard were underinterrogated by Hume, but they will affect both the generalized perspective and the perception of human nature that is meant to supplement it. Impartiality and equal respect require us to mitigate these limits as far as possible. The greater degree of equality and inclusion that comes with liberal-democratic legal and political institutions can attenuate the natural deficiencies of sympathy. We can imagine the sentiments of others much better if they are able to tell us about them, after all. The access to public deliberation that individual rights protect for members of minority groups facilitates such communication and supports regular contestation and debate, which extend the reach of the imagination and influence the contents of our judgments accordingly.[6] Hume did not exactly connect moral judgment to this notion of narrativity, but he did believe that judgments in "human affairs, and the Duties of common life" benefited immeasurably from "conversation" with others. Philosophy, he complained, "went to Wrack" by its "moaping recluse method of study." What else could be expected, he asked, from men who "never consulted Experience in any of their Reasonings, or who never search'd for that Experience, where alone it is to be found, in common Life and Conversation?"[7] Conversation—much like history, literature, and art—allows us to "correct" our "false tastes" and erroneous judgments by bringing the sentiments of others and the facts of human experience to bear on our sympathetic imagination. Yet for Hume the art of conversation is, or should be, well insulated from politics.[8]

We should not be bound by the limits of his vision in this regard. The incentive structure that follows from equal rights to political participation supports the extension of sympathetic imagination, both in citizens themselves and in their elected representatives and other officials. A liberal-democratic political system in effect forces us to extend the generalized perspective of judgment, to consider the sentiments of those who now have the power to obstruct our purposes or vote us out of office. It can therefore make moral sentiment and the judgments to which it gives rise more fully impartial than Hume's own account allowed. The right political context also can mitigate the tendency of the moral sentiment model to reify the status quo. The latter represents another common complaint about this approach; namely, that moral sentiment gives us a merely conventionalist account of judgment, one that is not amenable to social criticism or reform. Yet where public institutions are structured so as to permit different voices to raise issues of concern to them and to bring novel perspectives and interests into the public eye, the social fabric of moral sentiment may actually make individual judgment and deliberation quite responsive to reform— more responsive than a model that postulates a withdrawn, solitary judge reasoning in abstraction from the sentiments of others. Given the right political context, judgment in this form carries the potential to sustain the critical perspectives and motivating sentiments that generate social change and political reform.

It is perhaps worth emphasizing that the relevant context will include both liberal and democratic components. The separation of powers, rule of law, and individual rights that figure so importantly here are largely liberal mechanisms rather than democratic ones.[9] Yet in a polity in which the people ultimately are sovereign these liberal mechanisms assume democratic forms. Thus the liberal principle of protection against arbitrary power takes the form of democratic rights of equal participation, among other things. It is this distinctive mix of liberal and democratic elements in the law that tends to support the expansion of the generalized perspective within judgment; neither democracy nor liberalism in itself could achieve the same result. The problem with democracy in this regard is that it contains no principle for criticizing democratically decided outcomes, and so stands in tension not only with the generalized perspective but also with Hume's standard of human nature. For its part, liberalism contains no internal requirement to extend the rights of political participation universally, and so it may not stimulate an adequately wide expansion of the generalized perspective; hence one can envision (as Montesquieu did) an aristocratic form of liberalism that is characterized by a balance of powers, the rule of law, and individual rights against encroaching power but that lacks universal suffrage.

Does all this mean that the moral sentiment model of judgment is only feasible—and only safe—in liberal democracies? Practical judgment and deliberation inevitably have affective valence, and this will be true in any political context. Affective judgment will be most fully impartial, however, in democratic contexts. And democracy is rendered stable and secure by liberal mechanisms. Hence liberal democracy establishes conditions for generally optimizing evaluative judgment and impartial deliberation. This is not to say that individual judgments made in liberal democracies are always better than those made under other forms of government. The right political conditions are not sufficient to ensure impartiality. Nor are they always necessary. Exceptional individuals may manifest extensive sympathy and be able to achieve impartiality even in the face of countervailing political institutions and social practices. Think of Gandhi, with his great breadth of vision and feeling, emerging out of colonial India, for instance. So it would be wrong to say that good judgment is only possible in liberal democracies. Strictly speaking, liberal democracy is neither necessary nor sufficient for impartial moral judgment, but it is generally conducive to impartiality. Liberal democracy makes it possible for judgment and deliberation on the whole to be more impartial and hence more justified than they could be, on the whole, in other contexts. The fact that good deliberation is contingent on political context may strike some readers as a mark against the moral sentiment approach. But moral sentiment is no different in this respect from any other viable account of judgment and deliberation, although it is more open about its own contingency than many other approaches. The idea that we could judge and deliberate in abstraction from the patterns of interaction established by the political regime is based on a dream of transcendence—usually reason's transcendence—that does not fit who we are as human beings.

The dependence of impartial judgment on a liberal-democratic political context does raise a quandary, however. If sound judgment depends on (that is, is preceded by) liberal democracy, how does liberal democracy, in the absence of sound judgment, ever arise? Rousseau draws attention to a similar difficulty that exists at the founding of any legitimate polity. To rule itself, a people needs to possess a public-spirited character, but this character can only be produced with the help of the laws and institutions they are setting out to establish:

> In order for an emerging people to appreciate the healthy maxims of politics, and to follow the fundamental rules of statecraft, the effect would have to become the cause; the social spirit, which should be the result of the institution, would have to preside over the founding of the institution itself; and men would have to be prior to laws what they ought to become by means of laws.[10]

Rousseau's solution is to invoke the figure of the founder, or "Legislator," whose "sublime reason" and "great soul" allow him to identify the requisite laws and institutions, and to convince the people (with an appeal to divine authority) of their value.[11] The founding of legitimate states is therefore a sketchy operation, subject to the "miracle" of there being someone of such extraordinary capability in the right place at the right time.[12] There are good reasons to resist, as a normative matter, Rousseau's ideal of a single, godlike man who manipulates the people into accepting a constitution that serves (what he takes to be) their true interests. Yet Rousseau is surely right to think that the successful creation of new and just political orders requires unusual vision or judgment, and that the emergence of such vision is a highly contingent matter. Leaders with vision like this are few and far between, and no one can predict when they will arise.

Liberal democracy in the United States, for its part, initially got off the ground as a result of an imperfect but powerful vision on the part of the founders. Men such as Jefferson, Madison, and John Adams had the ability to see, however imperfectly, beyond the cultural horizons of the day. The political principles and institutions they formulated certainly had roots in previous practices but they also broke new ground. Since then, American liberal democracy has unfolded piecemeal over time, in fits and starts. It is the product of a dialectical relationship between individuals with unusual vision and commitment—the founders, the abolitionists, the suffragists, the civil rights activists, and so on—the groups in which they formed their thinking, the intellectual resources of their time, and the political order they generated and reformed. The new modes and orders they have introduced have given rise to ever more inclusive ways of thinking and feeling on the part of the general populace. Our political visionaries have had a gift for judgment that transcended conventional limits, and the liberal-democratic changes they brought about have established the conditions for increasingly impartial judgment among the public. The more impartial judgment becomes among the public, in turn, the more support there will be for institutions that more fully instantiate liberal-democratic ideals. There is an irreducible element of contingency in the generation and the rise of impartiality, much as there was in the birth of liberal democracy, but over time liberal democracy and impartiality are mutually supportive. The question of how liberal democracy arises is of course distinct from how it is justified. *Civil Passions* does not aim to elaborate a full justification for liberal democracy. Its purpose is instead to show that impartiality is possible even despite the inevitably affective dimensions of judgment and deliberation. As we have seen, to exercise impartiality in moral judgment and public deliberation is in effect to honor the principle of equal respect. This same principle underlies the value of liberal democracy as a form of political order that treats persons as free and equal, or as ends in themselves. Thus to the extent that equal respect can be justified on grounds of moral sentiment, so, too, can liberal democracy.

I have said that an open and contestatory context of discussion on public issues, which facilitates the exchange of sentiments among citizens, is important for the general cultivation of individual impartiality on a widespread basis. Individual rights to freedom of speech and association as well as a free press provide institutional supports for this exchange. The exchange also depends on the dialogic contributions of individuals and groups. These contributions sometimes take the form of carefully reasoned arguments that draw on the principles of public reason. Such arguments provide necessary justificatory grounds for formal decisions on the part of the state that issue in coercively enforced laws and public policies. As we shall see in chapter 5, reflective sentiments have a legitimate role to play even here. Yet not all the public dialogue through which the exchange of sentiments transpires issues in formal state decisions. Much of this exchange comes through more informal types of communication, as people find myriad ways to publicly voice their sentiments on the issues that affect them and the things that matter to them. These informal types of communication can help to extend the sympathetic imagination that makes impartial judgment among individuals possible.

The demands of impartiality therefore recommend in favor of a capacious conception of public deliberation as opinion-formation, one that includes a greater diversity of expressive forms than most contemporary accounts of deliberation allow. Many expressions that could not pass the test of Rawlsian public reason, for instance, can enlarge the scope and enhance the sensitivity of moral sentiment. They should be admitted as part of the deliberative process rather than being "gagged" or "bracketed out." In this respect, the moral sentiment approach makes common cause with the work of theorists such as Nancy Fraser, Jane Mansbridge, and Iris Young, who have argued for the importance within public deliberation of forms of expression that for one reason or another do not meet the criteria for rational argument on the basis of public reason. Fraser, for instance, has insisted upon the deliberative importance of "subaltern counterpublics" in which members of subordinated social groups "invent and circulate counterdiscourses to formulate oppositional interpretations of their identities, interests, and needs."[13] These discourses include forms of expression that are not directly argumentative, and they frequently contest the shared norms that ground public reason. The feminist subaltern counterpublic in the United States includes a "variegated array of journals, bookstores, publishing companies, film and video distribution networks, lecture series, research centers, academic programs, conferences, conventions, festivals, and local meeting places."[14] In these contexts, feminists have been successful in reformulating the experience, history, and conditions of women's subordination in terms that challenge the perspectives and concerns of the dominant public. In recasting the needs and identities of women, they have brought new sentiments onto the public stage, sentiments that have altered the public's horizon of concern and that today figure in the evaluative judgments of Americans as never before.

Along these lines, Young emphasizes the important role that activists play in bringing previously excluded sentiments to bear in dialogue on public issues, despite the fact that they often make their contributions through nondiscursive means: "Pictures, songs, poetic imagery, expressions of mockery and longing performed in rowdy and even playful ways aimed not at commanding assent but disturbing complacency. One of the activist's goals is to make us *wonder* about what we are doing, to rupture a stream of thought, rather than to weave an argument."[15] Expressions of sentiment can contribute in valuable ways to public deliberation even when they do not take an explicitly argumentative form. Plenty of deliberative democrats are willing to acknowledge that such forms of expression can support good deliberation by stimulating discussion on issues that might otherwise receive little attention, and by bringing marginalized interests to the table. Yet most insist on preserving a bold line between expressions that merely support or lead to deliberation and those that constitute deliberation itself. At stake in this distinction is the effort to protect rational decision making from the ostensibly unruly and distorting effects of the passions.

To be sure, it is important to distinguish between deliberative and nondeliberative forms of expression. Not every expression is deliberative, and we risk losing the clarifying power of analysis if we define the category too broadly. Yet the presence or absence of rational argumentation that is devoid of passions and desires is not the best basis for the distinction. In light of the role that sentiment always plays in practical deliberation, it makes more sense to define deliberative expressions as those that express and engage sentiments to make claims—whether through the logical presentation of reasons or in some other fashion—about justice or the common good, or that are tied to an agent's effort to advance such claims. The public display of mock coffins by members of ACT UP in the early 1990s was meant to convey not only the grief of those affected by AIDS but anger at the injustice of a public that had refused, because of prejudice against gay people, to allocate resources commensurate with the scale of the public health crisis that AIDS presented. Something similar holds true for animal rights demonstrations that strategically spill red paint to represent the spilled blood of animals used in testing or the food industry. The aesthetic expression is not an end in itself but makes a moral claim: Causing the suffering or extinction of other species for human convenience or commercial profit is wrong. We can distinguish such acts from mere expressivism because they represent (a) efforts to change the minds and hearts of the public, (b) on some matter of law or policy, and (c) with a view to justice.

In the same way, the personal testimonials of activists in the gay-marriage debate are more than merely self-expression. They represent efforts to bring the sentiments of a marginalized (but affected) group into the generalized standpoint of moral sentiment and to link these sentiments to publicly shared horizons of concern, specifically to principles of justice and notions of the common good. This articulation of one's experience and concerns may seem to be more expressive than deliberative in the strict sense of the word, for it appears to eschew formal argument, or the positing of contestable validity claims. Instead, it often takes the form of narratives in which gay couples publicly communicate the personal experience of their lives together.[16] Likewise, cultural productions such as public service announcements, advertising, television shows, movies, and the theater have begun to portray gay relationships in ways that convey the usefulness and agreeableness (in Hume's terms) of gay unions for the partners themselves and those affected—but without making actual arguments. Yet these expressive (often aesthetic) appeals do not stand on their own. They are part of a larger, recognizably deliberative argument on behalf of gay marriage: Here is love, which we all have grounds to value;

here the fundamental human purposes of friendship, loyalty, mutual understanding, shared goals, and physical companionship (and increasingly the rearing of children) are realized; here as elsewhere, then, these goods should be honored and protected.[17] Thurgood Marshall adopted a similar strategy in arguing *Brown v. Board of Education*, using "compelling biographical narratives" to show "the specific effects of segregation on the life history of African American children."[18] He meant to engage the sentiments of the Court and to extend the range of sentiments included within the moral judgments of average Americans. As James Bohman notes, this forceful presentation of sentiments was connected to a general claim about "fairness" and to bringing "school segregation under the norm of equal protection."[19] The symbolic expressions and testimonials of activists do more than merely lead to deliberation, then. They are themselves deliberative if they press (however implicitly) justice claims, or claims about the common good, and thereby contribute to individual and public reflection on matters of law and policy.

In a related vein, Jane Mansbridge has argued for the deliberative importance of "everyday talk."[20] Everyday talk occurs "when a nonactivist takes an action in order to change others' actions or beliefs on an issue that the public ought to discuss."[21] The act of calling someone "a male chauvinist," for example, clearly "falls far short" of the deliberative ideal as it is usually construed. Yet the use of the term makes two claims: "Descriptively, it claims that the behavior in question results in part from a structure of gender relations that extends beyond the particular individuals engaged in this interaction. Normatively, it claims that the man's behavior is not merely disagreeable but also unjust."[22] The use of the term, even when it arises in informal venues such as the home or office, contributes to public deliberation as opinion-formation because it presses individuals to reflect not only on their own behavior but also on the relations of gender inequity that are underwritten by existing social norms. This account encourages us to think more capaciously about the forms of expression that deliberation may legitimately take and about the contexts in which it may occur. "Everyday talk" happens in the nonpublic or informal places that friends and families and co-workers meet, rather than in the courtroom or the halls of Congress. Many issues that eventually become the subjects of formal public deliberation as will-formation begin by being discussed in everyday talk, or Fraser's "subaltern counterpublics." Informal deliberative communication not only allows marginalized groups to formulate and then develop their novel claims in ways that will ultimately engage common sentiments and intersect with the public's prevailing horizon of concern. It also can stimulate, at the grassroots level, widespread reflection on matters of law and public policy, reflection that over time often comes to influence the decisions that citizens make in more formal political arenas such as the voting booth. And if it presses claims about justice or the common good, if it stimulates reflection on prevailing norms, if it seeks the reform of widely held sentiments, then everyday talk is surely a form of deliberative engagement.

Everyday talk occupies one end of a larger continuum that constitutes public deliberation as a whole. As Mansbridge puts it, "the venues for deliberation fall along a spectrum" from official representative assemblies producing binding decisions to "the most informal venues of everyday talk."[23] Together these different venues comprise "the deliberative system." A single set of criteria apply to all deliberation within the system (these criteria include equal access, accountability, publicity, and reciprocity) but the criteria are to be applied more or less loosely depending on where a particular instance of deliberation falls within the system as a whole. Deliberation that results in binding decisions or political obligations, such as that which generates laws and public policies, should be held to the strictest standards. Deliberation within public advisory bodies may be somewhat less stringent; and deliberation in the many forums of the nongovernmental public sphere, including everyday speech, will be even more inclusive. A truly deliberative democracy will welcome deliberation along the whole spectrum represented by the "deliberative system."

A deliberative-system approach has the benefit of allowing for more open and wide-ranging public discussion than do the standard models of public reason. It will be less vulnerable to the charge, frequently levied against deliberative democrats as well as liberals, that regulatory ideals of public deliberation systematically exclude the deeply held beliefs and values of many citizens, not least religious believers.[24] The more expansive conception of deliberation makes a place for these citizens and welcomes their contributions to public dialogue and debate. To be sure, it will not permit the religious beliefs of some portion of the populace to provide the sole justification for state decisions that are coercively enforced on all citizens.[25] And even at the level of opinion-formation it will incorporate the ideal of equal respect as a resource for reflecting critically on the sentiments conveyed. The sentiments of marginalized groups are not always warranted in extending the public's horizon of concern, after all. When they manifest bigotry or hatred, for instance, other citizens should reject them. Yet the expansive account of deliberation will allow for policies to be proposed and debated in terms of sentiments and concerns that are not, at least initially, widely shared among citizens. Through the layered process of public debate in the many different venues of the deliberative system, the arguments defending particular policies will either gain wider acceptance or they will gradually fade from the public agenda. By the time a policy is ready to be voted up or down we can expect—and require—that the arguments on either side do appeal to sentiments and concerns that are generally shared by citizens, or to publicly accessible reasons.

What counts as a publicly accessible reason shifts over time in response to new claims, changing social conditions, and the deliberative process itself. This fact reinforces the importance of making space within the deliberative system for reasons that are not (or not yet) publicly accessible. Because it can accommodate more diversity of sentiment than do the standard accounts of public reason and democratic deliberation, the deliberative-system approach will be more responsive to social and political reform. By allowing informal, symbolic, and testimonial types of deliberative expression, it can enrich citizens' reflection on public issues and thereby improve public deliberation. Such expressions are also tremendously important for the cultivation of moral sentiment. They can enhance impartial individual judgment by bringing more sentiments—especially those of marginalized groups—into the public eye and extending the reach of sympathetic imagination. The deliberative-system approach thus supports the cultivation of an enlarged generalized standpoint and an enriched faculty of moral sentiment among citizens, and so helps sustain impartiality.

Moral Sentiment and Opinion-Formation

If the deliberative practices of liberal democracy can enhance moral sentiment and the impartiality of judgment, it is also important to see the contributions that moral sentiment can make to these practices. The process of opinion-formation in the deliberative system is in large part a function of the communication of sentiments. Recent arguments for gay marriage present a case in point. Many activists and supporters defend gay marriage by emphasizing the positive moral value of loving and committed same-sex partnerships—both for gay people and for society as a whole. These arguments appeal to a newly expansive faculty of moral sentiment within the American populace, and seek to further extend the operation of citizens' sympathetic imagination. In fact, part of the effort on the part of activists has been to bring about this more expansive moral sentiment. Activists have focused attention on the idea of loving, committed unions and have sought to engage public sentiments to respond to this object rather than respond to ideas about gay people that reflect habitual prejudice. The hope has been to make visible the agreeableness and usefulness (in Hume's terms) of gay unions for the partners themselves and those affected by them. In effect, the idea of "loving relationships" is constructed as the relevant object of sympathy. By articulating this positive experience, the aim has been to make the sentiments of gay people who wish to marry accessible to the imagination of the general public, and thereby to enlarge the generalized perspective of moral sentiment so as to include these sentiments.

In framing the debate this way, activists connect the value of gay unions, which is a novelty, to the value of the more familiar unions that are central concerns for most people. In effect, they have accepted the Humean point that we always judge within a horizon of concern, and they are hoping to extend the majority's horizon by showing how its existing concerns are conceptually connected to this new one. This is another way that intellect functions within a moral sentiment model of judgment. Rather than subduing affective concerns, it reveals relations of identity or resemblance between our existing concerns and new claims. It illuminates the ways in which new claims intersect with the things that matter to us. In this way, the intellect can help to modify our horizon of concern even though it does not lead us to step outside this horizon entirely. There is nothing automatic about the development of greater inclusiveness, of course. In the last several years, forty-five states have passed state constitutional amendments or statutes prohibiting gay marriage, which demonstrates that the generalized perspective of moral sentiment has not been much transformed on this matter so far, even though toleration of gay people in general has increased significantly.

Particularly in light of public recalcitrance on such issues as gay marriage, one might wonder whether it is wise to put so much stock in people's feelings. One of the great contributions of modern liberalism, after all, has been to turn the state away from its intrusive interest in the souls—and hence the psychological lives—of citizens. Does affective judgment, with its emphasis on the inner workings of sentiment and desire, run afoul of liberalism in this regard? A defender of gay rights, for instance, might think that appealing to the principle of liberal neutrality is a wiser approach than the sentiment-based one. Neutrality has been defined in various ways by liberal theorists, but the form most pertinent for present purposes is what Rawls has called "neutrality of aim."[26] This principle holds that "the state is not to do anything intended to favor or promote any particular comprehensive doctrine rather than another, or to give greater assistance to those who pursue it."[27] In this case, neutrality asks that the law refrain from favoring one type of loving relationship (heterosexual) while disadvantaging another (homosexual). So conceived, the neutrality argument requires only that persons be treated equally by the law. It ostensibly asks us to step outside affective modes of consciousness and to make decisions in a way that relies only on an intellectual assessment of what equality under law requires. The ideal of neutrality in this sense is intended to be dispassionate and emotionally disengaged. Instead of encouraging us to affectively affirm the moral value of gay unions, it appears to allow us to avoid passing moral judgment entirely on the matter of homosexuality. Neutrality in law seems to set aside our feelings about right and wrong, even to make judgment itself obsolete in such cases.

Yet while legal neutrality has a crucial place in liberal-democratic societies, it cannot function alone, for neutrality cannot replace our moral judgments or the sentiments that shape them.[28] Indeed, neutrality leans on these sentiments. In practice, the state's obligation to be neutral in its legal treatment of different ways of life is balanced by its obligation to protect citizens and society as a whole from harm. Thus courts have recognized exceptions to the neutral treatment of religious practices (for example) on the grounds of a compelling state interest.[29] In other words, the only legitimate candidates for neutral treatment by the law are persons and causes that bring no harm to society. Yet when the persons under consideration are pressing novel claims, they sometimes find that their status in this regard cannot be taken for granted. To establish this legal status, something other than arguments championing the principle of neutrality will be necessary. In other words, liberal neutrality finds its limit at the margins of public recognition, where the sympathetic imagination of the majority has not yet been engaged. Consequently, neutrality may be least effective, when taken on its own terms, in the cases in which reform is most needed. Such cases call for a revision of the background beliefs and values, including the generalized standpoint of moral sentiment, that portray certain persons or practices as harmful and hence shape our judgments of them.

Once again, the issue of gay rights offers a case in point. Today it is more or less viable to argue that the state should exercise neutrality in its treatment of gay and straight citizens by legalizing homosexual acts between consenting adults, for instance, and prohibiting discrimination in jobs and housing on the basis of sexual orientation. Even those who oppose gay marriage largely support equal treatment in regard to these other civil liberties. But the viability of the neutrality argument in this context today follows on a generation of substantive moral debate about the nature and consequences of homosexual life, which has significantly revised the American public's horizon of concern. Although many dissenters still exist, the weight of opinion in the United States now recognizes that homosexuality in itself brings no harm to society and that gay persons are sufficiently like their straight counterparts in the respects relevant to citizenship as to legitimately share a common civil and political status.[30] However disappointing the recalcitrance of the American public may be on the specific question of gay marriage, no one can deny the very real gains in the status and the freedom enjoyed by gay citizens over the past twenty-five years. Yet public sentiment had to change in order to make this possible—and in order for the principle of liberal neutrality to be invoked successfully on behalf of gay rights. If one considers the various movements for greater inclusion in American citizenship pressed by marginalized groups over the course of U.S. history, one finds evidence that reform often operates in just this way. The greater inclusiveness of the American polity over time is not the result of the public having become more "rational" and less passionate. Instead, it illustrates how the exercise of sympathetic imagination in the presence of political contestation has generated new moral sentiments and gradually transformed the public's horizon of concern—and with it the laws. Our minds are changed when our hearts are engaged.

More generally, appeals to the formal liberty rights of citizenship and to the liberal principle of toleration turn out to be empty in practice unless underwritten by the sympathetic (in Hume's sense) communication of sentiments, which facilitates public recognition of one's commonality or equal status. Hume once said that all government is founded on opinion.[31] How power is exercised and how it is limited depends a great deal on the prevailing opinions of the populace, even where constitutional government, individual rights, and the rule of law are in place. Constitutions, rights, and laws are not self-activating, after all, but must be interpreted, and interpreted not only by judges but also by legislators and by citizens themselves. Under the reign of the opinion represented in *Bowers v. Hardwick* the neutrality argument could not succeed and basic freedoms of gay Americans were denied; under the new regime represented by *Lawrence v. Texas* neutrality has a chance. The change reflects the rise of a more inclusive faculty of moral sentiment within the American populace. The intervening years have seen a surge of activism and public discussion—not to mention the proliferation of cultural expressions (in movies, television, and print media) representing the experience and concerns of gay people—that have brought gay and lesbian sentiments into the public eye as never before, and have significantly extended the generalized perspective of judgment within many Americans so as to include these sentiments. Along these lines, polls indicate that Americans are more likely to support civil liberties for gay people when they have friends, family, or co-workers who are (known to be) gay. In this way, moral sentiment in conjunction with democratic contestation and public debate can usefully step in to supplement and support the principle of neutrality and to bring substance to the constitutional promises of liberty and equality.

And what if such efforts do not succeed? Does the moral sentiment approach hold individual judgment hostage to the often biased, sometimes stubborn sentiments of the majority? Is there any perspective, for instance, from which gay people might affirm the value of their committed unions, even when substantial majorities react to the prospect of gay marriage with sentiments of aversion rather than approval? Such a perspective does exist. If one adopts the generalized standpoint and reflects on the usefulness and agreeableness of gay unions for the partners themselves and those affected by them, one has cause to affirm their value, whatever the majority may feel at present. The sentiments of those averse to gay unions will be properly excluded from the generalized standpoint if they are based on prejudice, ignorance, or superstition. They will carry less weight, too, if those holding such sentiments are not themselves directly affected by gay unions, as is the case for most people who oppose such unions.[32] The moral affirmation of gay unions also is compatible with a Humean, minimalist standard of human nature, conceived in terms of common, empirically verifiable needs and purposes. This affirmation supports rather than thwarts the common needs for love, companionship, sexual gratification, and the sharing of a life; and it answers to the empirical fact that a portion of the population best satisfies these needs with members of the same sex. Consequently, one whose sentiments are structured by the generalized perspective and sensitive to what empirical experience informs us about human nature, including its diversity of sexual orientations, can affirm the value of gay marriage. This conclusion is compatible with the ideal of equal respect, as well. The moral sentiment account thus allows for a critical perspective on existing legal conventions and social practices, and makes it possible to mount principled challenges to the de facto moral judgments of a majority.

It is true that a person exercising sound affective judgment could, in principle, reach a different conclusion on this matter than the one just articulated. The line of reasoning laid out here is intended to rebut the concern that deliberation from reflective sentiment allows of no principled perspective from which one could affirm the value of a position in the presence of public sentiments to the contrary. My example shows that a critical perspective is possible, but this is not to say that the conclusions one might reach through this perspective are incontestable. It is conceivable that some sentiments of aversion to gay unions may not arise from prejudice, ignorance, or superstition. Where such sentiments and the character that stands behind them are themselves endorsable from within a suitably structured generalized perspective, and compatible with equal respect and with what empirical experience tells us about human nature, they will legitimately figure in judgment. As we saw in chapter 3, impartial judgment can sometimes point in different directions. The fact that sound judgment may not always yield one and only one legitimate conclusion should not be alarming. A theory of moral judgment need not (and should not) aspire to the perfect determinacy that Rawls associates with his "moral geometry."[33] The aspiration to perfect determinacy in judgment is not true to the nature of moral or political life, which regularly are characterized by dilemmas in which no single, perfectly right answer exists that would render all other possible answers perfectly wrong. Human goods are genuinely plural. Some judgments will be better than others, and a theory of judgment should provide the criteria for distinguishing sound from unsound judgments; yet two equally sound judgments on a single issue can sometimes yield different conclusions. Still, if we must live with a measure of indeterminacy in moral life, *political* life often demands determinate decisions. The possible grounds for making such decisions in the face of moral indeterminacy will be explored in the next chapter.

The appeal that the moral sentiment model of judgment makes to common, empirically verifiable human concerns may seem to be at odds with an important principle of liberal-democratic life—namely, toleration. One might worry that the appeal to *common* concerns will lead to an assimilationism that undermines liberal protections for diversity. In addition, the appeal to *empirical* concerns may appear to systematically foreclose a role for religious beliefs within individual judgment on public matters. The gay-marriage case brings out the first danger. I have argued that in light of the endorsable sentiments of those affected by gay marriage, as well as the principle of equal respect and the common human concerns that such marriages would serve, there are grounds to endorse gay marriage. In appealing to common human concerns, this account implies that the justification of new claims must proceed in part by invoking familiar feelings and shared values. Does this mean that there is no possibility of respecting or protecting people whose identity sets them so far apart from the majority that no common concerns exist between them? Must we show that gay relationships are uniformly like straight ones in order to sustain a defense of gay-marriage rights?

The moral sentiment approach does presuppose that common ground usually can be found among diverse human identities. We should not let the real differences between us blind us to what we do share. Social coordination would be impossible without any common ground, and social coordination is clearly not impossible. Still, it is equally important to recognize that common concerns are often expressed in different ways. For instance, Americans respect the right to freedom of religion because they recognize both that religion represents a very common human concern and that religion takes diverse forms. If religious convictions did not take so many different forms, we would have no need for the right of free exercise; but neither would we need it if religious conviction were not such a common concern. Because religion is commonly important, but important in different ways, we let people practice it in their own ways (or not at all). A similar argument could be made about marriage. The desire to form intimate associations, often including the raising of children, is a common and often quite powerful one. Yet this desire can take a variety of forms. To argue for the right to gay marriage is not to force gays and lesbians to assimilate to a single, heteronormative model of intimate association. It is rather to extend the right of marriage to another form of intimate association, one that serves, in its distinctive way, needs that are very common among human beings.

Marriage among heterosexuals in contemporary liberal democracies hardly represents a single fixed ideal of intimate association anyway. The character and purposes of heterosexual marriages vary significantly. People marry for all kinds of reasons in free societies: romantic love, sexual passion, friendship, social status, money, the desire to reproduce and raise children, pressure from parents, social conformism, professional ambition, religious piety, the fear of loneliness, accidental pregnancy, and on and on. Different marriages combine and prioritize these (and other) purposes in different ways. The character of the marriage relation also differs. Among other things, marriages may be egalitarian or inegalitarian, communicative or quiet, cooperative or combative, passionate or tame, and they may involve lots of time together or a great deal of independence. In this sense, "traditional" marriage is itself not one thing but many different ways of forming intimate partnerships. Gay marriage would add to this existing diversity even as it answered to certain common concerns. We no more need to show that gay relationships are uniformly like straight ones to defend gay marriage than we need to show that straight relationships are uniformly alike to sustain the rights of heterosexuals to marry. Nor does the right to marry (whether for gays or straights) imply a duty to do so. The fact that one can approve gay marriage from within a sentiment-based account of judgment need not entail that all gay people should marry. The desire for lasting intimate associations is common enough to justify making marriage available to all but it offers no justification for making it mandatory.

The other worry about moral sentiment that goes to the question of toleration involves the place of religion in moral judgment. Given that religious convictions, though diverse in their content, constitute common areas of concern for many people across cultures and over time, it seems that a theory of moral judgment that would exclude these convictions out of hand would itself be at odds with something fundamental in human nature. Does the moral sentiment account of impartial judgment discount the convictions of religious believers? We must distinguish, of course, between the role of religiously motivated sentiments in formal public deliberation as will-formation and their role within opinion-formation and individual judgment on public matters. When it comes to the formal decision-making procedures that issue in binding law, democratic legitimacy precludes religiously motivated sentiments from providing the sole justification for decisions that will be coercively enforced on all citizens. As we shall see in chapter 5, such decisions need to be justified in terms that have wider appeal, although it is true that religiously motivated sentiments often overlap with sentiments that are commonly held and consistent with shared public values. With respect to the more informal processes of public deliberation that result in nonbinding opinion-formation, we have already seen the importance of incorporating the widest range of sentiments. Here religiously based sentiments should have free play. They can potentially contribute usefully to the cultivation of an inclusive faculty of moral sentiment and ultimately to impartiality in deliberation. They can also provide a valuable critical perspective on prevailing social values and the public's existing horizons of concern.

The proper role of religiously motivated sentiments within individual moral judgment, including judgment on public matters of justice, raises a different set of questions. In particular, should such sentiments carry weight within the generalized perspective of moral sentiment? The empiricism of Hume's own philosophy seems to recommend against their incorporation. Must we go along with his view in this regard? No single answer to this question could fairly cover all cases, but some general principles are relevant here. Recall that the sentiments that properly figure in the generalized standpoint are themselves subject to critical evaluation. They must be endorsable from within a suitably structured perspective of evaluation, they must be compatible with equal respect, and they must be consistent with what empirical experience tells us about human nature, supporting rather than thwarting common human concerns. This is a reflective process in which the intellect clearly has a role. If reflection reveals that the sentiments in question are grounded in mistakes of fact or are in conflict with the ideal of equal respect, they should be excluded. Religiously motivated sentiments will be subject to the same standards of critical evaluation as are other sentiments that are candidates for inclusion in the generalized standpoint. Some of these sentiments will meet the standards, others will not.

We should also note that there are real differences, even for most religious believers, between faith, on the one hand, and practical judgment and deliberation, on the other. Faith explicitly rejects the evidence of the senses; it rests on an appreciation of the mystery of God's nature and will. The central articles of Christian faith, for example, which defy the laws of the empirical world, are just that: articles of faith, not conclusions of judgment. One comes to believe them, if one does, as the result of a leap of faith in which one is asked to suspend the otherwise legitimate conditions of good judgment. Faith by its nature operates outside the usual constraints of empirical evidence. By contrast, decisions about action generally do involve empirical considerations, even for religious believers. I may believe, based on my faith, that I have an immortal soul that will live on after the death of my body, but most likely I would not decide, based on this conviction, to cross a busy street without checking for approaching cars or to jump off a third-floor balcony in lieu of taking the stairs. When it comes to action-guiding judgment and deliberation of the sort being considered here, even most religious people look to the evidence of their senses for guidance.[34] This is true, or should be true, for the moral evaluation that serves to guide action.

A theory of moral judgment that simply ruled out the influence of religiously based sentiments (or reached to the reformation of religion) would face difficult challenges. At the very least, it would require a long argument to justify universally discounting something that operates as an important source of moral inspiration and guidance for so many people. The moral sentiment account need not make this demand. On the other hand, it will indeed define some religiously based convictions as examples of poor judgment—namely, those that fly in the face of what empirical experience tells us about common human concerns and the causes of human suffering, or those that discount on principle the value of empirical evidence. The decision to disbelieve the theory of evolution despite the preponderance of scientific evidence that supports it is a right of citizens and a prerogative of persons, but it is also a case of poor judgment. The same is true for the people who believe that homosexuals are possessed by demons (as one placard on election day in 2004 read), despite all that their eyes and ears could tell them to the contrary, should they choose to attend to the empirical evidence. Most religious people do not take their religious beliefs as a justification for ignoring the evidence of the empirical world or turning a blind eye to the actual joys and sufferings of other persons, of course, so demarcating as unsound those judgments that do ignore empirical evidence or the sentiments of others need not entail a wholesale rejection of religiously informed moral evaluation.

The deepest difference between religious and sentiment-based accounts of moral judgment concerns the sources of normativity. The moral sentiment approach takes common human concerns and the sentiments of affected persons, when impartially arrived at, to be intrinsically normative. There is nothing mysterious or otherworldly about morality on this view; morality is grounded in who we are as human beings and in what we need to sustain social coordination. Theological views, which see God as the source of normativity, necessarily dispute this claim. Whether this metaphysical dispute needs to affect the practice of sound moral judgment is another question, however. It is conceivable that the two views could coexist as a practical matter. One can imagine a religious believer who thinks that the reason human beings typically share certain fundamental concerns (the desire for friendship or intimate association; the aversion to being enslaved or humiliated) is that God made us this way, or that God wills it to be so. God's authority thus underwrites the authority of the moral sentiments that incorporate these common concerns. Yet the way we gain access to God's will for us, this believer thinks, is by attending (in an impartial fashion) to such concerns. God is mediated by, or made manifest in, the empirical world, and moral sentiment properly construed is the voice of God speaking to, and through, human beings. The practice of moral judgment on this view thus takes the form identified by the moral sentiment model, although it sees the authority of judgments as ultimately undergirded by the authority of God.

The full articulation of such a position would require the development of a theological view that is well beyond the scope of this study. My speculation here is meant to suggest the possibility of a rapprochement between the empirical approach to moral judgment and certain religious approaches. If we accept that reflective sentiments, when properly arrived at, carry normative force, and if we agree that our actions should be guided by such sentiments, we can remain agnostic about *why* they are normative for us. We can leave to one side the vexed metaphysical question of whether or not there is a God that authorizes them, and agree that even if God stands behind moral sentiment, the only way to deliberate well about what we ought to do is to engage it. Even in looking to God for guidance, one might say, we must always engage the evidence that the world has to offer. This position surely will conflict with some religious doctrines. The rapprochement offered here is only partial, for some believers will insist that knowledge of God's will comes to them by way of revelations that have nothing whatsoever to do with the facts of this world. Evaluations that follow from such doctrines—and are therefore willfully blind to the evidence of the senses and the sentiments of other persons—will fall outside the scope of sound judgment. The exclusion of some views is inevitable, of course. On any viable account of sound judgment, there will be some examples of judgment that do not make the grade. Yet the moral sentiment approach will be practically compatible with plenty of the moral judgments carried out by religious believers. We can criticize the soundness of some religiously based judgments without excluding religious beliefs per se or nullifying the basis of all religious belief. And even where the moral sentiment model implies that a particular, religiously motivated judgment is a poor one, we need not seek to exclude it from the informal practices of public deliberation. The interest that we all have in impartial deliberation, which requires an inclusive form of moral sentiment, argues for public policies and cultural practices that welcome into informal public discussion the voices of all those affected, and that make available sentiments that may fruitfully challenge or reform existing sensibilities.

One final consideration worth mentioning before we proceed involves the relationship between moral sentiment and individual rights. We have seen that moral sentiment must incorporate a critical perspective, that the sentiments that properly figure within the generalized standpoint must be limited to those that can themselves be endorsed from within a suitably structured generalized perspective (in light of the value of equal respect and the sentiments of those affected) and that support rather than thwart common human concerns. On these grounds, the prejudiced aversions of a racist ought not be factored into the standpoint of moral sentiment in arriving at an impartial judgment of Martin Luther King's courage, for instance. Likewise, the fact that some people in previous eras (and some even today) have found it desirable to hold slaves in no way legitimates this practice. The iterative character of moral sentiment and the principle of equal respect thus impose certain constraints on impartial judgment. These constraints may seem to resemble rights since they force us to consider the legitimate sentiments of all affected (but only their legitimate sentiments) and hence to treat persons with equal respect. Indeed, one might think that much of the normative work being done by moral sentiment in fact results from an implicit theory of rights, one that may stand in tension with the moral sentiment approach. On this interpretation, impartial judgment and deliberation turn out to rest on knowledge of fundamental rights as much as on the sympathetic communication of sentiments. And it is only to the extent that moral sentiment respects the limits imposed by individual rights that this account of judgment can be compatible with liberal democracy—or so one might argue. Does the moral sentiment model of judgment quietly bring a Kantian notion of rights in through the back door? Must it do so to avoid running afoul of the fundamental commitments of liberalism and democracy?

As we saw in chapter 3, Kantianism is not the only basis for establishing the principle of respect for persons and the deliberative constraints it imposes. The constraints on the generalized perspective that help constitute impartial judgment can be explained and justified in broadly Humean terms, although it may indeed make good sense to call them rights. There are first of all pragmatic grounds for these constraints. As Hume pointed out, partiality and ignorance, or an overly narrow faculty of moral sentiment, lead us into continual conflict and contradiction with others and with ourselves. The fact of our interdependence means that we need to be able to coordinate our actions with others if we are to satisfy our own purposes, and this requires coordinating our evaluative responses or judgments. Such coordination is only possible if our judgments are relatively consistent, and consistency requires impartiality. As a general matter, then, the more impartial we are in judgment and deliberation, the more successful we are likely to be in the long run in achieving our most important purposes.

Furthermore, we cannot identify in advance those with whom we may need to coordinate in the future, and consequently we should always incorporate as many (endorsable) perspectives into our judgments as possible. It is true that great inequalities and large distances may disrupt the experience of interdependence. Wealthy Americans insulate themselves in many ways from the poor. Likewise, the citizen of a prosperous Western democracy rarely thinks about, much less interacts with, the average Sudanese villager. In many cases, it seems, one can achieve one's purposes without attending at all to the sentiments of others. And although one cannot always predict exactly whose cooperation one will need in the future, one *can* predict, in light of long-standing patterns of inequality and large territorial distances, that certain groups of persons are not likely to be very relevant. Granted, if distances are so great that no interaction or mutual dependence exists at all, then it is difficult to see why the views of others should figure in one's judgment. After all, impartiality requires incorporating the sentiments of all *affected* others. Where others are truly not affected, their sentiments have no grounds to carry weight in one's deliberation. But what about cases where one's personal or political actions would affect others, but where the relevant others are weaker persons or peoples? Why should we consult their sentiments? Why be impartial where the power differentials are so great as to disrupt the experience of interdependence? As a pragmatic matter, we should take seriously Hobbes's insight that even the weak often have strength enough to disrupt the purposes of the powerful. In the United States, the rich tend to avoid direct contact with the poor but they pay the costs of poverty in countless ways, from the alarm systems they install to secure their property to the private school tuition they pay to education their children. At the international level, the later history of colonialism and the unfolding consequences of new imperialisms suggest that "dominant" peoples are never invulnerable to those they dominate and cannot afford over the long term to forsake the sentiments of others in their judgments. The fact that people sometimes turn a blind eye to these costs and vulnerabilities does not make them go away, and it does not undermine the prudential justification for respect for persons and the impartiality it supports.

In a more explicitly normative vein, recall that Hume also insisted that an overly narrow sympathy reflects a "want of humanity," a vice that will tend to elicit feelings of disapproval when considered impartially. The kind of person we can admire is one who is sufficiently well educated in the human sentiments and conversant enough with others to be capable of extensive sympathy. Ignorance, prejudice, and partiality cannot themselves be endorsed from within the generalized standpoint of moral sentiment; they tend on the whole to thwart rather than support common human concerns. Therefore we have moral as well as pragmatic grounds to consider the endorsable sentiments of all affected others in moral judgment, or to treat others with equal respect in evaluation and deliberation. The ideal of equal respect can also be established with reference to the fact of reflective autonomy, as we saw in chapter 3. To be clear, the principle of equal respect in this context does not mean that the actual sentiments of all parties are to be automatically weighted equally in the deliberative process. As we have seen, there may be grounds for weighting the sentiments of different parties differently in any given case. Equal respect instead requires that the sentiments of all affected be considered impartially, and that where they do not themselves thwart the principles of equal respect, or the common concerns of human nature, or the sentiments of those affected by them, they be incorporated into the generalized perspective of moral sentiment and reflected in our judgments.

Insofar as honoring the principle of equal respect, or acting on the virtue of humanity, is a condition of moral excellence and a component of impartial moral judgment, it makes sense to see it as an obligation. And as a general obligation, the principle of equal respect yields a basic right to be respected on the part of all individuals. In this sense, we can say that the individual right to equal respect constrains the operation of moral sentiment. The principle of equal respect constrains moral sentiment but it is justified with reference to common concerns and by means of moral sentiment. So even if we must look to the principle of equal respect to reconcile moral sentiment with the norms of liberal democracy, we need not conclude that the moral sentiment model rests on a hidden Kantianism or incorporates a theory of rights with which it is fundamentally at odds. One need not be a Kantian to be committed to impartiality, or the liberal right to equal respect, or to democracy itself; there are good Humean grounds for these commitments. There are also Humean resources available for sustaining the practice of equal respect. First among these is sympathy, which facilitates the communication of sentiments and thereby enables us to enact respect for others in the sense most relevant to moral evaluation. As we have discussed, however, the practice of sympathy is naturally partial in its scope. To successfully support the virtue of humanity and the obligation of equal respect, sympathy needs to be cultivated in the direction of greater inclusiveness and to be educated in the sentiments of persons whose identity or experience may be unfamiliar.

Cultivating Moral Sentiment

The moral sentiment account of individual judgment and deliberation thus suggests that the cultivation of impartiality will require the education of moral sentiment and the development of sympathy. This cultivation will need to go beyond the common accounts of the virtues required for liberal-democratic citizenship. Socializing persons to recognize the rational ideals of mutual respect and toleration, which is the focus of many civic liberal accounts, is important but it cannot replace the education of moral feeling. We need to cultivate the capacity to feel with the widest range of others, not merely familiarize ourselves with their cultural practices. As we understand better the affective dimensions of judgment, our schools, youth organizations, and families can be more effective in developing the appropriate capacities in children, in fostering the affective as well as intellectual faculties that sustain impartial judgment. In civics classes, for instance, we should be teaching students about the institutions of American government and the principles that underlie them, but we should also be educating the imaginative capacities that figure so importantly in moral sentiment.

Biographies and movies can be effective tools in this regard insofar as they represent in affectively engaging ways the sentiments of persons whose life experiences may be unfamiliar but whose concerns must be included if judgment and deliberation are to be impartial. More generally, school reading lists should strive to balance classic works of literature with works that consciously reflect the experiences of marginalized groups. Note that the moral sentiment justification for this practice differs from more familiar ones, which emphasize the self-esteem of marginalized persons. From the standpoint of affective judgment, the purpose of including such literature in educational curricula is not so much to enhance the self-esteem of those in the minority as to educate the moral sentiments of the majority. And history should never be neglected, for it helps educate us to the common human concerns that cross time and culture as well as alert us to the ways in which our own public horizons of concern may be distinctive or new. Finally, a renewed commitment to strong and integrated public schools is called for. In conjunction with this, we should consider establishing incentives for private primary and secondary schools to encourage a greater measure of socioeconomic, cultural, and racial diversity in their student bodies. Sympathy needs exposure to difference if it is to serve impartiality. This is not to say that exposure to difference inevitably extends our sympathies, but without such exposure the extension of sympathy would be impossible.[35]

The right public policies can also have a positive impact upon the judgments and deliberation of adult citizens. Efforts to encourage, or even require, greater participation in national service programs such as Americorps are worth considering in this regard. Such programs have the potential not only to get citizens from different walks of life working together on public projects but to facilitate the education of moral sentiments in the process. The citizen advisory boards championed by Amy Gutmann and Dennis Thompson might also be effective in bringing more sentiments to bear on public decision making in certain contexts.[36] Legal and institutional mechanisms that increase access to public deliberation and that give voice to the sentiments of persons who might otherwise remain outside the majority's frame of reference are key. Affirmative action policies, as well as greater sensitivity to the representation of minority voices in legislative districting, may help expand the imagination not just of legislators but of citizens more generally. The more that minority voices are formally represented in electoral bodies, the more likely it is that minority sentiments will find their way onto the public stage, whether it is on the floor of Congress or (perhaps more likely) in the pages of the local newspaper. The dynamics of deliberation—even as will-formation—extend beyond what happens on the floor of Congress, of course. The media responds when elected officials speak or write about an issue. Consequently, congressional representatives can put an issue on the public agenda and stimulate debate about it among the citizenry at large even when they do not succeed in passing a particular piece of legislation relevant to it. To the extent that elected officials can be especially effective in introducing marginalized sentiments into the public consciousness, greater diversity among them may serve to educate the moral sentiments of members of the polity as a whole. This effect is independent of any one representative's ability to change the mind of another in actual congressional debate. Moreover, we know that legislative representatives and other elected officials respond to public opinion and the expressed concerns of their constituents, if only because they wish to win re-election. To the extent that greater diversity in congressional membership can help to educate and extend the moral sentiments of the general public, then, congressional decisions are likely to reflect, indirectly through the pressure of public opinion, this diversity of membership. So while there is reason to think that greater diversity in Congress could have a salutary effect on moral sentiment in the general public— even if it does not directly affect legislative outcomes—we should also expect these outcomes to be affected by the greater impartiality among average citizens that congressional diversity fosters. Here the requirements of impartial judgment add new considerations to the usual justification for policies such as racially sensitive legislative districting, which typically center on fairness.[37] The moral sentiment model of judgment suggests that these policies may be important not only as matters of fairness but also because they may support the cultivation of moral sentiment and the development of impartial deliberation among us.

Another place where institutional mechanisms might help facilitate the development of moral sentiment is in jury deliberation. Tocqueville treated the jury as a key site for the education of civic virtue in democratic societies.[38] More recently, Jeffrey Abramson has remarked on the fact that deliberating jurors cross "all kinds of racial and ethnic lines to define a shared sense of justice," and for this reason he insists that the jury "is more crucial than ever in a multiethnic society struggling to articulate a justice common to U.S. citizens."[39] To be successful in this regard certain conditions need apply. First, the cross-sectional approach to jury selection needs to be combined with new limits on peremptory challenges. The heavy use of peremptories too often results in juries that represent an insufficiently broad range of personal experience and sentiment. It permits attorneys on both sides to select juries according to their perceived favorability instead of the capacity for broadly extended sympathy.[40] In addition, we need to abandon the idea that impartiality is best secured through ignorance.[41] Knowledge about matters relating to the case at hand ought not in itself constitute general grounds for dismissal, unless it can be determined that a particular juror is indeed biased as the result of this knowledge. Juries need information—sometimes extralegal information—to reach sound verdicts, and studies show that the personal knowledge jurors bring to deliberation can be crucial.[42] This is especially true in cases where a just verdict depends on the jury's grasp of the sentiments of the defendant. Ignorance of the perspectives of others undercuts impartial judgment because it prevents sympathy from operating effectively. This is also true in cases where community sentiment is called upon, for jurors cannot hope to embody the conscience of the community on some matter if they are in the dark about (or indifferent to) the range of feelings that constitute it.

For these reasons, in cases where empirical evidence demonstrates the existence of a systematic negative sympathy index for members of a particular group, it may be important to ensure that several persons from the same group are included on the jury.[43] More generally, the importance of cultivating an extended sympathy suggests that we should prefer twelve-member juries to the smaller ones that have arisen in many jurisdictions in the last generation since larger groups are likely to contain a wider range of personal information and diverse sentiments.[44] Moreover, the principle of unanimity should replace majority-rule juries where the latter have taken hold. For there is a good deal of strong evidence that demonstrates unanimous-rule juries are more deliberative.[45] In particular, unanimity imposes an incentive on jurors to engage the widest range of relevant sentiments. And because juries educate the moral faculties of citizens, the institutional mechanisms that extend sympathy and foster moral sentiment in jurors may also support greater impartiality in the moral and political deliberations of persons more generally.

A vibrant civil society with strong civic associations and legal protections for cultural, religious, and other identity groups is likewise crucial. As we have seen, such associations are often vehicles for the effective communication of sentiments among citizens. This consideration suggests that the state should adopt positions in law and public policy that allow for the flourishing of the greatest measure of diversity in this regard that is compatible with basic civil liberties and social justice. Public arts programs represent another opportunity to support the development of moral sentiment within the venue of civil society. Robert Goodin has emphasized that art and literature are important means for communicating the sentiments of others and thereby extending citizens' imaginations in ways that expand the moral standpoint and generate greater impartiality. Beyond well-stocked public libraries and public funding for the arts, he encourages us to press for real diversity in the projects we fund and display. This means accepting the fact that some of these projects are bound to be controversial, or "sad or depressing or downright obnoxious."[46] Too often public funding is regarded as legitimately reserved for works of art that do not offend prevailing sensibilities. Why should citizens have to pay for paintings that defile their deeply held religious beliefs, for example? But this approach is misguided. Art and literature are tremendously powerful educators of the deliberative faculties because of their effectiveness in conveying to us the sentiments of others, and often the sentiments that offend existing sensibilities are the ones about which we most need to be educated if we are to deliberate impartially. A key purpose of public programs that fund the arts (as well as public television and public radio) is to probe and explore the status quo, and, not infrequently, to challenge it in ways that expand the moral sentiments and enhance our deliberative capacities.

Much more could be said about the cultural programs, social practices, and political institutions that might support moral sentiment and help cultivate impartiality. My comments here are intended to be suggestive only. To specify in a compelling fashion the range of policy initiatives likely to foster moral sentiment and impartiality would require extensive empirical research that is beyond the scope of this study. For our purposes, it is enough to emphasize that the right political context matters for moral judgment, even individual judgment. Democratic rights and representative political institutions give citizens an incentive to take seriously the sentiments of others. Public policies regarding education and the support of the arts, electoral mechanisms such as legislative districting, and legal practices regulating the constitution of juries, among other things, may affect the extent to which persons develop the deep and broad faculty of moral sentiment that supports impartiality and leads to sound deliberation. Freedom of association and speech give us access to the sentiments of others, of which we might otherwise remain ignorant. And the continuing practices of democratic debate and contestation—ranging from public demonstrations to arguments at the office water cooler to weblogs—make these sentiments present to the public consciousness and available to individual judgment in important ways. The sentiment-based account of judgment and deliberation thus recommends a deliberative-system approach to public deliberation, which makes room (at the level of opinion-formation) for many sentiments that fall short of the strict demands of public reason. Expansive informal deliberation supports affective impartiality.

By the same token, the moral sentiment model of impartiality has much to offer our theories of public deliberation. It helps illuminate how the process of deliberation as opinion-formation actually proceeds, and how social criticism and reform unfold. Some will worry that by recognizing the ways in which sentiment-based responses figure in judgment and deliberation we may inadvertently unleash the ugliest and most dangerous parts of human nature. Sympathy communicates sentiments of aversion as well as approbation, after all. And when people act on their aversions in politics, things can get ugly very fast. This concern has a long and distinguished lineage in the history of Western political philosophy, and it is not without merit. Hume himself was sensitive to the dangers of certain passions in politics, and we should be, too. Liberal-democratic political institutions, individual rights, and the rule of law all set limits on what we can do to one another, and they may force us to show consideration for the sentiments of other persons even when we contemplate such persons with aversion. These factors are crucial both to a decent society and to sound judgment and deliberation. The Humean approach does not deny the value of liberal-democratic protections against the influence of untutored passion. As we have seen, such protections can be justified from the perspective of Humean judgment and are required for its fullest flourishing. What the Humean approach denies is the possibility of deliberating in a way that fully abstracts from passions and the horizons of concern they constitute. It also denies the viability of a sanitized theory of moral sentiment, along the lines defended by one recent commentator, which welcomes "positive emotions" such as benevolence and fellow-feeling but seeks to exclude such "negative emotions" as shame and disgust.[47] Our aversions, when they result from a properly structured moral perspective, can tell us as much about how we should act as our feelings of approbation do. The fact that people sometimes will feel (and try to act on) aversions that do not result from impartial judgment is not a reason to turn away from the sentiment-based model of judgment—because no sentiment-*free* form of practical judgment is available to us. In this sense, there is no real choice to be made between the sentiment-based model and the rationalist one because we cannot deliberate about practical ends without affect. So to argue for a sentiment-based model of judgment and deliberation is not to recommend bringing more passions into politics, or to encourage people to be more emotional and less reflective in their judgments. It is rather to defend a clearer understanding of what is already happening (and what cannot help but happen) when we deliberate about what we ought to do. In the next chapter, we turn to the role of moral sentiment within the formal procedures of public deliberation as will-formation, and explore how it supports the impartiality that makes democratic decisions legitimate.

CHAPTER FIVE

Public Deliberation and the Feeling of Impartiality

CHAPTER 4 SHOWED how liberal-democratic institutions and practices can enlarge moral sentiment, thus enhancing the impartiality of individual judgment among citizens on important public issues that raise questions of justice. Impartial moral judgment on the part of individuals plays an important role in the process of opinion-formation in liberal democracies, but when it comes to the formal procedures of will-formation, something more than the impartial judgment of individuals is needed. Public deliberation differs from moral judgment in the sense that it operates under distinctive constraints. Because it issues in decisions that are coercively enforced on all citizens through law, public deliberation in a democratic state must build in mechanisms to ensure that those subject to the outcomes of deliberation are also in some real way its authors and masters.[1] Important as individual impartiality is, public deliberation will need to meet additional criteria if it is to generate legitimate decisions.

Public deliberation also differs in structural ways from the judgments of individuals because it involves collective rather than individual evaluation and leads to collective decision making.[2] To a significant degree, public deliberation happens between persons rather than within persons. It is true that individual acts of judgment and deliberation are intrinsically intersubjective in the sense that they build upon the history of communicated sentiments.[3] If persons never communicated with one another about their responses to the world, then moral judgment could not arise. Yet any single act of moral judgment or deliberation is a function of the mind and heart of an individual human being. By contrast, democratic public deliberation transpires only between persons and as a process of active communication. Thus Benjamin Barber insists that "political judgment is defined by activity in common rather than thinking alone."[4] Public deliberation is "in essence political and not cognitive," he says, because "*I* cannot judge politically, only *we* can" do so.[5] Along these lines, some deliberative democrats even speak of "subjectless communication," to use Habermas's term, to emphasize the idea that public deliberation cannot be construed in terms of the faculties and internal experiences of individual subjects but exists only in the public, communicative interactions that transpire between persons.[6]

Furthermore, unlike individual moral judgment, public deliberation must answer to the fundamental political values that govern the exercise of power in the specific polity in which it arises. In a constitutional liberal democracy, this means that public deliberation is subject to the legal constraints of a constitution, a tradition of constitutional interpretation, and a set of basic rights, all of which codify in law the public values. Beyond that, political deliberation typically takes place in the context of the need for determinate decisions, usually on matters of some dispute, which will affect the lives of people who may disagree deeply about them. The need for determinate decisions and the fact of disagreement thus set additional constraints on public deliberation in liberal democracies. Finally, public deliberation is subject to constraints arising from the particular institutional settings in which it takes place. The deliberative practices of legislators, for instance, will differ in some measure from those of judges, executives, and members of the general public. In the American context, the institutional structure and function of each branch of government and those of civil society set different types of constraint on deliberation in each domain, although some core features will be consistent across domains. These core features establish impartiality and are best characterized as aspects of reciprocity.

Reciprocity is the guiding light of most theories of deliberative democracy. It entails that "citizens owe one another justifications for the institutions, laws, and public policies that collectively bind them."[7] Deliberation guided by reciprocity is typically understood as a process of seeking "mutually justifiable reasons, and reaching a mutually binding decision on the basis of those reasons."[8] The ideal of reciprocity is indeed important, but as usually conceived within theories of deliberative democracy it is marred by an excessive rationalism. By the same token, previous attempts to make the theory of public deliberation more receptive to affect have lacked principled criteria for specifying the proper role and limits of affect, or have unwittingly subjugated it to the intellect; and they have tended to eschew the important deliberative ideal of impartiality. This chapter argues for an alternative understanding of reciprocity—and with it, democratic deliberation—that incorporates sentiments within an ideal of impartiality and provides principled criteria for the proper inclusion of sentiment but without subjugating it to the rule of reason, where reason is understood to be independent of sentiment. Reciprocity rightly conceived involves the communication of appropriate sentiments and an attachment to the common, affective concerns that are constitutive of the political order. The intellect has a role in reciprocity but its function is not to transcend the influence of sentiment. The dominant accounts have acknowledged the perspective-taking dimension of reciprocity but not the affective elements of this practice. On the moral sentiment view, impartial deliberation will be guided by reflective concern rather than by a form of reason that leaves affect behind. This account of reciprocity makes it possible to distinguish between sentiments that rightly have a place in the deliberative context and those that should be excluded. It provides further evidence that affect and impartiality need not be mutually exclusive; indeed, real impartiality in public deliberation depends on the proper incorporation of sentiment.

Reasons and Passions in Deliberative Democracy

The theories of deliberative democracy that proliferated among political theorists and philosophers in the 1990s sought new ways of understanding the practices of democratic decision making. They meant to provide a corrective to the long-dominant aggregative model of democracy, which treated political decisions as the outcomes of procedures (above all the vote) that were intended to collect and represent the individual preferences of citizens, but which did not attend to the deliberative process leading up to such procedures. The aggregative view had already begun to come under fire in the preceding decade from social-choice theorists who argued that voting fails systematically to produce outcomes that accurately represent citizen preferences.[9] This claim called into question the feasibility of majority will as the sole basis of democratic legitimacy. It also opened the door to other criticisms. Some questioned the aggregative model's assumption of established preferences on the part of individual citizens. Bernard Manin, for example, challenged the idea that citizens enter the process of collective decision making with a coherent set of fixed interests. Instead, he said, whatever initial preferences citizens may have at the outset of deliberation are inevitably transformed in the process of decision making. The result is that the true source of political legitimacy in democratic societies must be "not the predetermined will of individuals, but rather the process of its formation, that is, deliberation itself."[10]

Other theorists pointed out that the representation of individual interests is only one part of democratic decision making. On many issues citizens vote on the basis of principled commitments so that their votes express "beliefs about what the correct policies are . . . not personal preferences for policies."[11] On this view of what citizens do in the voting booth, the aggregative model misses the mark entirely, for it fails to capture the epistemic character of public choices. Decision making is not a matter of aggregating preferences but rather a process of forming common judgments based on the principled beliefs of participants.[12] Another objection to aggregative democracy concerns the fact that it "fundamentally accepts and may even enforce existing distributions of power in society," and consequently that it leaves basic questions of justice vulnerable to being settled by the competition for power among interest groups and elites.[13] Finally, some theorists have held that the aggregative approach has become obsolete in view of changes in the nature of the issues that have crowded the public stage in the United States in recent years. As Seyla Benhabib puts it, the 1980s and 1990s saw a "shift from 'issues of distribution,' " where preference-based decision making had a natural place, to "a concern with 'the grammar of forms of life,' " which involve conflicts of moral values. As struggles over wealth and political position were supplanted in politics by debates about abortion, gay rights, environmentalism, and the like, the competition of interests gave way to a clash of values, and consequently aggregation became less relevant as a model for democratic decision making.[14] So the critics have challenged aggregative democracy on practical, conceptual, moral, and historical grounds. At some point, of course, decisions must be concluded, and here aggregation in the form of voting is a necessary part of the democratic process. The point pressed by deliberative democrats is that the aggregative moment ought to be preceded by real deliberation.

Thus the heart of deliberative democracy is the idea that political decisions, if they are to be legitimate, must reflect the deliberation of citizens and public officials, where deliberation is defined as "communication [that] induces reflection on preferences [and, we could add, values] in non-coercive fashion."[15] Moreover, to yield legitimate decisions, the procedures of deliberation must themselves be democratic in the sense that they instantiate respect for persons as free and equal. The deliberative dimension of democratic politics is indeed a crucial one, and for all the reasons that deliberative democrats identify. Above all, while interests have a place in political decision making, questions of law and public policy that involve justice should not be left to interest-group competition or the play of power. Such matters demand deliberation that is informed by a moral standpoint, for we could never endorse (from within the moral standpoint) the practice of deciding questions of justice on the basis of prevailing relations of power alone. And while acts of pure altruism are relatively rare, most of us regularly vote on the basis of our convictions about what is right and not only as an expression of self-interested preferences for particular candidates or policies. This is often true even when the issue at hand is one of distribution, but it is virtually always the case when the issue involves a conflict of values. Moreover, as we saw in chapter 4, public deliberation in the domain of opinion-formation usefully extends the individual moral imagination and thereby enhances the impartiality of our moral judgments. So, for both political and moral reasons, democratic deliberation is important. We should support procedural mechanisms in political institutions and in the wider practices of civil society that facilitate a deliberative approach to public decision making, at least so far as this is consistent with protections for constitutional rights and basic civil liberties.

Yet we should be more skeptical than are most deliberative democrats about the power of reason, conceived as an intellectual faculty that is disengaged from passion, to motivate and legitimate public decisions. It may seem strange to champion the importance of deliberation while challenging the power of reason so conceived. After all, deliberation is almost universally regarded as an exercise of disengaged reason. The more deliberative a decision process is, the more insulated it will be from the influence of affective attachments and desires—or so the common view has it. Thus the procedural criteria for legitimate decision making that figure so importantly in theories of deliberative democracy are typically intended to ensure that decisions "answer to reason" as opposed to sentiment. This is especially true of the reciprocity requirement, which demands that deliberation be conducted in terms that all "have reason" to accept, and which is meant to establish the impartiality of deliberative processes. The reasonableness of decisions makes them impartial and gives them legitimacy because in theory it protects decisions from the influence of passions.[16] Legitimate public deliberation therefore "will engage the mind rather than ignite the passions."[17] Political discussion "unsullied by irrationality" is the ideal.[18] In fact, if "the force motivating the decisions is passion rather than reason," then the decisions are not to be counted as deliberative at all.[19] Discussion will be rational, and hence impartial and deliberative, only if participants justify their claims in terms of reasons rather than in terms of sentiments and desires, reasons that may conflict with such concerns. Impartial deliberation exists only where the force of the better argument—and that alone—prevails.[20] This account clearly contains a significant measure of truth, as no one would say that decisions brought about by threats and coercion are deliberative. And passions can indeed obstruct sound judgment. Yet the idea that giving reasons to one another renders decisions subject only to the force of reason, where reason is conceived as a mental faculty that transcends the passions, is a mistake.

References to the reasons that are supposed to move participants in impartial public deliberation, as required by reciprocity, are marked by a certain ambiguity. This ambiguity derives from the different but related meanings assigned to "reasons" as justifications for action and "reason" as a cognitive faculty of the mind associated with thought and understanding.[21] One cannot give a reason for something without having thought about it, and consequently we tend to regard reasons as issuing from the faculty of reason. For deliberative democrats, reasons carry normative weight in a way that mere interests and preferences do not, and this normativity seems to come from their association with the faculty of reason, which (following Kant) is often considered to be the very source of normativity.[22] In other words, our reasons present themselves as particular embodiments of the general capacity for reason, and this status sets them apart from mere sentiments, which are not exclusively intellectual and sometimes not reasoned at all. Because of the special normativity-conferring function of reason, the story goes, our reasons have the power to turn assertions into arguments that justify claims rather than simply express them. By the same token, in the context of public deliberation the act of justification based on reasons seems to make the cognitive faculty of reason the basis for decisions, and hence the determining ground of the collective will. And because sentiments and desires are still commonly seen as forms of passivity while reason is thought to be active, the reasonableness of deliberation—its detachment from affective concerns by means of reason-giving—is thought to make it free. This explains why deliberative democrats insist that decisions must be reasonable in order to be legitimate, for political legitimacy on the democratic view requires that decisions reflect the free choices of those bound by them. Decisions that are justified with reference to reasons are free because reason itself, which generates reasons, is free and is the source of human freedom.

But what are reasons, really? According to Joshua Cohen, a notable contributor to the deliberative democracy literature, reasons in the general sense are "considerations."[23] Cohen does not define considerations, but we may infer that they include anything that can be a determining ground of the will. At first glance, this notion of considerations seems to capture yet another meaning of reasons—namely, the explanatory (that is, non-normative) sense of reasons as the causes or motives of actions. If you ask me why I oppose the war, for instance, I might tell you that my brother is a soldier and I fear for his life. My love for my brother is the consideration that motivates my position, or the reason for it. Reasons-as-causes will include all sorts of interests and preferences, and more generally all kinds of unreflective sentiments and desires. Cohen rejects the explanatory notion of reasons, however, or at least he insists that reasons of this sort should have no role in public deliberation. Deliberative democracy presupposes rather that "the notion of a reason is essentially normative—a term of justification and criticism—and that a reason is not a kind of motivation. Practical reasoning, then, is a matter of reflecting on what one is to do, not what one is motivated to do."[24] Reasons that are normative in public deliberation are still considerations—what else could they be?—but they are not mere causes. Reasons do not explain our claims in light of the affective attachments and desires that constitute our personal motives for action. To count as a reason, a consideration must instead justify our actions or choices in terms of "considerations that others have reason to accept."[25]

The phrase "have reason to accept" introduces more ambiguity. On the one hand, it might refer to the cognitive faculty of reason so as to convey the idea that this faculty authorizes certain considerations as rationally acceptable, or reasonable. This would imply that reason bestows normativity upon these considerations and thereby turns them into "reasons." Cohen's use of "reason" as opposed to "reasons" here points in this direction, as it suggests that reasons are considerations that others will accept *if they have reason*, meaning if they are exercising the faculty of reason. It fits together with his insistence that public deliberation is a matter of reflecting on "what one is to do" (as in, what one is rationally required to do) rather than on what one happens to be motivated to do. On the other hand, his phrasing also points back to the idea of reasons as considerations. It suggests that reasons are considerations that others can accept if they have reasons for doing so, meaning if they are committed to considerations that recommend in this direction. To count as reasons, however, the considerations that recommend in this direction must also be ones that others can accept. In other words, reasons are considerations that others can accept in view of considerations they hold that others can also accept, in view of considerations *they* hold that others can also accept . . . As a practical matter, what this infinite regress means is that reasons are considerations that others can accept given the considerations they hold. If this is the case, then it is not clear what role reason as a cognitive faculty is playing in the generation of reasons as normative, since considerations in themselves may be nonrational, as we have seen. It is true that the cognitive faculty of reason allows us to ascertain whether the considerations that others hold permit them to accept the considerations we are putting forward. Yet what allows them to accept these considerations is not reason itself but the considerations they hold. From this perspective, it is the fact that the considerations are shared—not the faculty of reason—that establishes the status of certain considerations as "reasons" and so makes them normative. On this interpretation, Cohen's invocation of "reason" in the definition of normative "reasons" is something of a red herring since reason as a cognitive faculty is not actually conferring normative value. Yet the association he suggests between reasons and reason lends an air of dignity to the considerations that count as reasons, the dignity traditionally associated with reason as a cognitive faculty and its putative role in generating normativity.

Reason exercises its normative authority, on Cohen's account, by establishing "reasons" that justify decisions independently of the affective concerns that agents actually have. In the background of this account lies the assumption that reason can yield decisions about action in the absence of any connection between the concerns of the agent and the action.[26] Recall Cohen's forceful distinction between what one ought to do and what one is motivated to do. The radical disjuncture between norms and motives is intended to establish and protect the rationality of public deliberation. In fact, for deliberation to be rational it is necessary that our motives (or preferences, as he puts it) be "sensitive to reason" in the sense that "merely believing that I have . . . a reason may suffice to refashion preferences."[27] To illustrate, Cohen invokes the example of a person who sees no reason to help others and has no desire to do so but who does believe that she has reason to avoid harming them. If reflection leads her to see that the explanation for why she has reason to avoid harming others logically implies that she has reason to help them, then she has reason to help and this reason is totally independent of her desires, which (by stipulation) do not include the desire to help.[28] What Cohen concludes from this example is that the faculty of reason generates reasons for action independently of affective concerns or the passions that motivate action, although he adds that reasons so conceived can motivate.[29] So the intellect on its own can motivate decisions, and it can also change affective concerns. Cohen emphasizes that such changes

> are not simply changes of *induced* preference that result from the acquisition of new information through discussion. . . . [T]he kinds of preference changes I am contemplating reflect a sensitivity of motivations—understood as behavioral dispositions—to reasons, understood as standards of criticism and guidance, and not simply a sensitivity of some preferences to information about how most effectively to satisfy other preferences.[30]

In other words, reason yields decisions about action that do not rest on relations between affective concerns (or any previously existing motives) and the action. And only when reason determines decisions in this way are the decisions impartial. So Cohen treats the normative reasons that guarantee impartiality in deliberation as grounded in a faculty of reason that abstracts from affective attachments and desires.

We have seen in previous chapters that there are powerful grounds to doubt this view. Cohen's own example of the person who has no desire to help others but can be persuaded to do so on the basis of a certain belief alone is unconvincing as a statement of reason's power in this regard. The example obfuscates the key role that affective concerns play as background for the justification of the relevant belief. What persuades the agent in this instance is reflection on why she has reason not to harm others; this reflection leads her to see that the justification for that position also justifies helping others. But the "why" here is established in part by the horizon of concern that makes certain things, such as not harming others, *matter* to the agent. These concerns are what carry the justificatory—and motivating—force of the (as she now sees it) injunction to help others. Deeply settled, constitutive concerns like these sometimes conflict with immediately occurring desires. In cases of such conflict, impartiality requires that momentary desires cede to the force of more settled concerns. What happened in the course of the reflection that Cohen describes here is not that reason spontaneously produced a new desire but that the agent came to appreciate in a fuller, deeper way (with the help of reason) the range and implications of her more settled desires, or reflective concerns.

Elsewhere Cohen himself gives us grounds to doubt that motives could be as sensitive to reason as he sometimes suggests, or sensitive in the way he suggests. For in remarking that practical reasoning "may proceed along deliberative paths with only the most attenuated connections to the agent's current aims,"[31] he in effect acknowledges that practical reason cannot abstract *entirely* from the agent's actual aims (which he associates with desires) however "attenuated" the connection between them may be.[32] Human motives are sensitive to reason but only insofar as reason makes contact with existing concerns. This caveat means that it is not reason per se to which our motives are sensitive; instead, our motives are sensitive to our existing concerns. Reason allows us to see that our existing concerns make us sensitive to certain new considerations. Yet the only power that reason itself has in changing occurrent motives is given by the force that our concerns hold for us, and if reason did not connect up with some of these concerns it could not change occurrent motives—as Cohen himself is forced to acknowledge in the passage quoted above, albeit without saying so directly. This point has more than motivational significance. It raises doubts about whether reason, conceived as a strictly cognitive faculty, can generate "standards of criticism and guidance" without reference to at least some of the affective concerns that agents actually have. Given that behavioral dispositions are sensitive only to a combination of reason and existing concerns, reason on its own will never be the determining ground of our decisions about how to behave. If reason by itself cannot determine the conclusions of practical deliberation, then it cannot be the sole source of whatever normative force these conclusions carry. This is why claims about reason (conceived independently of affect) as the source of moral and political justification are untenable. Unless practical reason is understood holistically, in a way that fully integrates affect and cognition, it can neither motivate nor justify decisions. The effort strictly to divide normative reasons, which justify and obligate action, from the psychological considerations that motivate action is misguided.

Most deliberative democrats, including Cohen, acknowledge the fact that "background constrains what can count as an acceptable reason within a process of deliberation."[33] Yet few elaborate the consequence of this fact, which is to shift the source of normative authority within deliberation away from an ideal of reason that transcends sentiment. The truth is that reasons are constituted by the things we care about, and public reasons are constituted by the things we *all* care about—not by things that "reason itself" tells us we *should* care about. How do we arrive at the values that make up the background after all? The moral judgments and evaluations that form the background for public deliberation are not the progeny of intellect alone. Rather they are expressions of what we care about, the considerations that matter to us when viewed from an impersonal standpoint. All this suggests a philosophical explanation for Damasio's neuropsychological findings, canvassed in chapter 2. His affectless subjects cannot reach determinate conclusions about what to do because deliberation is not an exclusively cognitive activity. Only insofar as it incorporates sentiments and desires (properly arrived at) can practical reason determine our decisions and generate obligations. The fact that psychological dispositions have a role here need not imply that anything goes, of course. It need not subjugate deliberation to the passing fancies of untutored individual passion. But it should encourage us to look beyond our old notions of reason for the sources of impartiality. If practical reason entails affect, then any viable model of impartial deliberation will need to make a place for it.

Integrating Affect

A number of recent theorists have attempted to incorporate affective modes of consciousness into the practices of public deliberation. These efforts typically have been subject to one of two limitations, however. The first is to treat affective modes of consciousness simply as motivational catalysts for deliberative procedures that themselves remain highly rationalist, thus leaving untouched the deeper issue of the role of affect in the generation of public norms. Secondly, the theorists who do incorporate affect into deliberation itself tend to lack convincing criteria for precisely how affect should be incorporated and when its contributions are sound, and they often treat affective judgment as an alternative to impartiality.

Gutmann and Thompson offer a good example of the first approach. They are sensitive to concerns raised by critics about the ways in which deliberative democracy appears to privilege "cool reason-giving" over "heated appeals" and "emotional rhetoric" generated by passion. To the extent that the critics connect this apparent marginalization of affect to bias against disadvantaged groups, however, Gutmann and Thompson object. The notion that the rational "style of argument" required by deliberative democracy builds in an advantage for those with more power implies that members of disadvantaged groups "are less reasonable in their appeals than their more advantaged counterparts." But this, say Gutmann and Thompson, would be difficult to prove.[34] In addition, they rightly point out that supporters of the status quo "show no reluctance to use passionate appeals."[35] In fact, they go even further here, charging that "the critics assume a dichotomy between passion and reason that deliberative democracy need not and should not accept."[36] Their reluctance to dichotomize reason and passion looks promising. Yet in the paragraphs that follow it becomes clear that Gutmann and Thompson see affect as a potential motivational support for deliberation but not as a constitutive feature of deliberation itself. Although they want to recognize "the legitimacy of modes of persuasion in politics that combine reason and passion," they relegate these modes of persuasion to "nondeliberative" activities. Political demonstrations, sit-ins, and workers' strikes, for instance, can be important if they bring issues of injustice onto the political agenda and thereby spur public deliberation about them. But insofar as these activities are driven by passions and issue in "statements and declarations rather than developing arguments and responses," they belong in the class of "nondeliberative politics" rather than being a part of deliberation itself. Gutmann and Thompson acknowledge that affective expressions may be "justifiable" in the political arena but they never say that such expressions are justifiable in deliberation. Indeed, they are politically justifiable only so long as they serve to promote the separate, higher end of rational deliberation, from which they are apparently to be excluded.[37]

Some other theorists have attempted to incorporate affective modes of consciousness more directly into deliberation itself. Iris Marion Young, for instance, has criticized deliberative democracy for "expelling desire or affectivity from reason,"[38] and has argued instead for a model of "democratic communication" that does not demand the "absence of emotional expression."[39] Likewise, James Johnson insists that that there are points at which affective "factors such as anger, frustration, humor, fear, joy, and humiliation quite reasonably and justifiably enter political argument."[40] Robert Goodin shows that the generalized perspective associated with reciprocity in deliberative democracy depends on "the expanding of people's sensibilities" and that this expansion would be impossible without engaging affective modes of consciousness.[41] Finally, Jane Mansbridge has argued that public deliberation "should be enlarged to encompass a 'considered' mixture of emotion and reason rather than pure rationality,"[42] if only because "reason can proceed only rarely without emotional commitment."[43]

These efforts to incorporate affect more directly into deliberation are welcome but they have not gone far enough to develop the precise role(s) of affect in this regard. Too often references to the place of emotions and desires within public deliberation lack standards for their legitimate incorporation. They fail to specify the conditions under which affective modes of consciousness support and enhance the ideal of impartiality to which sound deliberation aspires. Indeed, affective judgment is sometimes presented as an alternative to impartiality. Young, for example, associates affect with partiality, and she sees her defense of it as part of a larger critique of impartiality.[44] Benhabib has criticized her in this regard, insisting that "Young's attempt to transform the language of the rule of law into a more partial, affective, and situated mode of communication would have the consequence of inducing arbitrariness" and would "create capriciousness."[45] Benhabib's concern for impartiality is warranted but her response, which is to relegate affect to informal modes of discussion while precluding it from public deliberation proper, is misguided.[46] She is right to defend impartiality but wrong to suggest that it is necessarily threatened by affect. Mansbridge's insistence on the value of affect within public deliberation proper is a step forward, then, but her account stops short of providing criteria for exactly when and how emotions contribute to the "normative legitimacy" of public deliberation.[47] Not all emotions that people feel should carry equal weight in public deliberation, but Mansbridge offers little guidance for how to make the relevant distinctions. The invocation of emotion without standards for differentiating legitimate from illegitimate contributions to deliberation understandably raises hackles among those who adopt a more rationalist approach. As a general matter, efforts to identify the role of affect in deliberation have been too thin normatively to constitute a significant advance over existing rationalist models.

Martha Nussbaum's work on the role of emotions within deliberation is unique in having elaborated principled criteria for distinguishing between legitimate and illegitimate expressions of affect. Certain emotions, such as compassion and (appropriate) anger, she argues, have an important place in political and legal deliberation. Other emotions, such as disgust and shame, should always be excluded. In assessing particular emotions we should consider whether it is reasonable to value the object of that emotion. Anger, for instance, legitimately figures in deliberation if it responds to violations of rights, liberties, and opportunities that can be justified by reference to a "standard of reasonable appraisal."[48] Shame and disgust, on her account, can never be so justified because they are based on dangerous and unrealistic aspirations.[49] They are "repositories of unreasonableness" and should never figure in deliberation.[50] One difficulty with this approach, as a recent commentator notes, is that it "makes reason the tribunal that reviews the emotions and decides which the law should encourage."[51] The appeal to a form of reason that stands apart from and judges the emotions undercuts the force of her argument on behalf of the normative value of emotions themselves. And as we saw in chapter 2, there is a strong current of rationalism in Nussbaum's theory of emotion. The concept of emotion that she employs too often loses touch with the affective mode of consciousness that distinguishes emotions from cognitions such as thoughts and beliefs. Much like earlier rationalists who sought to exclude the emotions from sound judgment, she, too, marginalizes affect, however unintentionally.

In a similar way, John Dryzek appears to champion the role of affect within public deliberation but ultimately he holds affective expressions to a standard of "rationality" that undercuts their distinctive contributions to deliberation. To illustrate the right role of affect he invokes Martin Luther King's rhetorical references to the Declaration of Independence and the U.S. Constitution:

It was the place of the Declaration of Independence and the Constitution in the *hearts* of white Americans that King could reach. The attachment to these documents and the processes that created them is largely, though not exclusively, emotional, rather than a matter of prudent calculation. King's achievement was thus to lead adherents of the established discourse of liberalism to question and ultimately redefine some key terms of that discourse. Certainly there was rational argumentation here too, but the transmission was aided, perhaps even made possible, by the accompanying rhetoric. Without the emotional appeal the argument would have fallen on deaf ears.[52]

Dryzek usefully presses us to think about the process of what he calls "transmission," or the transformation of beliefs and values that accompanies social change within a deliberative democracy; the role of moral sentiment in this process was discussed at some length in chapter 4. Dryzek helps us to see the ways in which affective attachments and desires contribute to making reasons become publicly convincing.[53] And he gives us a standard for distinguishing between legitimate and illegitimate forms of affect. Unfortunately, however, the standard he offers is reason, conceived as an intellectual faculty that rises above the emotions. Because emotion can be coercive, he says, "in the end it must answer to reason."[54] Like Nussbaum, Dryzek insists that any emotions that figure in public deliberation must be "capable of rational justification."[55] Emotions can be subjected to rational justification because "emotions often rest on beliefs."[56]

The problem with invoking rational justification to establish the criteria for legitimate affect is that, as we have seen, there is no such thing as rational justification in the absence of affective modes of consciousness. Justification always proceeds by appeal to the things we care about. So the "rational" justification of affective modes of consciousness is bound to draw upon affective modes of consciousness. This is not something to regret; it is simply how justification operates. It does undercut the force of the standard found in the work of both Nussbaum and Dryzek, however, because it means that one could never make emotion "answer to reason" as an independent source of normative authority, as their presentations suggest. Given the limits of these previous efforts to incorporate affect into public deliberation, new thinking and additional resources are called for.

RECONCEIVING RECIPROCITY

So far we have seen that affective concerns inevitably figure in the reason-giving practices of justification that constitute public deliberation. We still lack an adequate account of how such concerns *should* figure in deliberation, however, or how they might serve deliberation that is sufficiently impartial to generate legitimate, publicly enforceable decisions. We need a normative account of affective deliberation, one that can specify the difference between right feeling and wrong in the deliberative context and that supports the ideal of impartiality. Most deliberative democrats see reciprocity as the key to impartiality, and the present account accepts this association. The reciprocity requirement ensures that public deliberation yields decisions that can be endorsed by those subject to them. It is meant to protect decision making from the prejudice and partiality that privilege some citizens at the expense of others. By making deliberation impartial, reciprocity makes decisions legitimate. The principle of reciprocity is therefore crucial to democratic deliberation. Yet it incorporates more affect than the standard accounts suggest. Reciprocity properly conceived involves two practices in particular that bring sentiments into deliberation in a way that supports impartiality. The first is the practice of framing arguments in terms of the common concerns that underlie the political order and that often, though misleadingly, go by the name of "public reason." The second is the practice of perspective-taking, which incorporates the endorsable sentiments of affected parties into decision making. Affect thus figures in two distinct ways: it involves devotion to public principles and the desire to see them realized, and it involves sympathetic (but critically informed) identification with the sentiments of relevant others.

Public Reason as a Horizon of Concern

The notion of public reason has generated much discussion in recent years. Critics worry about its exclusionary quality, the fact that it systematically (though sometimes unintentionally) rules out the kinds of claims that are central to many citizens' cherished moral and religious doctrines.[57] Additionally, the requirements of public reason strike many interpreters as too utopian to have any value for the real business of public deliberation. As a practical matter, our legislative assemblies seem to be hard-pressed merely to enforce standards of elementary civility, much less enact the kinds of reciprocity that public reason calls for. There are nevertheless grounds to insist on the value of public reason as a standard of legitimacy in the specific context of deliberation that yields laws and policies that are coercively enforced on all citizens (that is, deliberation as "will-formation," as contrasted with deliberation as "opinion-formation"). The deliberative democrats are right to say that democratic legitimacy requires that laws and policies that are enforced on all of us need to be capable of being justified in terms of principles and concerns that are shared. The mistake that is often made here is to treat all deliberation, including opinion-formation, as if it were will-formation. The present account avoids this error. Moreover, while it may be true that the ideal of public reason sets a high bar, it would be wrong to dismiss the ideal as utopian. Legislators, for example, do not exercise public reason consistently in anything like perfect fashion, but they rarely stand up on the floor of Congress and defend a proposed law solely on the grounds that it suits their personal interests, or serves the interests of some select group, or accords with the commands of some particular religious tradition. To the extent that legislators and other public decision makers do make reference to such considerations, these references are usually supplementary, and what they supplement is public principles of right, public values, and widely shared public sentiments—in short, public reason. If the only grounds for justifying a particular law are personal or private or shared only by a few, we do in practice question the law's legitimacy and the fairness of the process that produced it. What this suggests is that even though few people exercise public reason perfectly, as a practical matter most of us in liberal democracies do implicitly accept the idea that public reason is meant to capture as a criterion for decision making—namely, that it is unfair to use state power to coercively impose what is merely one person's (or group's) private interest or personal perspective on everyone else.

So the ideal of public reason is in principle valuable. Yet the standard accounts do not adequately capture its affective content. The moral sentiment model of impartial deliberation suggests that to understand reciprocity rightly, we need to reconceive the nature of public reason so as to acknowledge the importance of sentiments within it. Like other uses of the term "reason" within theories of deliberative democracy, the notion of public reason trades on the normative authority commonly associated with the faculty of reason conceived as devoid of passion. But what is public reason, really? To engage the faculty of public reason in deliberation is essentially to frame one's arguments and make one's evaluations in terms of principles and evaluative standards that are constitutive of the polity and are therefore sources of common commitment, things that citizens *care* about. Public reasons reflect the shared horizons of concern that are implicit in the political culture of a particular community. The relevant horizon of concern for deliberation in the American context, for example, includes commitments to the principles and ideals enshrined in the Constitution and Bill of Rights, as well as the Declaration of Independence. Such commitments are by no means devoid of intellectual content. To care about the principles of liberty and equality for all requires sophisticated cognitive capacities. And if asked why we value the principles of liberty and equality, we may have a very reasonable answer. Yet affective at-

tachment or desire is fundamental to our orientation to these principles. The principles are not simply ideas that give cognitive meaning
and intellectual order to our experience.[58] They also mark out forms of
interaction that we wish to see instantiated in the world. As democratic
citizens, we desire them in the sense that we want the world to embody
them.[59] We have a conative, not merely a cognitive, orientation to public reasons, and as such they are forms of reflective desire. And as we
have seen, there is good reason to think that the principles of public
reason must have this affective character if they are to be capable of
motivating decisions and action.

Reflective desires such as these are partly a function of socialization
and education, which shape citizens' dispositions in ways that support
public norms. But as Hume saw, there are no legitimate norms without
related, pre-existing motives, no properly socialized obligations in the
absence of prior desires and aversions that link them to who we are as
persons.[60] Without this link, our obligations would lack meaning and
value. This is not to say, of course, that one must first desire to perform
a specific action before she can be obligated to do so. I may have no
particular desire to respect your right to express views on immigration
that I find objectionable, but your right to do so imposes an obligation
on me nonetheless. Yet this obligation is not unconnected to desires
that I do have. It is underwritten by the principle of free speech, an
element in the shared horizon of concern that constitutes liberal-democratic citizenship. The right to free speech in turn expresses the values
of equal liberty and respect for persons. These values make possible
peace and prosperity in a pluralistic context. They therefore satisfy fundamental human concerns. On reflection, then, I can be brought to see
that I have grounds to care about your right to speak freely in view of
the various public and private concerns it serves. These concerns sustain my obligation to respect the right to free speech even in the face
of other opposing desires that I may have. This example thus parallels
Cohen's case, discussed earlier, in which reflection reveals that one's
settled concerns entail a commitment (and a motive) to help others,
even though one initially had no immediate desire to do so. The process of so reflecting involves practical reasoning in the holistic sense.
It includes perceiving the logical connections between my obligations
and the things I care about as a citizen and as a human being. But it
involves more than merely the perception of logical links. It also involves the faculty of caring, the feeling of the importance of free
speech, of equal liberty, and ultimately of peace and prosperity. This
mode of reflective caring distinguishes the affective account of public
reason from more rationalist approaches.

Not only is our commitment to the principles within public reason a form of reflective concern, but the principles themselves rest on, and can be justified in terms of, sentiments. No principles could ever be normative for us if they did not connect up with who we are as persons. Standards that lacked such a connection would be arbitrary and the obligations they imposed capricious. Who we are is, most fundamentally, a function of what we most care about, the constitutive concerns that shape our identities and orient our life plans. Therefore the norms that obligate us ultimately must be justifiable with respect to the things that matter to us. To identify the concerns that underlie general obligations, we need to be able to distinguish common, constitutive concerns from idiosyncratic desires and passing fancies, however. The generalized perspective of moral sentiment, detailed in chapter 3, answers to this need. It yields an impartial standpoint for the purposes of norm justification. Even common concerns can go wrong, of course. Consider the widespread support in the United States today for the aggressive defense of "homeland security" despite its well-documented threats to civil liberties. This support is underwritten by Americans' common, and perfectly legitimate, concern for safety in the new world of global terrorism. Even though it is grounded in common concerns, however, we can criticize the rush to security at any price, and we should do so. Still, any justified and persuasive criticism will make reference to other elements in our shared horizon of concern, as persons and as Americans. The values of equal respect and individual liberty provide powerful resources for correcting public desires, but they are not unconnected to desire. Our affective attachments to liberty and equality express the deeper desires and aversions—the sentiments of those affected—that justify these principles. And it is only because of their status as affective concerns, or things we care about, that the appeal to these principles makes arguments publicly convincing and enables the deliberative process to arrive at determinate decisions. Public deliberation, even at its most impartial best, is not only not free of passions and desires but relies heavily on them, and it relies on them for more than merely motivational support.

So public reasons are considerations that incorporate common concerns, and the practice of public reasoning involves a combination of caring and reflection.[61] When public deliberation is conducted in terms that answer to public reason, so conceived, it achieves a significant measure of impartiality. It helps ensure that deliberative outcomes will in principle be endorsable by those who are bound by them because the outcomes are justified in terms of concerns that all citizens, as citizens, can be expected to share. Such deliberation is impartial in the sense that it does not privilege the special concerns of certain individuals or groups over others but incorporates concerns that are widespread. Remember that we are talking about decisions that will be coercively enforced on all citizens, about the formal process of collective will-formation rather than the more informal discussions that are associated with opinion-formation. Although we should be quite permissive about the kinds of claims and arguments that figure in the opinion-formation aspect of public deliberation, as we saw in chapter 4, will-formation should be more constrained. And even in a pluralistic polity such as the United States *some* common political values are available. No polity could exist without them. Every shared political value is subject to dispute by someone, of course. The politics of difference that emerged in the 1990s offered an important corrective to what were then relatively uncritical liberal (and communitarian) assumptions about shared beliefs, values, and interests among citizens. But the real differences among us should not be allowed to obscure altogether what we actually do have in common. Social order—not to mention stable, democratic government—would be impossible if we had nothing at all in common, either as citizens or as persons. True, the interpretation in particular cases of common values can open up fissures in the ostensibly shared convictions of citizens. As such conflicts arise, however, they are appropriately argued out in terms of other elements in the public's horizon of concern, elements that are, for the moment, subject to agreement. Should the balance of public reason in any polity come to be contested all at once, real instability would ensue. Indeed, it is difficult to see how any political order could survive under such circumstances. Yet this extreme scenario does not describe the normal public deliberation in relatively stable, albeit pluralistic, liberal democracies with which we are concerned here. This deliberation regularly proceeds on the basis of public principles that are widely shared and that reflect common concerns.

It is worth noting that the notion of public reason offered here is tied to an account of public deliberation in the context of liberal-democratic societies, and as such it draws on principles and concerns that are constitutive of such polities. Public reason so conceived always operates in medias res. Although it is capable of reflecting on particular elements in the background of values and concerns that give it content, it cannot ever transcend this background fully. This feature is what makes public reason *public*, after all; it is embedded in a particular public, or a particular political community. Thus even when we deliberate publicly about particular constitutional amendments that are intended to revise certain core public principles, we do so in light of other public principles. The latter principles are for the moment held constant and are subject to general agreement, although they may in time come to be contested, too. Sometimes new principles are introduced into public dialogue, principles that previously were external to public reason. Yet in order for a new principle to revise public policy effectively and legitimately, it must connect up with some principles that are already subject to public agreement. Consider nineteenth-century abolition efforts or the contemporary movement for gay rights. In both cases, activists introduced new ideas (that blacks are fully human; that gay people are not a threat to social order) but they linked the new ideas to old and familiar elements of public reason—the promise of liberty for all, for instance, and the principle of equal treatment under law. The question of what justifies laws and policies within a liberal democracy is different from the question of what justifies liberal-democratic political institutions and principles. The latter question cannot be answered by reference to public reason alone. To justify liberal democracy itself, a more independent faculty of moral judgment is needed. As we saw in chapter 4, however, moral sentiment theory can provide valuable resources in this regard.

So the existence of common concerns supports the practice of reciprocity and helps sustain impartial deliberation. To be sure, impartiality in deliberation is not the same thing as universalism. Deliberation that answers to public reason will be impartial with respect to the treatment of different individuals and groups of citizens, but it will be partial to the concerns contained in public reason, and it will treat these particular concerns with special deference. The kind of impartiality that public reason makes possible may not be sufficient to generate truly universal norms of the sort that apply with equal force to all of humanity, but it does address the demands of democratic legitimacy. And when properly conceived, it does so without abandoning the affective mode of consciousness in favor of a mythical ideal of practical reason that transcends sentiment. The practice of reciprocity rightly understood fosters the greatest measure of impartiality we can hope for in politics, and it does so while remaining affectively engaged. Again, it must be acknowledged that the constitutive concerns that sustain reciprocity will not always be shared—or shared in the same way—by every last member of the polity. The class of things that are commonly felt or commonly believed with respect to a given issue often leaves someone out. Difference is part of the human condition, and hence it is common for some of us to be uncommon on any particular measure. The fact of human diversity recommends in favor of political institutions that protect individual liberty as well as the democratic practices of contestation that give voice to the marginalized among us. And it is crucial that prevailing understandings of the common concerns that constitute public reason be open to dispute of the sort discussed in chapter 4. The contestability of ostensibly common concerns also points to the need for perspective-taking. There is no better way to ascertain which concerns are common than to consult the sentiments of those affected. In addition, perspective-taking provides a mechanism for reflecting critically on the existing concerns of persons and groups, and even for reforming them, as we shall see.

Perspective-Taking as the Communication of Sentiments

The perspective-taking dimension of reciprocity is an important key to impartial public deliberation. It means that deliberating citizens must be prepared to consider things from the standpoint of all those affected by the law or policy in question. As presented in existing models of democratic deliberation, however, what the generalized standpoint of reciprocity involves is not always clear. Are we imaginatively to inhabit the identities of others as well as their situations? Or should we instead imagine what we ourselves, retaining our own identities, would think and feel under similar conditions? The first option is patently impossible because we can never sufficiently abandon ourselves or know enough about others to really *become* who they are in the relevant psychological sense. But if we cannot fully become who they are, perspective-taking so conceived will fail, and judgment inevitably will be partial rather than impartial. The second formulation is more feasible but less optimal. Its defect is that it does not push us to go beyond the limits of our private convictions and personal prejudices. Consider the case of abortion, for example. If I am a staunch anti-abortion advocate, to place myself imaginatively (with all my own beliefs and values) in the shoes of an unwed pregnant teen may bring home to me the ways in which my views are at odds with her interests, but cognitive awareness of this conflict is not likely to bring about any meaningful shift in my view.[67] Instead of concluding that her situation gives me reason to re-evaluate abortion rights, I may simply decide that there are good reasons to avoid getting into her situation. This example suggests that there is nothing in perspective-taking, construed as a purely intellectual act, that effectively moves us to think beyond the limits of our personal convictions. Yet laws and policies that will be coercively enforced on all citizens could never be justified in terms of anyone's personal convictions alone.

A better way to understand perspective-taking is as an exercise of moral sentiment. This standpoint is impartial in that it abstracts from private interest and personal prejudice so as to judge in light of common concerns, but it remains affectively engaged because it rests on sentiments and desires. And in contrast to many of the recent efforts to bring affect into public deliberation, the moral sentiment approach specifies criteria for properly incorporating affect within impartial judgment. For not every sentiment is relevant on this view; not all the emotions and concerns that people happen to feel are legitimately included. In evaluating a proposed law or public policy, I am to consult not my personal responses (as in Nussbaum's account) but the sentiments of those affected.[63] The impartial feelings of approval and disapproval, which emerge through this generalized perspective, constitute an intersubjective response rather than a personal or idiosyncratic passion. In cases where those affected cannot communicate their pleasures and pains to me directly, I must rely on indirect evidence of their sentiments or make inferences from like cases and from general rules, conceived as commonly accessible patterns of human concern. Many of these patterns of concern are already consolidated in the form of familiar principles of right, and consequently the moral sentiment model of deliberation makes a place for principled reasoning. But the source of our principles and their justification is to be found in common concerns and reflective sentiments.

Moreover, we must approach the sentiments that figure in the generalized perspective of moral sentiment with a critical eye. Only those sentiments that could themselves be endorsed from within a suitably structured moral standpoint and that are consistent with the principles of public reason are legitimately included in formal public deliberation. As with individual moral judgment, what makes the relevant sentiments endorsable in this context is that they can be affirmed by those affected by them from within a deliberative perspective that manifests equal respect. A key difference between individual moral judgment and public deliberation, however, is that the common concerns that constitute public reason supplement, as additional criteria, the ideal of human nature. The facts are also relevant to defining good deliberation. The sentiments of a man who is mistaken about the causes, character, or consequences of a law or public policy should carry little weight in our assessment of it. Whether the relevant sentiments are legitimate in these ways is subject to dispute, of course. Although not infinitely malleable, the content of moral sentiment is fluid rather than fixed, subject to revision based on new, empirical information and the incorporation of new or previously overlooked sentiments. In this respect, as we have seen, moral sentiment itself depends on the practices of democratic deliberation, which generate discussion and contestation about its proper content and scope. When sympathy is well cultivated and broadly extended, the generalized perspective of moral sentiment takes us out of ourselves in the right way; it does not demand the wholesale abandonment of our identities or an unattainable level of knowledge about the lives of others. Yet it does make our judgments more than self-referential. It causes us to register directly in our own minds and hearts the expressed (and sometimes inferred) sentiments of those affected.

Understanding perspective-taking in terms of moral sentiment brings to the fore what is really at stake in perspective-taking and what true impartiality actually requires. If reciprocity is effectively to serve practical deliberation, it must involve more than merely understanding the concerns of others; it must also include appreciating, even being moved by, these concerns. What one commentator calls "uptake and engagement" are needed.[64] Only if the concerns of others are taken up as a matter of affective engagement can they function as premises in the practical deliberations of citizens. For practical reasoning to be action-guiding, as we have seen, its premises must incorporate affective concerns. Therefore if I am to deliberate in a way that takes your sentiments into account, it is not enough for me to know cognitively what they are; they must also be (or become) objects of concern for me, or at least they must connect up with concerns that I have. Affective uptake is the only way that arguments about practical ends can become convincing to us. It is also the only way that decisions can become the objects of personal commitment. And it is only under these conditions—that citizens are convinced by the arguments and committed to the outcomes—that deliberation and its results can achieve democratic legitimacy.[65]

The uptake and engagement of others' concerns typically proceeds by way of association with our own existing concerns. In this respect, perspective-taking often goes hand in hand with appeals to public reason, conceived as common concerns. Consider once again Martin Luther King's use of rhetoric. King and other activists publicized the sentiments of African Americans living under segregation and made them available for perspective-taking by the wider public. His rhetoric then connected these sentiments to concerns shared by many people within the white majority. King's arguments for racial equality became convincing to white Americans not because of their logical structure alone or even because they led to greater understanding of African American sentiments. Instead, they were convincing because they appealed (in a logical fashion) to things most Americans really cared about: security, opportunity, and dignity, not to mention the aspiration to liberty and equality for all found in the Declaration of Independence and the promise of fair treatment made by the Constitution. In this way, and in so many others, King made the connection between the reflective concerns of the white majority and those of African Americans. He could not have been convincing—and public deliberation on this issue could not have produced conclusive and legitimate results—in the absence of this connection. In effect, King facilitated the uptake and engagement of African American sentiments by whites, and thereby nurtured the deliberative practice of reciprocity as perspective-taking. Political activists are midwives for the communication of sentiment. They help us to feel with others, and in this way they can be crucial to the practice of reciprocity and the development of impartiality.

The notion that we must *feel* with others to arrive at legitimate decisions in democratic politics will strike some as excessively demanding, or naïve. If empirical experience suggests that sympathy regularly communicates sentiments between persons, history clearly shows that sympathy often fails in this regard. Modern liberalism, with its emphasis on the motive of self-interest and the mechanisms of representative government, checks and balances, and ambition that counteracts ambition, was intended in part to compensate for this kind of failing. It was meant to make decent government possible in the absence of sympathetic identification among persons—possible even, as Kant said, for a nation of devils.[66] It is true that plenty of the questions that arise in political life can properly be decided on the basis of a competition of interests without recourse to a highly cultivated capacity for moral sentiment. And public decision making always should transpire in the context of institutions that constrain political power in principled and predictable ways. When it comes to questions of justice and basic liberties, however, citizens owe it to one another (and themselves) to decide on the basis of something other than who has more power. So liberal democracies will always have need of impartial deliberation, and consequently we cannot turn away from the challenges that impartiality poses. The psychological demands are indeed high. To meet them citizens must cultivate a broad and sensitive faculty of sympathy. Yet when compared to the standard accounts of impartial deliberation in theories of deliberative democracy the moral sentiment view is no more demanding, and it is far more realistic. For the demands it makes take account of the irrepressible place of affective attachments and desires within practical reasoning. Because it does not rest on a mistaken conception of the nature and capacities of practical reason, affective impartiality is a challenge that we can, with effort, meet.

Residual Worries

One might still wonder about the wisdom of placing so much stock in people's sentiments. Sentiments can be full of prejudice and marked by ignorance, after all. Reciprocity asks us to consider the sentiments of all affected by the law or policy in question, but what if these sentiments reflect bigotry, or personal animosity, or mistakes of fact? When it comes to formal procedures of decision making, whether in the voting booth or on the floor of Congress, the perspective-taking dimension of reciprocity needs the constraints of a critical standard. We need to be able to distinguish right feeling from wrong in the process of making public judgments. The common concerns that constitute principles of political right within public reason provide support here, as they suggest a standard for the legitimate incorporation of sentiments. Sentiments of relevant parties that would violate these principles or thwart the common concerns that underlie them are properly excluded from the perspective-taking required by reciprocity. On these grounds, for instance, we should discount, on reflection, the pain the racist feels in the face of anti-discrimination laws.[67] Racism flies in the face of equal liberty, a constitutive concern of public reason in constitutional liberal democracies such as the United States. The sentiments it generates have no place in public deliberation. Likewise, we should exclude sentiments that rest on mistakes of fact. The aversion for immigrants among some citizens, which grows out of the erroneous belief that immigrants are likely to be terrorists, should carry little weight with us. Decisions governed by such sentiments could not be legitimate. Insofar as they thwart the common concerns that comprise public reason or are based in error, they could not themselves be endorsed by all those they affect. These considerations demonstrate that reciprocity is not to be equated with blind empathy. It does involve feeling with others but not in a way that forsakes critical thinking. Reciprocity requires the cultivation of a deliberative standpoint that engages the sentiments of those affected, inclusively and without prejudice, but not uncritically.

Whether or not a given sentiment is politically legitimate in the sense of being consistent with public reason may be contestable, in part because prevailing interpretations of public reason are themselves contestable. In a liberal-democratic context, the line between arguments that are acceptable to public reason and those that are not may be less distinct than some would wish for. What seems to count as an acceptable argument at one moment in time may come to be seen as unacceptable at a later time (or vice versa). The *Plessy* doctrine of "separate but equal" is one example of how a policy that we now consider to be inconsistent with core public principles was for a long time thought by most Americans to be fully consistent with the Constitution. This particular interpretation of the Constitution could only be sustained by excluding the perspectives of those on the losing end of the doctrine, however. "Public" interpretations of constitutional principles and other political values that systematically exclude the sentiments of certain groups of citizens are not fully impartial, and they violate the norms of equal respect and democratic legitimacy.[68] Still, the fact remains that constitutional principles must be interpreted, and it is theoretically possible for conflicting interpretations of some principle to be equally legitimate. A certain measure of contingency in liberal-democratic public deliberation is ultimately unavoidable. There is nothing automatic about the interpretation of public reason; it requires sensitivity and careful consideration. Our public horizons of concern offer general standards for judgments, not an automated decision mechanism. For example, what equality means to us as citizens and why we care about it is something that unfolds over time in the context of new and continuing disputes. In the future, the principle of equality may come to cover cases (and therefore to have new meanings) that no one has yet conceived. The intrinsic contestability of this principle does not prevent our concern for equality from being an ordering principle of our deliberative practices here and now, however. It is also important to leave room for sentiments that offer principled challenges to the status quo and hence contest certain parts of the public's horizon of concern, challenging the dominant view of public reason. Without this, marginalized groups could have no chance of one day making their sentiments count in the perspective of public reason. Under such conditions, social and political reform would be impossible, and we would never see moral progress in politics. Nevertheless, liberal-democratic decision making needs political legitimacy, and this means that it needs public reason. We can acknowledge the moral fallibility of public reason (and we should encourage social and political practices that support critical reflection on it) while still affirming its importance in the domain of public deliberation, at least when it comes to decisions that will be coercively enforced by the state.

Moreover, it makes good sense to ask those who wish to reform particular elements of public reason to frame their arguments in terms of concerns that are shared among those who are subject to public reason. Without some common points of reference, no collective evaluation can take place. And insofar as we always deliberate in light of things that matter to us, to deliberate together we need some shared concerns. These shared concerns may take the form of other (not currently contested) principles within public reason, or they may reach instead to sentiments that, as Hume said, human nature makes common. If those contesting particular aspects of public reason are also seeking specific legal or political reforms (in addition to advocating for new moral insight), their claims will need to connect up with at least some of the concerns that constitute public reason. Advocates of gay rights criticize common values and established laws surrounding marriage, for instance, and in doing so they dispute key elements of the prevailing interpretation of public reason. Yet they do so in the name of core American values, such as equal protection under the law, as well as common human concerns, such as the desire for intimate partnerships and the need for respect. What all this suggests is that it is possible to constrain perspective-taking by means of common concerns without closing the door to social and political reform.

Some will remain skeptical about the value of sentiments within deliberation. Sometimes we want to say that a particular law or public policy is simply *wrong* (or, alternatively, that it is obligatory) regardless of what anyone may feel about it. This conviction surely is an admirable one, but what does it really amount to? If the claim is that we need some established principles of political right to give us critical leverage against the passing fancies of majorities, then the moral sentiment model of reciprocity already allows for this. It combines sensitivity to the legitimate sentiments of those affected with a commitment to the common concerns of public reason as codified in fundamental law. On this basis, we can say that a proposed law institutionalizing gender inequity would be illegitimate because it is contrary to the Fourteenth Amendment, whatever the majority might at present feel about it. If the claim goes beyond a concern for political legitimacy—if it implies that we need universal standards of right that rise above the limits of public reason (conceived as a horizon of concern) and perspective-taking among citizens—then it will indeed require something more than reciprocity. Political legitimacy is not synonymous with justice. In a society that aspires to justice, citizens will answer to moral ideals that sometimes go beyond, and even rise against, the public agreements that establish political legitimacy. Yet while moral ideals can help us gain critical perspective on existing public sentiments, these ideals are not themselves free of sentiment. If what we have said so far is accurate, then ideals that are to guide moral action must have a footing in common human concerns and must be endorsable with reference to the impersonal but affectively engaged standpoint of moral sentiment. Moreover, while such ideals can supplement political legitimacy in important ways, political legitimacy matters when it comes to the public deliberation that leads to enforceable decisions. Legitimacy may not be the sole standard relevant to deliberation in this form but it is an important one because in liberal democracies the moral value of one's purpose is not sufficient on its own to justify coercing others into complying with it.[69]

One might also worry about the misrecognition of sentiments. Sympathy is fallible, and I can be wrong about what your sentiments are. In addition, insincere expressions of sentiment, engaged through perspective-taking, may distort public deliberation and lead to unjust outcomes. Yet while the dangers of misrecognition and insincerity are real, they are not unique to the affective account of reciprocity. Reciprocity on any model will depend upon effective communication and the sincerity of participants as they bring their concerns to the common table. More unsettling is the specter of sentiments that are clearly conveyed and sincerely felt but based on self-conceptions that have been distorted by systemic inequalities of power—what once went by the name "false consciousness." Prior to the 1960s many American women seemed to be satisfied with social norms and public policies that relegated them to the domestic sphere and precluded them from pursuing the range of life experiences that were open to men. As the barriers have come down, the large numbers of women who have pursued opportunities outside the home suggest that many women of earlier generations may not have been as satisfied with the old arrangements as they themselves once thought.[70] Should we accept the sincere (and endorsable) sentiments of others at face value in public perspective-taking, even though they may be based on false consciousness? The obvious danger in doing so is that deliberation may legitimate and reinforce patterns of social and political organization that systematically disadvantage certain groups. Yet there are also dangers involved in rejecting sentiments on the basis of their putative false consciousness. We risk an indefensible paternalism if we discount other people's sentiments for failing to express our own ideas of their "true" interests.

The better way to deal with the danger of sentiments based on false consciousness is to attack false consciousness at its source, to challenge the laws and policies that systematically disadvantage certain groups and the social norms that make these disadvantages seem acceptable. Moreover, we can certainly question and challenge the sentiments of others, in the context of informal debate, if these sentiments seem to be based on false consciousness. A good deal of social reform operates in just this way, as some of the things that matter to us change over time in response to prodding and argument from others. There is no reason to think that one's settled concerns are any more intractable than one's settled beliefs. Here again the deliberative-system approach is important because it supports the inclusion of divergent views at the level of opinion-formation that stimulates critical reflection. And the problem of false consciousness is no more unique to the sentiment-based approach than are the dangers of misrecognition and insincerity. Unless one postulates a Kantian-style noumenal subject behind every deliberative choice, it is inevitable that practical reasoning will be affected—and sometimes distorted—by features of the empirical context and by our fallibility as human beings. Again, beliefs are no less prone to this problem than are sentiments. Human fallibility in all these forms is another reason to value liberal-democratic politics, which opens up opportunities for correction through its protections of continuing communication and contestation.

Another issue associated with perspective-taking in public deliberation concerns how the various sentiments represented are to be integrated into a coherent viewpoint. As one recent writer points out, "perspective-taking by itself contributes little to successful deliberation if participants are not able to coordinate all the various perspectives into one in a dialectical process of constant enrichment and new articulations."[71] It must be acknowledged that in most cases, at least in a complex, pluralistic society such as the United States, the perfect integration of all perspectives into a single one is unlikely. Residual disagreement is an ineradicable feature of democratic deliberation even in the best cases, and public decisions must be made despite it.[72] Still, the affective account of reciprocity does provide grounds for ordering various sentiments within a coherent perspective. For one thing, the degree to which particular persons are affected by the law or policy in question will be relevant to how their sentiments are to be weighted within the generalized standpoint.[73] Public reason as a shared horizon of concern can also help with the integration of sentiments. As the sentiments of those affected by a law or policy are brought to bear in deliberation, reciprocity requires that they be articulated in ways that connect up with core public values. Perspective-taking does not happen in a vacuum. As we have seen, sentiments that themselves violate the principles of public reason are politically illegitimate and properly excluded. So, too, are sentiments based on factual errors and ignorance of empirical realities. Those sentiments that remain in play after the first two hurdles have been crossed are subject to a third kind of discipline by the public horizon of concern. The specific influence these sentiments have on deliberation about the law or policy in question is to be governed by relevant legal principles and public aspirations together with an empirical assessment of the circumstances of the case.

Consider the case of affirmative action, where equally legitimate sentiments exist on opposing sides of the issue. Here the desire that both sides express—the desire not to be subject to discrimination—is itself compatible with core public values. The parties to deliberation must consider the various sentiments in play in light of a reflective concern for the constitutional principle of equal protection under the law and for the American promise of equal opportunity. These concerns, together with the empirical reality of persistent racial discrimination, recommend in favor of a compromise solution. Ideally, we should aim for policies in educational settings and the workplace that provide affirmative impetus for decision makers to recognize and resist their (often unwitting) discriminatory assumptions but that do not systematically exclude any particular class of persons. Such a compromise would be sensitive to the legitimate sentiments of those affected, but the relative influence that the different sentiments carry in deliberation would be determined by the principles and aspirations contained in the public horizon of concern—and by the relevant empirical facts about the historical context of racial discrimination in the United States that bear on the realization of these principles and aspirations. Such considerations discipline deliberation and impose order on the relevant sentiments, making it possible to arrive at a coherent, albeit not incontestable, position.

It is worth emphasizing that it is possible for there to be more than one coherent, well-grounded position on an issue such as affirmative action. The sensible ordering of legitimate sentiments within the generalized standpoint of reciprocity is not the same thing as the generation of de facto consensus. Consequently, a certain measure of indefiniteness is endemic to deliberation. As Aristotle said, we do not deliberate about things to which there is one and only one right answer.[74] Thus we would not deliberate about whether two and two add up to four. The context of practical deliberation is the need to act in the face of moral uncertainty, conflicting interests, and competing goods. For this reason, it would be a mistake to demand of any theory of public deliberation that it generate singular, incontestable answers to specific questions of law and policy. In addition, a theory of judgment and deliberation that provided determinate answers to all policy questions would leave nothing for the people and their representatives to decide. It could not, therefore, be a theory for democratic politics. A model of democratic deliberation should provide general criteria for distinguishing good from bad deliberation, but it must allow for some range of "good" outcomes insofar as its function is to guide collective *choice*. To be sure, liberal democracy introduces some principled constraints on democratic choices, but it must still answer (within these limits) to the people's will, and hence even a liberal-democratic theory of public deliberation, such as the one offered here, must allow for some indeterminacy.

Instances of contestability within public deliberation also reflect the deeper reality of value pluralism. The diversity of persons and the plurality of human purposes worth pursuing is another reason why moral judgment is always imbued with a certain indeterminacy, and the same is true for public deliberation.[75] Gutmann and Thompson regard the public controversy over legalized abortion as an example, since "both pro-life and pro-choice advocates argue from fundamentally different but plausible premises to conflicting public policies."[76] The claims on both sides, they maintain, "fall within the range of what reciprocity respects."[77] Such indeterminacy reflects a real and ineradicable feature of moral and political life, which is that human goods are irreducibly plural. In view of this fact, and as we saw in chapter 3, the soundest moral judgment sometimes is a mixed one. Value pluralism suggests that we ought not expect public deliberation, even when well executed, to always generate singular, incontestable conclusions.

The indeterminacy that is endemic to democratic deliberation need not issue in paralysis or an inability to reach decisions when necessary, however. In cases where deliberation fails to yield only one legitimate conclusion and yet a publicly enforceable decision must nevertheless be made, the best course is to seek compromise and accommodation.[78] Sometimes guidance will come from other features of the decision situation itself. The current debate over social security reform offers a case in point. If we think about the proposed programs for privatizing social security in light of the sentiments of those affected and the public's horizon of concern, we find different but equally endorsable sentiments. People who are good at saving and who have the resources to do so would likely benefit from privatization and they tend to approve of it; those who lack either the personal habits of effective saving or the resources to do so would likely suffer from privatization, and these people typically contemplate it with sentiments of disapproval. Both sentiments are endorsable from the standpoint of political legitimacy insofar as neither one conflicts directly with core elements of public reason. Yet the relevant sentiments clearly point in different policy directions, so we will need to look to other considerations if we are to arrive at a decision. One thing that can be done in this case is to consider the purpose of social security. Historically its function has been to provide a safety net for persons who, whether through lack of resources or poor planning, find themselves facing abject poverty in their old age. By all accounts, social security has been tremendously successful in this regard.[79] In deliberating about the reform of social security in light of its historic function, it may make sense to prioritize the sentiments of those affected most directly by the dangers the program was uniquely designed to protect against. This consideration gives us grounds to weigh more heavily the sentiments of persons who oppose privatization, those who are least likely to enter retirement with enough savings to live above the poverty line. Again, this conclusion is surely contestable. There are coherent, well-grounded reasons to accept it, but there are no doubt reasonable considerations that could be brought against it. The point of the example, however, is not to demonstrate an incontestable conclusion so much as to show that decisions can be well grounded even when they are *not* incontestable. The implication is that the contestability of deliberative outcomes need not result in paralysis or the inability to reach politically legitimate, morally sound decisions.

Sometimes other kinds of considerations will come to the fore as a result of the decision situation, and these considerations can provide further guidance in choosing between equally legitimate alternatives. Reciprocity needs to be balanced with different kinds of obligations in different institutional contexts, and these obligations will affect decisions. Legislators must balance reciprocity with their duty to represent the interests of their constituents, for example. Executives must balance reciprocity with the obligation to provide for the common security. Judges must balance it with their commitment to the principle of stare decisis. More generally, if the deliberative process has been sound and the contemplated alternatives can be publicly justified in view of the two dimensions of reciprocity, then to select one of these alternatives on the basis of democratic practices, such as compromise, majority vote, or even bargaining, is not so bad. It may well be the best we can do. In such circumstances, we ask that public officials do their best to proceed with a spirit of impartiality, making themselves receptive to the legitimate concerns of those affected and answering to their best understanding of public interests and shared values. This assumes, of course, that the deliberative process remains open and that decisions can be revised over time in light of new information or further consideration. The lingering, ineradicable nature of contestability in public deliberation makes this procedural openness crucial.

So reciprocity rightly understood rests on reflective sentiment, on a form of practical reasoning that includes both cognition and affect. Too often the reciprocity requirement is treated as being simply synonymous with the requirements of "reason itself," conceived as a strictly intellectual faculty, which are thought to rationalize public deliberation. Yet reciprocity properly conceived is not a matter of subjecting deliberation to the putative authority of reason alone, public or otherwise. Instead it shows us how we are to bring our common concerns and the sentiments of one another to bear in deliberation about matters of basic law and public policy. We can specify criteria for the proper incorporation of affect within public deliberation, and when it is properly incorporated affect serves rather than thwarts impartiality. Intellect has a role here. Yet in contrast to other theorists, such as Nussbaum and Dryzek, the moral sentiment view does not make affect "answer to reason," if reason is understood to be free of feeling. We distinguish between legitimate and illegitimate sentiments—and we achieve impartial deliberation—through right feeling, or reflective caring, rather than through the transcendence of feeling.

The importance of sentiment in this regard reflects the fact that practical reason necessarily incorporates affective concerns in reaching conclusions about what we ought to do. Norms are intrinsically, not contingently, connected to human motivations, and moral sentiment embodies this connection. Hence the sentiment-based account of democratic deliberation helps to clarify how the conclusions of public deliberation can be both normative for us and motivationally compelling. By the same token, the practices of deliberative democracy so conceived help to expand moral sentiment. The relationship between moral sentiment and democratic deliberation is a reciprocal one. By establishing the political conditions of equality that incentivize concern for the sentiments of others, and by facilitating a wide-ranging deliberative system that brings the greatest diversity of sentiments onto the public stage, deliberative democracy has the potential to expand the imagination and educate moral sentiment. So while the path to impartial public deliberation proceeds through moral sentiment, the quality of our moral sentiments depends upon the presence of liberal-democratic institutions and political contestation in the wider society. Ultimately, what public deliberation needs is not more "reason" so much as a broader, more refined faculty of reflective concern and citizens who are skilled in the feeling of impartiality.

CHAPTER SIX

The Affective Authority of Law

IN LIBERAL DEMOCRACIES public deliberation operates within the legal framework established by the constitution, which embodies a large part of the public's horizon of concern. The framework is subject to critical evaluation, as particular elements of it sometimes become the focus of individual moral deliberation or collective political debate. As a general matter, however, the legal framework as a whole within which public deliberation transpires is authoritative in the constraints it imposes. Likewise, to the extent that the results of public deliberation take the form of laws and legally binding public policies, they draw on the authority of law for their effective implementation. In this sense, public deliberation depends heavily on the law's authority. The affective dimensions of public deliberation raise a new set of questions here, however, because the leading accounts of the authority of law today look to reason, conceived in opposition to sentiment, for the justification of this authority. How should we understand the binding quality of deliberation's results, as law, if they arise through the exercise of reflective sentiments? What does it mean to be obligated by law, and how do sentiments figure in this obligation?

Laws are fragile things in one sense, little more than words on the pages of statute books and judicial opinions. James Madison once referred to the Constitution itself—the fundamental law of the United States—as a mere "parchment barrier" to the abuse of political power.[1] It is true that laws are backed up by the coercive power of the state, and in any functional society this backing makes them a force to contend with. Yet their dependence on external support only emphasizes the weakness of the laws themselves. Moreover, the threatening hand of the sovereign cannot be everywhere at once, and innumerable opportunities for breaking the laws without any real fear of punishment are bound to arise. Still, Americans do generally comply with the law, and in this sense laws are not so fragile. One might say that what the law lacks in actual strength it makes up for in authority. The authority of the law, in contrast to its strength, is a normative condition. Laws impose obligations on us; they tell us what we ought to do and not only what we must do. For the law to be authoritative in this way, it must elicit both the respect and the allegiance of its subjects. Insofar as law's authority successfully establishes grounds for compliance that are independent of the fear of punishment, this authority also is a crucial condition of freedom because a polity in which social coordination was based only on fear could never be free.[2] So the authority of the law is a key to political liberty as well as to enforcing the outcomes of public deliberation. But where does this authority come from? What is the nature and basis of the law's authority?

The authority of law is tied to, but conceptually distinct from, the legitimacy of the political authority that generates it. Ostensibly legitimate political authorities sometimes pass bad laws, after all, laws that citizens may have a moral obligation to resist. In such circumstances, citizens challenge the authority of the law without contesting the fundamental authority of the government. By the same token, in constitutional regimes the rule of law sets constraints on what political authorities may do. Political authorities who act in flagrant disrespect of the law may be driven from office, even face legal prosecution, which is further indication that the two forms of authority may come apart. The relationship between legal authority, political authority, and morality has spawned a long and distinguished series of debates, beginning with the disagreement between nineteenth-century legal positivists such as Jeremy Bentham and John Austin, who treated the authority of law as synonymous with the government's power to coerce, and the natural lawyers who preceded them, who had insisted on the moral foundations of law and regarded legal authority as derived from these foundations.

Legal positivism insisted on drawing a sharp divide between law's authority and moral authorities because it wanted to preserve the possibility of moral criticism directed at existing law. The worry was that if law were defined simply in terms of what morality required, then this would leave no basis outside the law for criticizing it.[3] Yet to equate the authority of law with the government's power to coerce is to saddle the law with a normative deficit that is difficult to overcome. If law is in effect reducible to mere power, it is not clear that law can impose normative obligations on us. The proponents of natural law faced a different set of challenges. By equating law's authority with the authority of God or nature, they made the authority of law dependent on a highly contentious metaphysics.[4] Moreover, although the authority of law is not simply reducible to the legitimacy of the political authority that generates it, the two forms of authority are connected. In a democratic context this means that the authority of law does depend in some measure on whether this authority reflects the consent of those subject to it. Yet neither God nor nature normally looks to the consent of a populace to sustain its right to command. In this sense, the natural law theorists failed to account for the legitimacy dimension of law's authority, thus generating a normative deficit of their own.

Disagreement between positivists and moralists continues to dominate debates about the authority of law today, albeit in modified form. Both sides are plagued by difficulties. In part, these difficulties reflect the fact that scholars on all sides have almost entirely overlooked the role of affective concerns in establishing the authority of law. The neglect of affect is not surprising. The standard view of law in the history of the West has always associated law with an ideal of reason that resists the passions. Indeed, the whole purpose of law, it is often thought, is to regulate unruly affect through the application of cool-headed cognition. The current debates about the nature of law's authority reflect this long-standing view, and as a result the affective dimensions of this authority are not well understood.[5]

To be sure, no one denies that the law must engage the affective concerns of its subjects if it is to motivate adherence. What most theorists overlook is the place of sentiments in establishing the normative force of law's authority. In the course of this chapter we shall see that the two dimensions of this authority—the law's right to obligate and its power to motivate—are both grounded in the properly constituted concerns of its subjects. To show how such concerns generate normativity and why we cannot conceive of obligations, whether moral or legal, without affect, we return to the theory of moral sentiment. For the law to have normative authority (that is, to justifiably generate obligations) it must be endorsable from within the generalized standpoint of moral sentiment, a standpoint that rests upon the sympathetic communication of concerns among those subject to it. When it is endorsable in this way, the law also has motivational authority (the ability to animate allegiance). In this sense, the moral sentiments that enable us to justify law's authority also help generate allegiance to it, although the motivational authority of law depends upon other feelings as well, including mutual concern among citizens.

The first part of the chapter explores the meaning of authority as a general matter and explains in a preliminary way why affect necessarily figures in practical or action-guiding forms of authority. I then evaluate recent efforts by Joseph Raz, Jeremy Waldron, and Ronald Dworkin to explain the distinctive authority of the law, showing that none of them makes sense unless one posits a normative role for sentiment. In part three I sketch an alternative, sentiment-based account of law's authority. The moral sentiment approach charts a new course, one that avoids the difficulties raised by both positivists (such as Raz and Waldron) and moralists (such as Dworkin). Finally, I emphasize the importance of liberal-democratic political institutions and an inclusive political culture as necessary conditions of law's authority in liberal democracies. These practices support the expansive faculty of moral sentiment that underlies this authority. The affective sources of law's authority are crucial to understanding not only the efficacy of legal norms within political society but the nature of legal obligation itself. Because public deliberation depends on this type of obligation, both to constrain it and to make its results binding, the affective aspects of this obligation are important forms of civil passion.

AUTHORITY, ACTION, AND AFFECT

Some initial definitions and distinctions are in order. "Authority" in general refers to the power to affect human decisions, and it involves influence that is relatively stable and abiding. A power is not an authority if its influence is random or haphazard. We should also distinguish at the outset between "theoretical" and "practical" authority. Whereas theoretical authorities influence decisions about what to believe, practical authorities influence decisions about how to act.[6] The authority of experts is an example of theoretical authority. If an art historian tells me that the painting I thought was a Picasso really is a clever fake, I am apt to believe her. Her special knowledge of art makes her more likely than I am to ascertain the truth of the matter. Experts' special knowledge gives us reason to defer to their judgments, and our deference is a key condition of their authority. That is, deference is not merely a response to authority but a constituent of it. One can be an expert without ever becoming an authority, after all. Imagine a man who knows everything there is to know about penguins but whose penchant for solitude prevents him from engaging in the social and scientific activities that bring recognition to one's knowledge and influence to one's opinions. An expert only becomes an authority by actually influencing others. Authority is an intrinsically intersubjective phenomenon: deference matters. Indeed, the fact of deference partly establishes authority.

It also matters that this deference be justified. The special knowledge of experts that sustains theoretical authority gives us good reason to defer to their opinions. In the absence of reasons for respect, deference could only arise as a matter of caprice, or perhaps through the threat of force. Capricious deference will be too inconstant to generate the stable and abiding influence characteristic of authority, however. And threats of force, as Locke said, can compel action but not belief; hence they could never generate theoretical authority.[7] So theoretical authority is constituted through justified deference to the knowledge of others, deference that is informed by reason and therefore constitutes rational respect. In this sense, reason as the faculty that seeks to understand the world is what justifies our deference to theoretical authorities. The justifying power of reason is evident in the fact that experts' authority is contingent on their credibility, on whether it is reasonable to believe that they have represented the world correctly. The discovery that an expert is wrong tends to destroy her authority because it undermines the justification for deference as rational respect.[8]

Deference matters to practical authority, as well, but with some important differences. Authority in this form consists in the ability to influence others' decisions about what to do. Whereas decisions about what to believe need only appeal to intellectual criteria, decisions about what to do always involve a combination of cognitive understanding and affective concerns, as we have seen in previous chapters. The importance of affect for decision and action has recently been picked up by legal theorists as well. As Richard Posner puts it, "reason is not (*pace* Kant) motivational:"

> Knowing what is the right thing to do must be conjoined with a desire to do the right thing for action to result. When we say that a person did not allow himself to give way to his emotions (for example, he resisted that piece of chocolate), we mean that an aversive emotion ("self-control"—the aversion to being weak-willed) was stronger than the attractive emotion. There is no action without emotion.[9]

To the extent that practical authorities influence decision and action they carry motivational force, and hence they must engage the affective concerns of their subjects. This suggests that the basis of our deference to practical authorities is different from the basis of our deference to theoretical ones, which is solely intellectual.

Thus while the discovery that an expert is wrong destroys the grounds for deference to his authority, proof that a practical authority is mistaken about the facts in some case need have no effect on its status as authoritative.[10] Consider a parent who believes that playing outdoors on rainy days is likely to bring on the flu, and on the basis of this belief prohibits his children from playing in the rain. If it turns out that no connection exists between playing in the rain and getting the flu, this revelation will give him good reason to change his policy but it will not (or ought not) undermine his authority over his children. The grounds of his children's deference are unaffected by his mistake in this case. The same holds true for the practical authority of a legislature in passing, say, a speed limit law:

The implicit claim of the legislature is precisely the one that the expert cannot make: though the legislature thinks its judgment about the balance to be struck between energy, safety, and rapid transit concerns is correct, it claims that its judgment is to be followed even if it is wrong—indeed, even if it is based on incorrect factual assumptions about the effect on fuel conservation.[11]

Mistakes such as these do not destroy practical authority because practical authority does not rest exclusively on intellectual considerations, on the claim to produce greater understanding or to ascertain the truth of some matter. We do not defer to practical authorities for the reasons that lead us to defer to theoretical ones—namely, the belief that they will represent the world to us more accurately than we could represent it to ourselves. Thus it is not intellect alone, the faculty through which we seek truth and understanding, that justifies our deference to practical authorities. This deference has another basis, or at least it has an additional basis.[12]

It is often thought that deference to practical authority is supported mainly through the threat of punishment. Such threats, whether from parents (in the case of parental authority), from God (in the case of religious authority), or from the political sovereign (in the case of law), can indeed motivate obedience. The fear they generate engages our affective concerns, and so it has the motivational force needed to stimulate deferential action. But this is the wrong kind of deference. Practical authority as a general matter demands deference as allegiance, not simply deference as fear. Nowhere is this more evident than in the specific case of the law. The law is only truly authoritative for a population when it inspires compliance as a matter of respect and allegiance, so that its subjects comply even in cases where the failure to do so is unlikely to be punished. Otherwise compliance shows that the state has mastered the effective use of force but it tells us nothing about the authority of the law per se. Moreover, just as coercion cannot compel belief, it is incapable of establishing obligations. This was the problem with legal positivism in its original form. By treating law and morality as fully independent, legal positivism left itself unable to explain how the law ever can be obligatory in a way that carries normative force. In analyzing the authority of law, H.L.A. Hart insisted on the difference "between the assertion that someone was obliged to do something and the assertion that he had an obligation to do it."[13] If a gunman orders you to hand over your money, there is a sense in which you are obliged to do so. Yet it would be ridiculous, Hart said, to conclude that you had an obligation or a duty to hand over the money.[14] There is more to the authority of law than the force that stands behind it. Coercion cannot confer normativity. The deference we give to practical authorities, including the law, reflects respect for the normative force of these authorities. In deferring to them we acknowledge their right to command us and our obligation to obey.

Although Hart's distinction between being obliged and being obligated is sound and significant, his wider effort to sever normative obligations from psychological motivations (or concerns) is misguided. Hart believed that obligations were grounded in social rules, which he treated as independent of affective concerns.[15] He insisted that such concerns, or what he referred to as psychological "facts about beliefs and motives," were *not necessary* for the truth of a statement that a person had an obligation to do something."[16] To feel obligated and to be obligated were two different things.[17] Thus the fact that a swindler feels no obligation to pay the rent in no way dissolves his obligation to do so. Hart was right to say that obligations (whether moral or legal) cannot rest solely on the immediate, idiosyncratic psychological states of individuals. Passing fancies and personal desires cannot establish obligations. Yet he was wrong to think that affective concerns—or psychological states—have no role at all here. Indeed, his own account of the obligations generated by law's authority makes no sense independently of such concerns.

To see this, notice that on Hart's view the social rules that establish the normative structure of society and confer obligations of all types can be perceived from either an "external" or an "internal" point of view.[18] The external point of view is the perspective of an observer who, without accepting the rules himself, "is content merely to record the regularities of observable behavior in which conformity with the rules partly consists."[19] For him a red traffic light is simply a sign that there is a high probability that traffic will stop, in the same way that "clouds are a sign that rain will come."[20] By contrast, from the internal point of view a red light is "not merely a sign that others will stop," but also an imperative signal *to stop*—in effect, a command that imposes an obligation.[21] Hart emphasizes that we cannot comprehend the normative function of rules, or their status as practical authorities, on the basis of the external point of view alone. Normativity arises only with the internal point of view. This is surely true. Yet the internal point of view is more than just a different type of understanding. In contrast to the external point of view, which yields a detached form of observational knowledge, the internal standpoint is an affectively engaged psychological state, a motivational or dispositional orientation to the system of social rules. With the internal point of view the rules become concerns for participants, or the rules are seen by participants to reflect their concerns. And it is only participants—those for whom the rules constitute concerns—who are bound by the obligations these rules establish; on Hart's account there is no indication that the observer is so bound. Yet both the observer and the obligated participant posses the same knowledge of what the rules are. The difference between them is not one of mere cognition but also reflects a difference of feeling.[22]

So it cannot be true that the obligations imposed by practical authorities, including the authority of law, arise in a way that is fully independent of the "beliefs and motives" of their subjects. The imperative quality of the law's authority, which makes it action-guiding, is at least partly a function of the motivational states of those subject to it. Phenomenologically speaking, legal obligations differ from externally observed rules of a game because they have become reflective concerns for those bound by them. We cannot comprehend the meaning of law's authority without grasping this internal perspective of concern. Although not reducible to the passing fancies of individuals, legal obligations in any functional society will reflect the needs and purposes of the members of that society, the things people are generally motivated to care about. Legal norms grow out of motives in this sense, and consequently they cannot be respected as having normative force independently of the affective concerns of their subjects. Although it makes sense to distinguish between the normative-justificatory dimension of law's authority (its right to obligate) and the motivational dimension (its power to generate allegiance), we should recognize that both dimensions of this authority have affective valence, or so I shall argue in what follows. Hart was not the only one to overlook this fact. As we are about to see, the dominant views of law's authority today also neglect or minimize its affective sources.

The Sources of Law's Authority

One influential account of the authority of law emphasizes the justificatory dimension of this authority, which it grounds in reason. Authority in general is justified, according to Joseph Raz, "if it is more likely than its subjects to act correctly" in the sense that it serves "the reasons that apply" to its subjects better than they themselves do.[23] This "service conception of authority" holds that

> the normal and primary way to establish that a person should be acknowledged to have authority over another person involves showing that the alleged subject is likely better to comply with reasons which apply to him (other than the alleged authoritative directives) if he accepts the directives of the alleged authority as authori-

tatively binding, and tries to follow them, than if he tries to follow the reasons which apply to him directly.[24]

The law in particular has authority insofar as those subject to it are more likely to do what they have reason to do when they act because the law authoritatively commands them than if they simply tried to act for their own reasons.[25] For example, there are good reasons to refrain from stealing the property of others (provided that others also so refrain), but because our immediate interests may sometimes pull in the opposite direction we are more likely in the long run to comply with the reasons we have to refrain from stealing if we accept the authority of laws prohibiting it. The normative authority of law thus depends on its enabling subjects to act according to right reason.[26] In this way, law's authority mediates "between people and the right reasons which apply to them."[27] The law's ability to enable action in accordance with right reason justifies the obligations it imposes and explains why these obligations ought to prevail in our individual deliberations.

Raz's account is a positivist one. It holds that the law has no moral authority in itself; law has moral authority only in case there is moral reason to prefer its deliverances to one's own moral deliberations. The account is also a rationalist one insofar as it treats the intellect as the source of whatever normative authority the law has. To the extent that the reasons that determine practical or action-guiding deliberation always incorporate affective content, however, the "moral reasons" that establish law's authority will have this affective character. Where the law's authority prevails in the deliberations of its subjects, this authority inevitably rests on more than intellect. It requires a form of practical reasoning that also incorporates sentiment. Moreover, recognition of the appropriateness of deference to authority is one thing, but a full account of what the attitude of such deference consists in is something else again. Raz says next to nothing about this attitude. Just as he misses the inevitably affective content of the reasons that make law normative, so he neglects the law's motivating authority, the first-personal experience of respectful attachment and the feeling of allegiance, among other things, that generate compliance.

These two missteps are linked. They follow from the emphatic distinction that Raz posits between what he calls "value theory (which is concerned to establish which state of affairs is good or valuable and which is better than which) and normative theory (which is concerned with who should do what)."[28] Only the former covers the domain of human agency, he says, since "whatever people do they do because they believe it to be good or valuable"; only the latter explains the authority of law.[29] This distinction between normative theory and value theory, although not uncommon, should give us pause, especially when applied to the question of law's authority. For it is difficult to believe that standards of "who should do what" could be unconnected to our sense of "which state of affairs is good or valuable" and to the reflective sentiments that underlie these values. It is crucial for normative standards to answer to common concerns and be continuous with our reflective sentiments. Without this connection between norms (what we ought to do) and values (what we care about), as Rawls saw, "the sense of right lacks any apparent reason; it resembles a preference for tea rather than coffee,"[30] for it is unmotivated—and in a way that is normatively significant. Although such a preference might exist, to make it regulative of the basic terms of social coordination would be capricious. The right and the good must be congruent if they are to be motivating, and normative, for us.

By contrast, Raz seems intent on preserving a sharp divide between value theory and normative theory. And he insists that the terms "reason" and "ought" belong to the latter. Norms are operative reasons for action, on his view, but they are explicitly not values.[31] So when he defines legal rules as norms,[32] and when he further defines the authority of law as an ability to provide subjects with certain types of reasons for performing an action,[33] the effect is to disconnect the normative authority of the law from the motivating values of its subjects. Yet norms or obligations that have no footing in the things we care about (our goods, or values, or concerns) will be both normatively senseless, as Rawls said, and motivationally impotent, as Raz himself implies when he says that action is driven by values. What all this suggests is that the authority of law cannot be explained in the absence of careful attention to the affective concerns of its subjects. The reasons that justify the obligations that the law imposes must make reference to the things people care about if they are to influence action, which any practical authority must do, including the authority of law. Raz may be right to say that the reasons of subjects help justify deference to the law's authority, but we need to understand the affective content of these reasons and the affective experience of deference more fully than his own account allows if we are to grasp the phenomenon of law's authority as something that is both justified and motivating.

Another influential account of law's authority that follows in the positivist tradition is that of Jeremy Waldron. Waldron seats the authority of law in democratic societies in the fact of disagreement.[34] On this view the function of law is to provide a framework of rights and rules that order social interactions and enable us to make collective decisions in the face of persistent disagreement. In these "circumstances of politics," according to Waldron, the law cannot be based on

shared moral values and common understandings, much less on associative ties. Nor does it necessarily produce such commonality. Instead
law allows us to make definitive decisions in pressing matters of collective life without resolving the deep moral disagreements that often
give rise to them. Laws regulating abortion offer a good example in
that they establish definitive standards (for the time being) without
having settled our contentious moral debates about reproductive practices. The law ameliorates the problem of disagreement because it is
authoritative, and because its authority does not derive directly from
the principles of morality about which its subjects disagree.

This effort to distinguish between morality and the authority of law
is a mark of Waldron's positivism. But he is an ambivalent positivist.
For his account shows that the authority of law depends on more than
merely the fact of disagreement. Ultimately, the law draws what Waldron calls its "imperative" force from "our sense of the moral urgency
and importance of the problems that it is necessary for us to address—
the things that (morally) *need* to be done and must be done by us."[35]
This assertion cuts against Waldron's positivism. It also runs counter
to the picture of deep disagreement with which he began, for the
shared sense of moral urgency invoked here can only rest on some
agreement about what matters. Such agreement may be partial and too
abstract to resolve every particular dispute, but the fact that it is shared
and that it is commonly experienced as morally forceful is precisely
what gives the law the authority necessary to effect decisions in the
face of otherwise intractable conflicts. The fact of disagreement enhances the authority of law, but our disagreements can only run so
deep if the law is to have any authority at all. And without the sense
of moral urgency, the law would lack authority entirely; in this sense,
the authority it carries clearly has a moral character.

To ground the authority of law in a feeling of moral urgency is also
implicitly to give affective sentiments and desires a key place in establishing this authority, although Waldron does not develop this thought.
The "sense of moral urgency" clearly has normative as well as motivational implications. That is, the feeling of moral urgency and the felt
need for a common framework are not invoked by Waldron merely to
explain why citizens are motivated to comply with laws whose authority is established on separate grounds. The sense of moral urgency appears to justify the obligations the law imposes as well as to generate
a motivating feeling of allegiance to them. The suggestion in these brief
passages is that the feeling of moral concern on the part of citizens is
the key to what gives the law the quality of an imperative, what makes
it obligatory. It seems to explain why this authority ought to prevail in
our deliberations as well as why it does prevail (when it does). But

Waldron never says this. He remarks in passing that the circumstances of politics "deserve much greater attention than they have received in legal and political philosophy," and this is certainly true.[36] Yet while *Law and Disagreement* explores the circumstance of disagreement in significant detail, it leaves largely undeveloped another key circumstance of politics—namely, the sentiment of moral urgency that underlies the law's authority in democratic societies. For, aside from the brief comments noted here, this feature of the authority of law—its grounding in the affective concerns of those subject to it—remains untouched.

As against the positivist approach, Ronald Dworkin's theory of law as integrity is explicitly moral in nature. Dworkin treats the law as a coherent system of rules ordered by principles of political morality, including justice, fairness, and procedural due process.[37] Propositions of law are true "if they figure in or follow from" these principles, which "provide the best constructive interpretation of the community's legal practice."[38] In interpreting the law, judges (and citizens, too) should seek to promote "integrity" by thinking of new cases in terms of a single, unified "developing story," one that is true to both the precedents of existing law and the principles of political morality.[39] Law as integrity thus treats the normative authority of the law—its ability to obligate us—as being derived from its coherence as a whole and its consistency with these independent moral principles. For Dworkin, it is only when laws are guided by the principles that define the system of law and reflect political morality that they are authoritative in the sense of imposing legitimate obligations.[40]

A standard objection to moralist approaches of this sort is that they disconnect the authority of law from the consent of those subject to it.[41] At least in a democratic polity, the law's authority must rest in part on the willingness of subjects to be bound by it. In the absence of this willingness the law lacks legitimacy, and without legitimacy it cannot be normative for a population. Dworkin's account does provide some resources for answering this concern. Insofar as a polity operates according to the ideal of law as integrity, it will be what Dworkin calls a "true community." In a true community, people "accept that their fates are linked in the following strong way: they accept that they are governed by common principles";[42] that is, they share a commitment to collective decision making on the basis of law rather than bare power. A people "faithful to that promise, can claim the authority of a genuine associative community and can therefore claim moral legitimacy . . . in the name of fraternity."[43] Thus the nature of true community ensures that members assent to the norms that law entails. Their allegiance may not amount to actual consent, but it goes some distance toward addressing the legitimacy worry and to showing how the law as an independent moral standard could gain normative purchase and motivational authority for a particular collection of persons. The connection between law's authority and the sentiments of true community also suggests that this authority is partly a function of the affective attitudes of those subject to it, although Dworkin does not address this point directly. The relevant attitudes may not be limited to feelings about the law itself, either. The ideal of true community implies that deference to the authority of law is manifest in a particular type of concern for other persons—namely, respect for their rights.[44] Dworkin's account thus initially appears to allow for the legitimacy dimension of law's authority and to link this dimension of authority to the affective, social experience of community ties.

Yet in characterizing the relevant attitudes of citizens, he seriously understates both the affective and the social aspects of these ties. Indeed, he seems intent on distancing the notion of true community (and hence law's authority) from affective modes of consciousness. It is true that he refers to the ties that bind true communities as forms of mutual "concern."[45] He nevertheless insists that these concerns

> are not psychological conditions. Though a group will rarely meet or long sustain them unless its members by and large actually feel some emotional bond with one another, the conditions do not themselves demand this. The concern they require is an interpretive property of the group's practices of asserting and acknowledging responsibilities—these must be practices that people with the right level of concern would adopt—not a psychological property of some fixed number of the actual members.[46]

Dworkin suggests that the "interpretive property" of the group's practices of respecting the system of legal rights and duties is actually better established on the basis of individual reason, understood as independent of "psychological considerations," such as concerns. The idea seems to be that persons will identify for themselves, through the exercise of intellect, the principles of political morality that constitute their community's "scheme" of law as integrity, and that they will thereby endorse the law and act accordingly.[47] For Dworkin this caveat is crucial because it enables associative communities to be "larger and more anonymous" than they could be if they depended on real mutual concern, or affective ties more generally.[48] Still, the caveat undercuts a good deal of the force that the idea of associative obligations originally appeared to carry, which was to suggest that at least the law's practical authority, if not its normative force, consists partly in persons' feelings for (or attitudes toward) one another, thus on grounds that are affective as well as social. In the end, Dworkin eschews both these grounds, insisting on what one commentator has called the "more protestant idea" of the individual as oriented mainly to a set of abstract principles rather than to other persons,[49] and governed not by affective ties but by an ideal of affectless rationality. True community turns out to be a collection of rational individuals each of whom is primarily oriented to serving the principles of political morality. As a result, Dworkin's account proves to be limited in its ability to establish the legitimacy dimension of law's authority.

John Deigh's recent work on emotion and the authority of law represents an important departure from previous studies because it explicitly examines the nature of citizens' affective attachments to the law and the role of these attachments in establishing the authority of law. Deigh defines this authority as the ability to "set ends" for subjects that they do not set for themselves and that "dominate many of those ends that they do set for themselves."[50] Whereas the power to coerce compliance "is conditioned on the subjects' vulnerabilities to harm and capacities for fear," the authority of law "must be conditioned on something more." Specifically, it rests on subjects' "allegiance to the law, their willingness to be governed by the law ... to subordinate their own ends to the ends the law sets for them."[51] Allegiance addresses the legitimacy consideration because it captures subjects' affirmation of the law, or their endorsement of its authority. And this affirmation, Deigh maintains, can only come from "an emotional bond between them and the law."[52]

Deigh draws an analogy between this bond and the attachment children develop to their parents, which proceeds by means of socialization.[53] Whereas in the earliest stages of childhood development children obey their parents from instrumental motives (the desire for praise, the fear of anger), over time they become sensitive to the wrongfulness of disobedience in itself—in short, they develop the capacity for guilt and the semblance of a conscience. This leads to feelings of respect for the parents and the rules they set down. The new motives of conscience and respect "constitute a disposition on the child's part to do right even at the cost of forgoing pleasures."[54] Deigh maintains that legal subjects have an analogous disposition to obey the law, one that arises through similar processes of development and socialization. It, too, is grounded in emotional attachments and exerts a powerful affective pull. In fact, the emotional bond to the law begins within the family itself. The process of internalizing the authority of one's parents in childhood sets the stage for a continuing pattern of internalizing different authorities through "the subsequent bonds one forms to various other people and institutions as one gets older."[55] Attachments we develop at school, church, work, and in recreational and civic associations explain "the successively more mature dispositions to submit to the rules and dictates of these authorities and authoritative structures."[56]

This account of the emotional grounding of citizens' attachment to the law makes an important contribution, but it does not go far enough. For one thing, the complex character of law's authority, especially in a constitutional democracy, calls for further exploration of the distinctive attachments and concerns that figure in it. Although an emotional attachment is crucial, for instance, the law per se is not the only relevant object of this attachment. As we learned in connection with Dworkin's analysis, respect for the authority of law involves being attached in a particular way to one's fellow citizens—namely, with a feeling of concern for their rights and the duties that flow from these rights. Deigh's account implies that respect for law begins in attachments to others, but, once mature, consists in a feeling of filial allegiance directed at the law itself. Nor is it clear that filial allegiance is the best analogue for this respect. At least in a constitutional democracy, the law is supposed to reflect (however indirectly) the will of its subjects. In this sense, although the law has authority over people as individuals, the people together as political sovereign has authority over the laws. The reciprocity of this relationship differs fundamentally from the parent-child relationship. The attitude of respect for the laws felt by democratic citizens is not like filial allegiance. The two types of authority are too different in this regard to sustain the analogy that Deigh suggests.

More importantly, while the legitimacy dimension of law's authority is important, it is by no means sufficient. People may feel allegiance to vile laws and morally abhorrent legal systems. There must be more to the authority of law than mere allegiance. Its normative force depends in part on the validity of its claim to what Waldron calls "moral urgency." In addition, more needs to be said about the normative status of emotions. Although most people would agree that an emotional attachment to the law can support compliance by generating a motivation to obey, many would deny that emotions have a role in generating or justifying the normative obligations that the law entails. Does the feeling of filial attachment justify law's commands as well as motivate compliance with them? Deigh seems to want to insist that such emotions do have a justifying role but this view needs to be supported by an account of how emotions as a general matter can be normative. The standard view in legal theory, as in philosophy and political theory, is that affective concerns do not carry normative weight and cannot generate obligations. This view is reflected, for example, in Raz's sharp divide between "value theory" and "normative theory." From this perspective, Deigh's study of emotions could at most provide a description of some of the motivational supports of law's authority. It could never tell us anything about the law's power to obligate us or illuminate the normative question of what justifies these obligations. If a sentiment-based account of law's authority is to be anything more than a statement of the motivational supports required for the law to be effective in practice, if it is to say anything at all about why we *should* respect the law, it will need to be combined with an account of the normative value of sentiments.

So we need an explanation of law's authority that shows how legal and moral authority intersect (without simply collapsing the distinction between them) and that also attends to the legitimacy dimension of this authority. A moral sentiment approach answers these challenges. In contrast to the positivist view, it illuminates the moral dimensions of law's authority and shows why the law can obligate us. As against the moralist view, it shows that the allegiance of actual subjects matters to the law's authority, and matters to its normative as well as its motivational force. And in contrast to the emotion-based approach, the moral sentiment view allows us to distinguish between justified and unjustified allegiance to law, and to explain why certain feelings contribute to law's authority while others do not.

MORAL SENTIMENT AND THE AUTHORITY OF LAW

As we have seen, the great contribution of moral sentiment theory when it emerged in the eighteenth century was to establish a constitutive connection between norms and obligations, on the one hand, and the psychological motivations that generate action, on the other. It offered a powerful account of how the passions could be (or become) normative. The theory explained how affective responses to the world can be transformed into judgments of right and wrong, and how they generate the reflective values and obligations that govern (or should govern) human conduct. Not all feelings carry this normative weight, of course. Central to any viable theory of moral sentiment is a distinction between normative and non-normative forms of affect. We have all sorts of affective responses to the world: desires and aversions, hopes and fears, anger, love, admiration, disgust, and many more. So long as these emotions and concerns remain strictly personal they may motivate our actions but they cannot illuminate the concepts of right and wrong or generate obligations, with the implicit claim to general applicability that obligations entail. The function of norms and obligations is to regulate our conduct in relation to others, after all—to make it possible for different persons to coordinate their inevitable interactions in ways that are, for the most part, mutually satisfactory. Because of the general applicability of norms and obligations, and their function as serving general interests, they call for a means of evaluation that goes beyond the personal perspective of individual inclination or the partial perspective of group interests. The generalized standpoint of moral sentiment allows us to arrive at impersonal judgments of right and wrong on the basis of a reflective, impartial set of feelings. The notion of an impartial set of feelings may seem to be a contradiction in terms. In feeling with others, do we not forfeit our impartiality rather than extend it? This worry makes the mistake of equating impartiality with the absence of feeling, however. What impartiality really requires is the proper incorporation of feeling. It involves filtering out the distorting effects of self-interest and personal prejudice, and it demands sensitivity to the widest possible range of legitimate sentiments and to the principle of equal respect. The feelings we have when we contemplate an object from this impartial perspective, and in the light of the concerns that human nature makes common, form the basis of normativity. What we *ought* to do is what can be endorsed from within the generalized standpoint of moral sentiment and is consistent with equal respect and with what empirical experience tells us about human nature.

This account makes normativity itself an intersubjective phenomenon. We could not know what we ought to do if we were unable to feel the sentiments of others. The social character of moral sentiment can cause trouble when it leads to a herd mentality, or when individuals react uncritically to the sentiments of others. It also means that the moral stakes of political inequalities and social exclusions are very high. What distinguishes moral sentiment from non-normative feelings is that we arrive at them by adopting an impartial standpoint, one that rises above self-interest, personal prejudice, and narrow partiality to incorporate the sentiments of all those affected in a way that manifests equal respect. In this sense, there are good Humean grounds to worry about inequality and exclusion. Yet the rationalist view, which grounds normativity in a faculty of reason thought to transcend feeling, is as vulnerable as moral sentiment to the pressures of conformism and the effects of political inequality and social exclusion. As we saw in chapter 5, unless one posits a Kantian-style metaphysics of the subject, which has been resoundingly repudiated even by most Kantians today, the dream of perfect transcendence will be elusive. As long as human beings are interdependent, it is likely that our deliberative faculties will be sensitive to the sentiments of others. Moreover, while the norms that emerge from moral sentiment are always socially embedded, moral sentiment does allow for the critical evaluation of its own sources through the iterative, reflective stance of the generalized standpoint and the appeal to equal respect and common concerns.[57] And although the hope of perfectly transcending the social embeddedness of moral sentiment may be misguided, we can strive for an increasingly inclusive and impartial standpoint by means of the social and political practices discussed in earlier chapters.

Insofar as moral sentiment allows us to identify common concerns and the legitimate sentiments of relevant others, it can offer normative guidance and help us to see what we ought to do. Insofar as it rests on feeling, it has the potential to be practically motivating. Both features are important to the authority of law because of the fact that this authority generates normative obligations as well as motivates action. Moral sentiment theory suggests a new way of understanding the two dimensions of law's authority. It implies that for this authority to be justified (and therefore to have the normative force to generate obligations) it must be capable of being endorsed from within a suitably structured generalized standpoint. What do we feel when we contemplate the sentiments of those affected by the authority of a particular system of law? To what extent does the fact of the law's being authoritative for a population support rather than thwart common human concerns? Law as a general matter carries moral authority because it establishes social coordination, which is something endorsable from within the generalized perspective of moral sentiment. In any particular case, however, the authority of law will not elicit the sentiment of approval if specific laws, by thwarting common human concerns, elicit aversion. Nevertheless, the justification of law's authority in a particular polity is not synonymous with the sum of the justifications of all the laws of that polity. The normative authority of a particular legal system may be justified even if some specific laws fail the test of moral sentiment. It is not unreasonable to think that under a largely just collection of laws most people's lives will go better when they all defer to the general authority of law. Under these circumstances, reflective sympathy within the generalized standpoint will generate the sentiment of approval, which contributes to justifying law's authority, even though moral sentiment may also give us grounds to disapprove some particular laws covered by this authority. There is a difference between the justification of law's authority and the justification of the laws, although the two are closely related. In view of this distinction, public deliberation and debate about the justice of specific laws—which is a crucial activity of democratic citizenship—need not jeopardize the normative authority of law as a whole.[58] This consideration is important because public deliberation can be a meaningful activity only on the assumption that its final results (as law) will be authoritative.

The moral sentiment approach helps us to say why we should defer to the law, or why the law ought to prevail in our own deliberations about what to do. It justifies the authority of law with reference to the only sources of normativity that are practically available to us—namely, reflective sentiment and common human concerns impartially arrived at. This impartiality depends crucially on what Hume called "sympathy" and what contemporary legal theorists more often call "empathy," the capacity to feel with others differently placed.[59] In view of considerations raised earlier regarding the natural limits of sympathy and the social embeddedness of moral sentiment, the normative authority of law is intrinsically political. To establish this authority we must evaluate the law from within a generalized standpoint that incorporates the sentiments of all those affected, but we cannot know or feel their sentiments a priori. The sympathetic communication of sentiments—the operation of sympathy itself—calls for a deliberative democratic political order. In particular, it demands a critically engaged citizenry in which persons and groups regularly reflect on the justice of the laws, and voice their concerns and opinions; a free press and plenty of forums for the public debates that register these diverse sentiments and make them known to others; and a legislative system that generates laws in ways that respond to, and refine the outputs of, those deliberative processes. The justificatory dimension of law's authority is political not only because it must answer to the demands of democratic legitimacy, but also because it rests on democratic political practices and it presupposes empathetic citizens with broadly cultivated moral sentiments.

The practical authority of law—its ability to generate compliance for reasons that go beyond the fear of punishment—is sustained in part by means of its normative authority. At the same time, the affective valence of moral sentiment helps make sense of the legitimacy dimension of law's authority. To the extent that law can be endorsed from within the generalized standpoint of moral sentiment, it answers to fundamental human concerns and therefore can be expected to generate allegiance. This approach is better able to satisfy the demands of legitimacy than is Dworkin's, but it will generate *justified* deference and in this sense the view goes beyond what Deigh offered. It provides for a critical perspective on the actual allegiance of particular populations. To be justified, the obligations that the law imposes must serve shared concerns of citizens, for only in this way will reflection within the generalized standpoint give rise to impartial sentiments of approval. And insofar as the law serves these concerns, citizens will have an affectively engaged motivation to comply with its commands. Respect for law becomes a concern for me—the authority of law is something I care about—when the laws largely serve concerns that I already have. Here the moral sentiment approach calls to mind Waldron's implicit acknowledgment that the authority of law rests in part on the shared sense of moral concern about the goods that are secured by the rule of law. Yet this approach is more forthcoming than Waldron's about the dependence of law's authority on moral sentiments and common concerns. The connection between citizens' concerns and the authority of law means that in deeply unjust states, where the laws thwart key concerns, respect for this authority will itself have no place in citizens' horizons of concern. Under these circumstances, compliance can only result from coercion rather than respect or allegiance. In such cases, the law has little authority, although it may nevertheless be quite powerful if it is backed up by the force of the state. Needless to say, there is a continuum here with many gradations. Most states will fall somewhere between the two extremes.

It is worth noting that the practical authority of law also inevitably rests on reflective passions that go beyond moral sentiment itself. Certain forms of mutual concern among citizens, for instance, play an important role in establishing this authority. The main function of law, after all, is the regulation of interactions between persons. To respect the authority of law is to be concerned with the quality of our interactions, to care about how we treat others and are treated by them. Implicit in respect for the law, then, is a range of other socially oriented sentiments. Benevolence, or the desire to treat others decently, is surely one of these sentiments. In addition, the law's authority cannot be practically efficacious unless its citizens trust one another to generally comply with it. Only on the presumption of general compliance does individual compliance make sense. Part of the motivating authority of law is therefore a feeling of mutual trust among citizens. The desire to see justice done is yet another facet of our allegiance to law. This consideration recalls Dworkin's connection between the authority of law and respect for other people's rights. The feeling of respect for law's authority is not simply a matter of being attached to the law, but includes caring about justice and the rights of others. It also involves caring about how we ourselves are treated by others. Pride and the desire for recognition have a role here. Pride makes us feel that we deserve to be treated decently and inspires the ambition to claim our rights. The desire for recognition similarly reflects a sense that the character of our social interactions *matters*. To care about the quality of these interactions is to make the law, which regulates them, an object of our concern, hence to invest it with practical authority. This authority makes sense only in light of these other feelings. The motivating authority of law consequently goes beyond a sentiment of respect that takes the law itself as the direct object of feeling. This authority also rests on a range of feelings that citizens have for one another and for themselves. What commonly goes by the name of "respect for law" is more internally complex than is usually recognized.

The moral sentiment approach to law's authority clearly links this authority to morality as well as to politics. Does this mean that the authority of law derives from morality? In one sense the answer to this question must be affirmative. The law's authority rests on the fact that its subjects generally feel approval when contemplating it from within the generalized standpoint of moral sentiment. This approval in effect authorizes the obligations the law must impose if it is to be effective. Yet what generates the moral sentiment of approval is an object's ability to satisfy basic and common human concerns, and in this sense the sentiment is grounded in the whole range of desires, aversions, interests, and emotions that constitute the things we care about. There is no sharp line distinguishing moral concerns from nonmoral ones, no such thing as a fully autonomous moral domain or a set of norms that obligates us to certain forms of action without reference to the things we value. The authority of law is inextricably connected to morality not because law exists in some distinctive region called "the moral domain" or because it reflects the commands of an independent moral authority, but because the normativity of both law and morality derives from a common set of human concerns.

It may be useful to think about the class of human concerns from which practical norms (moral and legal) emerge in terms of Blackburn's "staircase of practical and emotional ascent," or the spiral of "emotional identifications and demands" that leads from simple preferences to compulsory obligations.[60] To be sure, in order for concerns to generate obligations they must be properly structured. Specifically, they must be insulated from private interest and personal prejudice, conditions that Blackburn himself does not adequately elaborate. This is where the theory of moral sentiment and the impartiality it establishes are useful. But for present purposes the interesting feature of Blackburn's staircase is that it is continuous. As we have seen, there is no one point on the staircase "before which we are not in the sphere of the ethical, and after which we are."[61] The temptation to mark out an autonomous moral domain, strictly separated from the more mundane concerns of practical life, including psychological attachments and desires, is a mistake that has long permeated Western philosophy.[62] It has often been thought that this domain is the only possible source of normativity. By disconnecting norms from the psychological sources of human motivation, this view gives rise to a motivational deficit. While this deficit poses a serious problem for moral theory, it is devastating for the authority of law, which is importantly constituted by its ability to motivate action.

In addition to the motivational problem, the claim that moral concerns are different in kind from (and independent of) psychological concerns raises normative questions. Why *should* we care about moral obligations so conceived? Because God wills it? Unless I accept as a matter of faith the authority of God (that is, unless the will of God is a concern for me), the normative force of the obligations will be unsupported. Nor can the threat of divine punishment establish the normativity of an obligation, no more than the coercive power of the state can establish political obligations. Threats can oblige but not obligate us. Perhaps we should care about moral obligations simply because "reason itself" requires it? But in what sense can reason require anything? Perhaps as a matter of logical consistency or deduction? Yet when it comes to practical deliberation, logical consistency and deduction always make reference to the things we care about. Reason conceived as detached from sentiment is incapable of imposing any requirements on action. Given a certain set of concerns, reason so conceived can show me, by means of logical deduction and appeals to consistency, what I should do in a particular case. The conclusions of practical deliberation in this sense are sometimes said to be "requirements of reason," but it would be more accurate to say that they are requirements of our reflective concerns, since these concerns are the real source of their normative force. Logical inconsistency has no moral significance in itself. What matters morally is not that I am acting inconsistently but that my actions are inconsistent with the things that should matter to me. And the things that should matter are not some special class of considerations. They are simply the things that *do* matter when considered impartially; they are the common concerns that can be endorsed from within the generalized standpoint of moral sentiment and that answer to human nature.

Still, there are real distinctions to be drawn between moral obligations and legal ones. Many legal obligations are concerned with things that must be coordinated if human lives are to go well but that in themselves are reasonably understood to be morally indifferent. They are *mala prohibita* rather than *mala in se*. If one reflects, from within the generalized standpoint, on the practice of driving on the right side of the road versus the left side, one is likely to be unmoved. In itself this practice simply does not touch on any significant human concerns. In this sense it lacks what we commonly think of as moral value. On Blackburn's staircase it occupies a relatively low step. Yet there are good reasons to legally regulate driving practices. If we left them to chance or personal preference, many people would lose their lives, and this *is* something of fundamental concern, something that occupies a relatively high step on the staircase. This concern explains why the law imposes certain obligations on automobile drivers. These obligations are in one sense quite far from what we conventionally think of as morality but in another sense they are closely connected to it. In this way, the moral sentiment account can accommodate the complex distinctions we commonly make between the different ways that legal obligations have normative force. It accounts for the fact that the authority of the law sometimes carries explicit moral authority and sometimes has only an indirect connection to what we conventionally conceive as morality. What it denies is that there is no necessary connection between the authority of law and the kinds of concerns that we usually think of as moral ones. It is because of this connection that law has normative authority to obligate that goes beyond its power to coerce. Insofar as the law serves basic human concerns, it can become a basic concern for us. And it is because the concerns that constitute law's authority engage affective modes of consciousness that the law can be a practical authority, one capable of effectively guiding action.

   If the moral sentiment approach clarifies the moral, political, and affective bases of law's authority, it also illuminates how and why the authority of law sometimes fails. In the absence of effective mechanisms to mitigate social inequalities, where the concerns of certain groups are systematically marginalized within the public consciousness, the generalized standpoint of moral sentiment will be incompletely realized in the minds and hearts of most citizens. Because the full justification of law's authority (and its normative force) calls for moral sentiments that are impartial, the lack of impartiality will undermine the normative authority of law, or at least set limits on it. If the generalized standpoint systematically excludes the concerns of certain (affected) classes of persons in justifying the law's authority, it will be difficult to say why this authority ought to prevail in the practical deliberations of these persons, or why it should override their concerns when these concerns conflict with what the law requires. The weakness of the law's normative authority under such conditions will tend to erode its practical authority as well, or to inhibit the feeling of respect for law among marginalized persons. One sees this dynamic at work in disproportionately high rates of law-breaking among members of socially and politically disenfranchised groups. These failures of law's authority may also generate cynicism about the political process as a whole and reinforce feelings of alienation, which can erupt in explosive ways.[63] The members of disenfranchised groups, lacking normative grounds to respect the law, will feel its threats more powerfully than they feel its authority, hence their relationship to the law is likely to be characterized more by fear than by allegiance. And living in fear is no kind of freedom. Hence those who have no feeling for law's authority will be less free than their fellows. If their numbers are small, the authority of law within the polity as a whole may remain largely intact. Where multiple such groups exist that together constitute a sizeable portion of the population, however, the law's authority may be significantly compromised. Informal and extralegal practices of discrimination, and a culture of exclusion and inequality, are therefore dangerous not simply to justice and social harmony but to the rule of law itself. Law's authority (both normative and practical) depends on the cultivation of an inclusive form of moral sentiment among citizens, one that brings to bear the concerns of all those who are subject to the law. The cultivation of this faculty will depend in turn on the political mechanisms and social practices that support the communication of feeling among citizens and foster reflective sympathy and mutual concern.

The role of moral sentiment in establishing the authority of law also means that this authority will never be complete, or perfectly authoritative. It will always be subject to the ways in which moral sentiment, at least in healthy liberal democracies, is itself continually contested and reconstituted. Moral sentiment in the best case is not only inclusive but self-critical. The periodic reconstitution of moral sentiment transpires in liberal-democratic societies through public debate and advocacy, political protests and other forms of activism, and the whole range of cultural expressions through which individual and group concerns are continuously conveyed to a wider public. These practices are crucial to impartial public deliberation; they are also important to the rule of law. Insofar as the law's authority rests on moral sentiment, the scope and strength of this authority in democratic societies depends upon an inclusive, contestatory, and deliberative political life that enlarges and enriches the moral sentiments of all its citizens.

We began this chapter by asking about how public deliberation, which rests on sentiment, could generate conclusions that have the authority of law. How can we make sense of the obligatoriness of deliberation's results, as law, if the source of these results is found in our reflective passions? After all, most legal theories today regard the authority of law as being independent of the passions. The theory of moral sentiment suggests, however, that both the normative and the motivating authority of law rests as much on feeling, properly conceived, as on intellect. Uneasiness about the dangers of emotionalism and fears about the power of the passions to destabilize social order have led us to overlook the affective sources of law's authority for far too long. We have good reason to be suspicious of affect, to be sure, but no action-guiding authority is possible without it. Consequently, these legitimate suspicions should not stand in the way of inquiry into the role that feeling properly plays. Moral sentiment theory helps us distinguish rank emotionalism and idiosyncratic passions from the reflective concerns that necessarily and rightly constitute our values, generate obligations, and sustain practical authorities, including the authority of law. As scholars continue to explore the ways in which passions, emotions, and desires properly interact with intellect to generate and sustain standards of right for political life, the affective sources of law's authority will need to be pursued further. For "the questions of why people obey the law and whether there is a defensible moral obligation to do so," as one recent commentator puts it, "are central to any understanding of the way the law works in society."[64] Understanding when and why the law does *not* work in society is equally important. Recognizing the moral, political, and affective sources of law's authority illuminates the conditions under which the authority of law fails, or fails some of us. And in a liberal democracy, for law's authority to fail some of us is for it to fail us all.

To avoid this failure, to sustain the authority of law and the freedom it promises, we need to cultivate a rich and inclusive moral sentiment as a habit of citizenship, and this will require liberal rights and a contestatory democratic political life. We need the continuing public debate that periodically reconstitutes the generalized standpoint of moral sentiment in ways that incorporate the concerns of marginalized persons and refine our collective sense of what matters. We also need a better philosophical understanding of the relationship between the legal norms that guide action and the psychological motives that generate it. We need to disrupt the myths of law's detachment from emotion and practical reason's independence from the passions. Moral sentiment theory shows us that the norms and motives that help constitute the authority of law come from a common source: the reflective concerns that constitute our values and move us to act. This insight is crucial to the practice of democratic citizenship, and specifically to the practices of public deliberation. To deliberate well as citizens, to reliably act on the results of our deliberations, and to enjoy liberal democracy's promise of freedom, we need to possess an impartial feeling for law's authority. Moral sentiment makes this possible.

Toward a New Politics of Passion:
Civil Passions and the Promise of Justice

To TALK ABOUT the politics of passion stimulates images of protesters smashing windows, zealots breathing fire in the public square, even the dreaded suicide bomber. It makes us think of smoky backrooms where public officials trade their votes to enhance their personal power or sell their influence for wealth and privilege. It calls to mind the police officer whose racism is barely concealed, or the judge whose decisions reek of his fears and his prejudice. But the politics of passion points to so much more. Women's suffrage, the end of Jim Crow laws, and the recent advances in freedom and equality for gay people in the United States are also products of the politics of passion. In the course of American history, the sympathetic communication of sentiments has extended the generalized standpoint of moral sentiment so as to include the feelings and the concerns of many previously excluded groups in new ways. This expansion of moral sentiment has powerfully influenced public deliberation on matters affecting justice in this country. At the international level, the rising influence of human rights since the end of World War II also testifies to the extension of moral sentiment. We have further to go—a long way in fact, and our gains are by no means fully secure—but we have come very far. And anyone who thinks that the American public has reasoned its way to these new views without help from the passions or the sympathetic communication of sentiments is willfully blind. Once again, our minds are changed when our hearts are engaged.

It does matter, of course, that our hearts be engaged in the right ways. The new politics of passion that moral sentiment suggests makes distinctions between the legitimate and the illegitimate influence of passions on public deliberation. It identifies criteria for the proper incorporation of sentiment. Passions can indeed be dangerous to liberty and equality, as all our negative associations with the old politics of passion suggest. For this reason, the old politics of passion is not obsolete; its dangers are always present and should never be minimized. But the way to prevent these dangers from materializing is not to abandon the passions for a form of reason that abstracts from feeling altogether. No such faculty is available to us, and the misguided pursuit of this idyll may discourage us from the important business of feeling with others. The cultivation of moral sentiment that is inclusive and sensitive enough to support genuinely impartial deliberation calls for affective engagement with others and with the pressing political questions of our time. This affective impartiality is the new politics of passion—the politics of civil passions. It points to a new model of citizenship, one that champions the faculty of reflective concern rather than disinterested, disengaged, and dispassionate intellect. Citizenship so conceived does not privilege care for particular others over the demands of justice, however. It treats impartial deliberation about what justice means and what it requires as a key political obligation and a moral duty. It asks us to feel with other citizens who are differently placed, to evaluate the laws and policies that govern us all in light of the legitimate sentiments and concerns of all.

The new politics of passion also connects impartial deliberation about justice to action on behalf of justice. In this sense, it should recall Hume's own theory of moral sentiment. He wanted a moral theory that would be not only "more correct in its precepts" but also "more persuasive in its exhortations" than the rationalist alternatives on offer in his day.[1] The rationalist approach could not generate effective exhortations, he thought, because the intellect on its own could never be a cause of action. A moral theory that founded knowledge of moral precepts on a form of reason that "excludes all sentiment" was bound to be impotent as a guide for action.[2] Hume envisioned a moral theory that would "represent virtue in all her genuine and most engaging charms" and therefore motivate us to "approach her with ease, familiarity, and affection."[3] The fact that moral sentiments, which generate judgment and guide deliberation, are grounded in the same range of reflective concerns that motivate action was intended to make the theory of moral sentiment practically efficacious. It rests on a more holistic—and therefore more realistic—account of practical reasoning, in which affective and cognitive modes of consciousness are deeply entwined. The model of affective but impartial public deliberation offered here reflects this same ambition. It escapes the motivational deficit that plagues rationalist accounts of judgment and norm justification, and that obstructs not only action but also decision making itself. The politics of civil passion avoids the motivational deficit by connecting the impartial standpoint of moral sentiment to the affective sources of human agency.

This does not mean that citizens always will do the right thing, but it does mean that the same considerations that move us in deliberation can also move us to action. In contrast, the parties to Rawls's original position are marked by a radically different moral psychology than that which characterizes actual persons and real citizens.[4] The result is that the concerns that move the parties in deliberation to arrive at the principles of justice do not themselves move citizens to support the principles of justice. In a similar way, Habermas acknowledges that the form of reason operative within the moral standpoint abstracts too fully from the sentiments and desires of actual persons to reliably motivate action on behalf of moral decisions. Moral principles therefore need to be enforced by the coercive power of law and by socialized identities, which give people new reasons to comply with the principles their "reason" has justified. This disjunction between the reasons for decision and the reasons for action is deeply unsatisfying. The principle of liberal-democratic legitimacy, as one recent writer has noted, entails that the basic motives required of citizens must arise freely if a liberal society is to achieve its ideals. A society in which citizens abided by the norms of justice only from fear of punishment or because of some program of "motivational indoctrination" could not be free.[5] This is not to deny the legitimacy of civic education or basic socialization, of course. It is to insist, with Hume, that the norms governing us should reflect motives that naturally animate us. The considerations that make something the right thing to do should also be considerations about which we care enough to act. In fact, our concern for them should be part of what makes these considerations relevant to determining what justice requires. The connection within moral sentiment between the concerns that guide deliberation and the concerns that motivate action answers to this aspiration. It does not guarantee just action, because additional motives may intervene that press in other directions. Moreover, citizens may not always achieve full impartiality. Yet the connection between norms and motives does establish an important link between dimensions of the self that tend to be fragmented on the rationalist accounts. It makes the self as public deliberator one with the self as political agent, a view that is much truer to how we experience ourselves as citizens (and as persons) and that better empowers us to enact the conclusions of deliberation. In this way, the politics of civil passion supports the practice(s) of justice.

Again, this approach does not deny the value of education and socialization. As we have seen, the exercise of impartiality requires the cultivation and refinement of moral sentiment. Chapter 4 identified some institutional mechanisms and policy options worth exploring further in this regard. Our education policy, for example, should seek excellence in student mastery of basic knowledge and skills but it should also aim to extend students' natural capacity for the sympathetic communication of sentiments. Likewise, finding ways to increase diversity in our legislative assemblies and executive advisory bodies as well as among judges and jurors may help promote the expansion of moral sentiment by bringing a wider range of sentiments into our deliberative contexts. And a vibrant associational and cultural life within civil society provides important support for the extension of sympathy and the education of moral sentiment. An extensive policy analysis centering on the demands of moral sentiment will have to wait for another day, however. Such an analysis might find that some current laws, policies, and institutions work against the cultivation of moral sentiment and ought to be reformed. *Civil Passions* remains agnostic on that question for now. Its purpose is not to argue for changes in how we order politics and social policy in the United States today but rather to suggest a fundamental rethinking of who we are as citizens and as persons. We are not who we thought we were, and we will never achieve what our old ideals tell us we should aspire to become. The very faculty of practical reasoning that makes us rational simultaneously engages us in feeling. Consequently, we cannot be the passionless, disengaged deliberators that we think we ought to be, even when we succeed in deliberating impartially. If this book advances our basic understanding of ourselves, our reflective passions, and our deliberative practices, it will have fulfilled its ambition. What it suggests is that any policy initiatives undertaken on behalf of impartial justice should aim not for the transcendence but for the civilizing of passions in public life.

In this regard, it is worth reiterating that the point of *Civil Passions* is not to bring more passions into politics. The aim is instead to illuminate the ways in which sentiment already (and inevitably) does figure in moral judgment, political deliberation, and the authority of law, and to articulate guidelines for accommodating it in ways that support rather than thwart the important ideal of impartiality. Moral sentiment theory reminds us that we can achieve a measure of impartiality in our judgments (and we should strive for this) but we cannot leave behind our passions and desires. When properly arrived at, these affective concerns figure centrally in our judgments about what justice means and what it requires of us. To abandon them would be to undercut our capacity for sound and impartial judgment. This would be a blow to democratic citizenship, because as citizens we are obligated not only to obey the laws but also to think critically about them. By clarifying the faculties of heart and mind involved in this critical reflection, moral sentiment theory gives us important tools for sustaining democratic citizenship and for properly orienting us, as citizens, to the laws and institutions that structure our common life.

Notes

INTRODUCTION
CITIZENSHIP, JUDGMENT, AND THE POLITICS OF PASSION

1. See, for example, Antonio R. Damasio, *Descartes' Error: Emotion, Reason, and the Human Brain* (New York: HarperCollins, 2000); Joseph LeDoux, *The Emotional Brain* (New York: Simon and Schuster, 1996); and V.S. Ramachandran, *Phantoms in the Brain: Probing the Mysteries of the Human Mind* (New York: William Morrow, 1998).

2. See, for example, George E. Marcus, W. Russell Neuman, and Michael MacKuen, *Affective Intelligence and Political Judgment* (Chicago: University of Chicago Press, 2000); Marcus, *The Sentimental Citizen: Emotion in Democratic Politics* (University Park: Pennsylvania State University Press, 2002); Rose Mc-Dermott, "The Feeling of Rationality: The Meaning of Neuroscientific Advances for Political Science," *Perspectives on Politics* 2 (4) (Dec 2004): 691–706; Ted Brader, *Campaigning for Hearts and Minds: How Emotional Appeals in Political Ads Work* (Chicago: University of Chicago Press, 2006); Jeff Goodwin, James M. Jasper, and Francesca Polletta, eds., *Passionate Politics: Emotions and Social Movements* (Chicago: University of Chicago Press, 2001); Neta Crawford, "The Passion of World Politics: Propositions on Emotion and Emotional Relationships," *International Security* 24 (4) (Spring 2000): 116–56; and Darren Schreiber, "Political Cognition and Social Cognition: Are We All Political Sophisticates?" in W. Russell Neuman, George E. Marcus, and Michael MacKuen, eds., *The Affect Effect: Dynamics of Emotion in Political Thinking and Behavior* (Chicago: University of Chicago Press, 2007).

3. The extent to which nonpractical (or theoretical) reason stands apart from sentiment is another question, one that I do not take up in this book. In what follows, I assume that theoretical reason is more independent of sentiment than practical reason, although nothing in the account of practical reason offered here requires this.

4. Michael Walzer, *Passions and Politics* (New Haven: Yale University Press, 2004), 126.

5. Ibid., 126–27. Walzer is somewhat ambivalent about the precise role that passions are to play within judgment. Although he sometimes (as here) implies that they rightly shape deliberation, at other times he treats passions as merely instrumental. In the latter instances he suggests that while passions motivate us to act, and perhaps to take up deliberation, they do not contribute to deliberation itself, which is rational in the sense of being detached from the passions, at least when it is well done (Walzer, *Passions and Politics*, 128).

6. Carol Gilligan, *In a Different Voice: Psychological Theory and Women's Development* (Cambridge, Mass.: Harvard University Press, 1982).

7. Virginia Held, *Feminist Morality: Transforming Culture, Society, and Politics* (Chicago: University of Chicago Press, 1993), 228; Joan Tronto, *Moral Boundaries: A Political Argument for an Ethic of Care* (New York: Routledge, 1994), 155; and Robin West, *Caring for Justice* (New York: New York University Press, 1997), 75.

8. Martha Nussbaum, *Love's Knowledge* (Oxford: Oxford University Press, 1990) and *Upheavals of Thought* (Cambridge: Cambridge University Press, 2001), 46; Iris Marion Young, *Justice and the Politics of Difference* (Princeton: Princeton University Press, 1990) and "Asymmetrical Reciprocity: On Moral Respect, Wonder, and Enlarged Thought," in Ronald Beiner and Jennifer Nedelsky, eds., *Judgment, Imagination, and Politics* (Lanham, Md.: Rowman and Littlefield, 2001).

9. Simon Blackburn, *Ruling Passions: A Theory of Practical Reasoning* (Oxford: Oxford University Press, 1998), 123.

10. Ibid.

11. Cheryl Hall, "Recognizing the Passion in Deliberation: Toward a More Democratic Theory of Deliberative Democracy," *Hypatia: A Journal of Feminist Philosophy* 22 (4) (Fall 2007), 91.

12. See Christine Korsgaard, *The Sources of Normativity* (Cambridge: Cambridge University Press, 1996) and "Skepticism about Practical Reason," in Elijah Millgram, ed., *Varieties of Practical Reasoning* (Cambridge, Mass.: The MIT Press, 2001); and T. M. Scanlon, *What We Owe to Each Other* (Cambridge, Mass.: Harvard University Press, 1998). Michael Smith has advanced an influential variant of the view that reason motivates in *The Moral Problem* (Malden: Blackwell, 1994). In political theory, the rationalist view can be found in Brian Barry, *Justice as Impartiality* (New York: Oxford University Press, 1995). It is also commonly associated with the work of John Rawls and Jürgen Habermas, although the analysis offered in chapter 1 complicated this common view.

13. Diego Gambetta, "Claro!: An Essay on Discursive Machismo," in Jon Elster, ed., *Deliberative Democracy* (Cambridge: Cambridge University Press, 1998), 23.

14. Walt Whitman, "Song of Myself," in *Leaves of Grass and Selected Prose*, ed. John Kouwenhoven (New York: Modern Library, 1950), 74, cited in Seyla Benhabib, "Judgment and the Moral Foundations of Politics" in Beiner and Nedelsky, *Judgment, Imagination, and Politics*, 198. Benhabib cites Whitman to illustrate her point that "Arendt was too quick in assuming that out of the self's desire for unity and consistency a principled moral standpoint could emerge." My point is somewhat different in that it refers to the limits of the intellect in practical deliberation rather than the limits of a particular concept of the self. Jennifer Nedelsky's argument is closer to my own when she insists that the mere recognition of logical inconsistency between different positions that one holds would not be enough to generate new deliberative conclusions. As she says, "it takes affect to change affect." Nedelsky, "Embodied Diversity and the Challenges to Law," in Beiner and Nedelsky, *Judgment, Imagination, and Politics*, 251. This general position is argued for at length in what follows.

15. David Hume, *A Treatise of Human Nature*, ed. L. A. Selby-Bigge (Oxford: Clarendon Press, 1968), 2.3.3, 417.

16. The leading examples of this literature (such as Damasio, Ramanchandran, and LeDoux) have been vetted by experts in the field. They include studies published in highly respected, peer-reviewed journals such as *Nature* and *Science*, and they have been extremely influential in shaping contemporary understanding of the operations of the brain.

17. It also goes beyond existing treatments of political judgment within political theory, many of them inspired by Hannah Arendt, and hence indirectly by Kant and Aristotle. See, for example, Ronald Beiner, *Political Judgment* (Chicago: University of Chicago Press, 1983); Beiner and Jennifer Nedelsky, *Judgment, Imagination, and Politics*; Andrew Norris, "Arendt, Kant, and the Politics of Common Sense," *Polity* 29 (2) (Winter 1996): 165–91; and Susan Bickford, *The Dissonance of Democracy: Listening, Conflict, and Citizenship* (Ithaca: Cornell University Press, 1996). For additional discussion of political judgment, see Peter J. Steinberger, *The Concept of Political Judgment* (Chicago: University of Chicago, 1993). The current study extends the exploration opened up by these works, but it takes the study of judgment in a new direction by bringing the resources of Humean moral sentiment theory to bear for the first time in a contemporary democratic context.

18. See Richard H. Popkin, "Hume's Racism," in Richard A. Watson and James E. Force, eds., *The High Road to Pyrrhonism* (San Diego: Austin Hill Press, 1980), 251–66; as well as Popkin, "Hume's Racism Reconsidered," *The Third Force in Seventeenth-Century Thought* (Leiden: Brill, 1992), 64–75, and John Immerwahr, "Hume's Revised Racism," *Journal of the History of Ideas* 53 (3) (July-September 1992): 481–86.

19. Immanuel Kant, "On the Proverb: That May Be True in Theory But Is Of No Practical Use," in Kant, *Toward Perpetual Peace and Other Essays*, trans. Ted Humphrey (Indianapolis: Hackett, 1983), 76 [295], 78–79 [298–300].

20. For a valuable treatment of this view of the difference between the right and the good, see Charles Larmore, *The Morals of Modernity* (Cambridge: Cambridge University Press, 1996), especially chap. 1. Larmore ultimately insists on the possibility of an attachment to the right, but he argues that this will require rethinking the nature of practical reason. The priority of the right "cannot plausibly be defended as a requirement of practical reason itself" (38), as it is in Kant and some of his contemporary followers. Instead, it depends on a more "contextualist" conception (38) of reason, one that is closer to the holistic account of practical reasoning argued for here. More generally, *Civil Passions* means to articulate the affective dimensions of the right, properly understood.

21. Gutmann and Thompson, *Why Deliberative Democracy?* (Princeton: Princeton University Press, 2004), 134.

22. One recent theorist has argued that the constitutive values of democracy itself provide justification for liberal rights and the constraints on democratic deliberation that they entail. I take no position on that here. See Corey Brettschneider, *Democratic Rights: The Substance of Self-Government* (Princeton: Princeton University Press, 2007).

CHAPTER ONE
JUSTICE AND PASSION IN RAWLS AND HABERMAS

1. Rawls once called for an examination of the substantive elements in these two ostensibly proceduralist views, and this chapter responds to that call. John Rawls, "Reply to Habermas," *Journal of Philosophy* 92 (3) (1995): 174.

2. Rawls, *A Theory of Justice* (Cambridge, Mass.: Harvard University Press, 1971), 30.

3. Ibid.

4. In this passage, Rawls gives two possible meanings for a "deontological" theory: it "either does not specify the good independently from the right, or does not interpret the right as maximizing the good" (*A Theory of Justice*, 30). His theory is deontological only in the second sense, he says. It does not meet the first condition because, as will become clear, justice as fairness does specify the good independently of the right in a variety of ways, and with important implications for the substance of justice.

5. Rawls treats autonomy as a good in part 3 of *A Theory of Justice*. Autonomy as "the realization of our nature as a free and rational being" (575) is a good made possible for the individual by her exercise of justice (577, 515).

6. Rawls's later work modifies the role this conception of the person plays in the moral background of justice as fairness. This modification will be discussed presently.

7. Rawls, *A Theory of Justice*, 142–44.

8. Rawls, *Political Liberalism* (New York: Columbia University Press,1993), 19.

9. Rawls, *A Theory of Justice*, 121.

10. Rawls, *Political Liberalism*, 52.

11. Ibid.

12. See Rawls, *A Theory of Justice*, 178. As Bernard Williams has remarked in regard to rationalist theories of morality, if morality "can and should have that much power against the heart's desire, it had better have a footing in the heart's desire" ("History, Morality, and the Test of Reflection," in Christine M. Korsgaard, ed., *The Sources of Normativity* [Cambridge: Cambridge University Press, 1996], 211). I concur with Williams in this view, but my analysis of Rawls is meant to show that at least some rationalist theories do aspire to have a footing in "the heart's desire," even if this aspiration is imperfectly realized or sits uncomfortably with other aspects of the theories.

13. Rawls, *A Theory of Justice*, 93.

14. This is not to deny the existence of *akrasia*, or weakness of will—not every desire determines the will or generates action. The relevant point here is to bring out the conceptual connection between goods and desires. In view of this connection, conceptions of the good, in contrast to the ideal of the right, are intrinsically attractive even if they are not in every instance motivating.

15. Rawls, *A Theory of Justice*, 51. This remark points to a neglected aspect of Rawls's theory—namely, that it has some debts to the moral-sense school, represented most famously by David Hume and Adam Smith. For further dis-

cussion of the Humean dimensions of Rawls, see Michael Frazer, "John Rawls: Between Two Enlightenments," *Political Theory* 35 (6) (December 2007): 756–80.

16. Rawls, *A Theory of Justice*, 505.

17. Rawls, *Political Liberalism*, 83–85; emphasis added. Conception-dependent desires incorporate principles into a larger conception or ideal, especially an ideal of the self. The sense of justice involves not simply an attachment to the two principles of justice and the prior ideal of reasonableness but an attachment to an idea of oneself as the kind of person who lives up to these standards (ibid.). The standards figure as elements in a more comprehensive self-conception that one desires to embody over time and in the different circumstances of one's life. The conception-dependent desire for justice is infused with affective feelings, such as self-respect in achievement and shame in failure, and is continuous with other moral concerns and indeed with the whole range of natural sentiments common among human beings. And while it is generally true that "persons tend to love, cherish, or support whatever affirms their own good" (Rawls, *A Theory of Justice*, 177), this does not mean that all human action is narrowly egoistic (Samuel Freeman, "Congruence and the Good of Justice," in Samuel Freeman, ed., *The Cambridge Companion to Rawls* [Cambridge: Cambridge University Press, 2003], 282). Once principles of justice are incorporated as conception-dependent desires into one's identity, the attachment to them is undergirded by the desires for self-respect and integrity. The principles are regarded as categorically right, not merely as expedient, and yet because they form the conditions for the fulfillment of our higher-order interests in self-respect and integrity, we cannot help but see them as good for us. They have become part of the system of ends that we rationally desire. Conception-dependent desires in effect bring the right and the good together. Susan Mendus remarks on the fact that Rawls treats the sense of justice as an "ideal of personal integrity," and although she does not connect it to Rawls's own discussion of conception-dependent desires, she develops this point in a fruitful fashion ("The Importance of Love in Rawls's *Theory of Justice*," *British Journal of Political Science* 29 [1999]: 72).

18. Rawls, *A Theory of Justice*, 478.

19. Rawls, *Political Liberalism*, 19. As Rawls notes, the sense of justice in this respect is close to T. M. Scanlon's "agreement motive" (see Rawls, *Political Liberalism*, 49n2; and see T. M. Scanlon, *What We Owe to Each Other* [Cambridge, Mass.: Harvard University Press, 1998).

20. Rawls, *Political Liberalism*, 49. The reasonable includes "the willingness to propose and honor fair terms of cooperation, and . . . the willingness to recognize the burdens of judgment and accept their consequences" (ibid., 49n1). The distinction Rawls makes in *Theory* between the two moral powers (the capacities for a rational plan of life and for a sense of justice) thus maps onto the distinction between the two faculties of reason found in *Political Liberalism* (the rational and the reasonable).

21. Susan Moller Okin remarks on the affective elements of justice in Rawls (*Justice, Gender, and the Family* [New York: Basic, 1989], 98–99), as does Cheryl Hall ("Passions and Constraint," *Philosophy and Social Criticism* 28 [6] [2002]: 745).

22. It is perhaps worth emphasizing in this regard that the veil of ignorance does not replace the sense of justice but rather expresses it.

23. Rawls, *A Theory of Justice*, 128–29.

24. Okin, *Justice, Gender, and the Family*, 101, and "Reason and Feeling in Thinking about Justice," *Ethics* 99 (January 1989): 238, 246, 248; Martha C. Nussbaum, "Rawls and Feminism," in *The Cambridge Companion to Rawls*, 496.

25. Rawls, *A Theory of Justice*, 587; emphasis added.

26. Strictly speaking, empathy itself is not a sentiment but a vehicle for the communication of sentiments. It is not especially misleading to refer to empathy as a sentiment, however, because the practice of empathy is always experienced in the form of feeling.

27. Ibid., 477.

28. Ibid., 570.

29. Brian Barry has complained along these lines that "some writers appear to believe that a theory of justice must somehow pick people up by the scruff of the neck and force them to behave justly," which is "an absurd demand" (*Justice as Impartiality* [Oxford: Oxford University Press, 1995], 114).

30. Rawls, *Lectures on the History of Moral Philosophy* (Cambridge, Mass.: Harvard University Press, 2000), 80.

31. Freeman reports that "Rawls has said (in conversation) that he thinks the congruence argument was one of the most original contributions he made in *A Theory of Justice* and that he is puzzled why it did not attract more comment" (Freeman, "Congruence and the Good of Justice," 308n2). For further analysis, see Freeman's discussion.

32. Rawls, *A Theory of Justice*, 574; and see *Political Liberalism*, 74.

33. Rawls, *A Theory of Justice*, 574.

34. Ibid., 574, 587.

35. Ibid., 476.

36. Ibid., 477–78. As Mendus points out, Rawls's interpretation of Ross is somewhat idiosyncratic, and cuts against the conventional view of intuitionism as "a theory about how we recognize something as right or wrong, not as a theory about what motivates us to act on that recognition" (Mendus, "The Importance of Love," 61). Whether or not Rawls was wrong about Ross, his objection to the doctrine of "the purely conscientious act" emphasizes his own commitment, as Mendus says, to the view that "there must be some motivational story, additional to the bare assertion that the thing in question is right," and that this story must show "justice to be congruent with the agent's own good" (Mendus, "The Importance of Love," 60). This conviction sets Rawls at odds with theorists such as Barry and Scanlon, both of whom reject the Rawlsian congruence argument (Brian Barry, "John Rawls and the Search for Stability," *Ethics* 105 [1995]: 889; T. M. Scanlon, "Contractualism and Utilitarianism," in Amartya Sen and Bernard Williams, eds., *Utilitarianism and Beyond* [Cambridge: Cambridge University Press, 1982], 105; cited in Mendus, "The Importance of Love," 63).

37. Rawls, *A Theory of Justice*, 476.

38. Freeman, "Congruence and the Good of Justice," 277–78; Mendus, "The Importance of Love," 59.

39. Rawls, *Political Liberalism*, xv-xvi.

40. Ibid., xvi.

41. Vestiges of the earlier argument do remain in *Political Liberalism*, but in modified form. Rawls now attributes the two faculties of rationality and reasonableness more narrowly to "the essential nature of citizens" rather than persons. In view of this nature, citizens of liberal democracies experience the exercise of these faculties as a good (Rawls, *Political Liberalism*, 203). Because the political conception of justice permits their exercise, a just political society itself counts as "a good for citizens," one that "secures their fundamental needs" (ibid.). "Congruence" now means only that justice is intrinsically good for persons as citizens, while no claim is made about the value of justice for persons in general.

42. Ibid., 12.

43. Ibid., 218.

44. Ibid., 147–48.

45. Jürgen Habermas, *The Inclusion of the Other: Studies in Political Theory*, ed. Ciaran Cronin and Pablo DeGreiff (Cambridge, Mass.: The M.I.T. Press, 2001), 54.

46. Rawls, "Reply to Habermas," 145.

47. Ibid., 146.

48. Ibid., 149; and see Mendus, "The Importance of Love," 75.

49. Rawls, *Justice as Fairness: A Restatement* (Cambridge, Mass.: Harvard University Press, 2001), 82n2.

50. Ibid., and 81–82.

51. Ibid., 19.

52. Ibid., 183.

53. Rawls, *Political Liberalism*, 82–83, 83n31.

54. Rawls, *Justice as Fairness*, 81–82; emphasis added.

55. Ibid., 140.

56. Ibid., 140–41.

57. Ibid., 103.

58. Ibid., 102.

59. Ibid., 103n26.

60. Ibid., 195.

61. Ibid., 196.

62. Ibid., 197.

63. Ibid.

64. For further discussion of the relationship between the rationalist and sentimentalist dimensions of Rawls's thought, see Frazer, "John Rawls: Between Two Enlightenments."

65. The moral sentiment account of judgment and deliberation developed later in this book bears an affinity to the Rawlsian view insofar as it involves adopting an impartial perspective in deliberating about justice. In this sense, there is a way in which my view also privileges the right over the good. The moral sentiment approach is, however, more direct about the role of sentiment within the perspective-taking that helps establish impartiality. It is also more unambiguously insistent that what makes something right is that it contributes

to a shared good. In this respect, the moral sentiment view of impartiality never lays claim, as Rawls does, to the absolute priority of the right over the good.

66. Habermas, *The Inclusion of the Other*, 50.

67. Ibid., 54.

68. Ibid.

69. Ibid., 55.

70. Ibid., 59.

71. Ibid.

72. Thomas McCarthy, "Kantian Constructivism and Reconstructivism: Rawls and Habermas in Dialogue," *Ethics* 105 (October 1994): 47.

73. Habermas, *The Inclusion of the Other*, 57.

74. Although the theories of Rawls and Habermas are often seen as competitors because of these and other differences, Donald Moon has argued that they are in fact complementary. Habermas, says Moon, seeks "to establish the moral constraints that Rawls takes for granted," while Rawls means to lay out the substantive principles of justice that follow from the moral point of view ("Practical Discourse and Communicative Ethics," in Stephen K. White, ed., *The Cambridge Companion to Habermas* [Cambridge: Cambridge University Press, 1995], 145). This is a helpful suggestion, as it brings into focus the somewhat different objectives of the two theories. Yet Rawls denies the viability of pure proceduralism (Rawls, "Reply to Habermas," 174); hence for him Habermas's effort to establish moral constraints (as Moon puts it) without reference to any prior moral substance would have to be untenable. In this respect, there is not only a difference of objectives between the two but a fairly fundamental disagreement about the grounds of moral life and the powers of moral and political philosophy.

75. Habermas, *The Inclusion of the Other*, 23.

76. Habermas, *Between Facts and Norms*, trans. William Rehg (Cambridge, Mass.: The M.I.T. Press, 1999), 107.

77. Ibid.

78. Habermas, *Inclusion of the Other*, 28.

79. Ibid.

80. Ibid., 32.

81. Habermas, *Moral Consciousness and Communicative Action*, trans. Christian Lenhardt and Shierry Weber Nicholsen (Cambridge, Mass.: The M.I.T. Press, 1996), 120.

82. Habermas, *The Inclusion of the Other*, 24.

83. Ibid., 26.

84. Ibid., 27.

85. Habermas, *Justification and Application*, trans. Ciaran Cronin (Cambridge, Mass.: The M.I.T. Press, 2001), 24, 120.

86. Habermas, *The Inclusion of the Other*, 35; and see *Justification and Application*, 75–76, 119.

87. Habermas, *Between Facts and Norms*, 95.

88. Habermas, *Moral Consciousness and Communicative Action*, 82–98; and see *Justification and Application*, 31, 76–77, 114.

89. Habermas, *Between Facts and Norms*, 4–5, 25, 113–14; and see *Moral Consciousness and Communicative Action*, 109, 179.

90. Habermas, *Between Facts and Norms*, 80, 114.

91. Habermas, *The Inclusion of the Other*, 29, 42; and see McCarthy, "Kantian Constructivism and Reconstructivism," 46–47.

92. Habermas, *Moral Consciousness and Communicative Action*, 202.

93. Ibid., 182.

94. Ibid., 50; emphasis in original.

95. Ibid., 67; and see *The Inclusion of the Other*, 57. For further discussion of the importance of reflexivity on Habermas's account, see Moon, "Practical Discourse and Communicative Ethics," 148, 157.

96. Habermas, *Moral Consciousness and Communicative Action*, 61.

97. Habermas, *Between Facts and Norms*, 135.

98. Ibid., 228.

99. Habermas, *The Inclusion of the Other*, 26–27.

100. Habermas, *Moral Consciousness and Communicative Action*, 65.

101. Ibid.

102. Ibid., 62.

103. Habermas, *The Inclusion of the Other*, 29.

104. Ibid.

105. Habermas, *Between Facts and Norms*, 36.

106. Ibid., 23.

107. Ibid., 22.

108. Habermas, *Moral Consciousness and Communicative Action*, 67.

109. Mark E. Warren, "The Self in Discursive Democracy," in White, *The Cambridge Companion to Habermas*, 181.

110. Habermas, *The Inclusion of the Other*, 34.

111. Habermas, *Between Facts and Norms*, 4–5, 25, 113–14; and see Habermas, Moral *Consciousness and Communicative Action*, 109.

112. Ibid., 183. Constitutional patriotism is the political embodiment of this moral disposition. Habermas describes constitutional patriotism as "the supportive spirit of a consonant background of legally noncoercible motives and attributes of a citizenry" oriented to universal principles of liberty and equality. See Habermas, "Citizenship and National Identity," appendix 2 in *Between Facts and Norms*, 499–500; Attracta Ingram, "Constitutional Patriotism," *Philosophy and Social Criticism* 22 (6) (1996): 1–18; and Patchen Markell, "Making Affect Safe for Democracy? On 'Constitutional Patriotism,' " *Political Theory* 28 (1) (February 2000): 38–63. This background mediates between the rational standpoint that justifies norms and the affective attachments and desires that normally motivate action.

113. It is also consistent with the Rawlsian notion of integrity as grounded in conception-dependent desires.

114. Habermas, *The Inclusion of the Other*, 26–27.

115. Habermas, *Moral Consciousness and Communicative Action*, 101; and see *Justification and Application*, 15.

116. Habermas, *Moral Consciousness and Communicative Action*, 104.

117. Habermas, *The Inclusion of the Other*, 27–28.

118. Ibid., 32; emphasis in original.

119. Ibid.

120. Habermas, *Moral Consciousness and Communicative Action*, 109.

121. Arash Abizadeh, "On the Philosophy/Rhetoric Binaries: Or, Is Habermasian Discourse Motivationally Impotent?" *Philosophy and Social Criticism* 33 (4): 462–63.

122. Habermas, *Moral Consciousness and Communicative Action*, 108.

123. Mark Warren makes a related point, saying that Habermas's ideal requires individuals to "question elements of their lives and lifestyles without drawing into question their own identity and value" ("The Self in Discursive Democracy," 181).

124. Habermas, *Between Facts and Norms*, 80, 114; and see Kenneth Baynes, "Democracy and the *Rechsstaat*: Habermas's *Faktizität und Geltung*," in White, *The Cambridge Companion to Habermas*, 208; and Markell, "Making Affect Safe?," 47, 49.

125. Abizadeh poses a similar criticism, pointing out that "the retreat to law either simply gives up on the possibility of rational practical discourse motivating action and belief, or it once again fails to tell us how it might do so" ("On the Philosophy/Rhetoric Binaries," 458).

Chapter Two
Recent Alternatives to Rationalism

1. Alasdair MacIntyre, *After Virtue* (Notre Dame, Ind.: University of Notre Dame Press, 1984).

2. Michael Sandel, *Liberalism and the Limits of Justice* (Cambridge: Cambridge University Press, 1982).

3. Iris Marion Young, *Justice and the Politics of Difference* (Princeton: Princeton University Press, 1990).

4. Carol Gilligan, "Moral Orientation and Moral Development," in Virginia Held, ed., *Justice and Care* (Boulder, Colo.: Westview, 1995), 33. See also Gilligan, *In a Different Voice: Psychological Theory and Women's Development* (Cambridge, Mass.: Harvard University Press, 1982).

5. Gilligan, "Moral Orientation," 43.

6. Ibid., 35.

7. Virginia Held, *Feminist Morality: Transforming Culture, Society, and Politics* (Chicago: University of Chicago Press, 1993), 77.

8. Ibid.

9. Ibid.

10. Ibid.

11. Ibid., 29.

12. Joan Tronto, *Moral Boundaries: A Political Argument for an Ethic of Care* (New York: Routledge, 1994), 109; and see Sara Ruddick, *Maternal Thinking: Toward a Politics of Peace* (Boston: Beacon, 1989), 13ff. For a contrasting view, which treats caring as "essentially nonrational," see Nel Noddings, *Caring: A*

Feminine Approach to Ethics (Berkeley: University of California Press, 1984), 25 (cited in Tronto, *Moral Boundaries*, 204).

13. Gilligan, "Moral Orientation and Development," 41.

14. Ibid., 36.

15. Held, *Feminist Morality*, 228.

16. Tronto, *Moral Boundaries*, 155.

17. Robin West, *Caring for Justice* (New York: New York University Press, 1997), 75.

18. Antonio R. Damasio, *Descartes' Error: Emotion, Reason, and the Human Brain* (New York: HarperCollins, 2000), xii.

19. Ibid., 52f, 191–92.

20. Ibid., 39, 43, 51, 54.

21. Ibid., 45.

22. Ibid., 36.

23. Ibid., 51.

24. Ibid., 43.

25. Ibid., 39.

26. Ibid., 173.

27. Ibid.

28. Ibid., 200–01.

29. Ibid., 195.

30. Ibid., 71.

31. Ibid., 185.

32. Ibid.

33. Ibid., 172.

34. See, for example, George E. Marcus, W. Russell Neuman, and Michael MacKuen, eds., *Affective Intelligence and Political Judgment* (Chicago: University of Chicago Press, 2000); Marcus, Neuman, and MacKuen, eds., *The Affect Effect: Dynamics of Emotion in Political Thinking and Behavior* (Chicago: University of Chicago Press, 2007); Marcus, *The Sentimental Citizen: Emotion in Democratic Politics* (University Park: Pennsylvania State University Press, 2002); Rose Mc-Dermott, "The Feeling of Rationality: The Meaning of Neuroscientific Advances for Political Science," *Perspectives on Politics* 2 (4) (Dec 2004): 691–706; Ted Brader, *Campaigning for Hearts and Minds: How Emotional Appeals in Political Ads Work* (Chicago: University of Chicago Press, 2006); Jeff Goodwin, James M. Jasper, and Francesca Polletta, eds., *Passionate Politics: Emotions and Social Movements* (Chicago: University of Chicago Press, 2001); and Neta Crawford, "The Passion of World Politics: Propositions on Emotion and Emotional Relationships," *International Security* 24 (4) (Spring 2000): 116–56.

35. Marcus, Neuman, and MacKuen, *Affective Intelligence*, 10.

36. Ibid., 95. Marcus, Neuman, and MacKuen emphasize the important distinction (also noted by Damasio) between emotion and "extreme emotion" (20). Emotions that are not extreme or that do not result in highly agitated states of mind often get classified in other terms. Specifically, they frequently are associated with reason or with "rational interests," and thus set in opposition to emotion. It is crucial to see both that emotions can be quiet or calm

rather than extreme and that "emotional reactions have important effects even in their quieter states" (38).

37. Ibid., 10.

38. Ibid., 1.

39. Ibid.

40. Ibid., 95. Anxious voters rely less on partisanship to make their choices and pay more attention to the positions and characteristics of the candidates. Their dominant concern is "which candidate's position on the issues is closest to theirs." They learn "far more about where the candidates actually stand on the issues and learn more accurately than complaisant voters do." Marcus, *The Sentimental Citizen*, 103.

41. Marcus, *The Sentimental Citizen*, 78.

42. Ibid., 108–9.

43. Marcus, Neuman, and MacKuen, *Affective Intelligence*, 129.

44. Ibid., 129–30.

45. Another recent effort to bring Damasio's findings to bear on the study of politics is William E. Connolly, *Neuropolitics: Thinking, Culture, Speed* (Minneapolis: University of Minnesota Press, 2002). Drawing on Damasio and others, the book offers an account of thinking that shows the "feedback loops that connect bodies, brains, and culture" and demonstrates the relationship within thinking between affective and cognitive modes of consciousness. Important as it is, however, *Neuropolitics* says virtually nothing about affect within the specific process of moral judgment. Still less does it illuminate the practices of political judgment and democratic deliberation. Connolly suggests that the dominant models of democratic deliberation should be modified in light of his findings but he does not specify how they should be modified or what would constitute good affective deliberation. For further discussion, see Sharon R. Krause, "Brains, Citizens, and Democracy's New Nobility," *theory & event* 9 (1) (2006).

46. For other cognitivist accounts of emotion see, for instance, Ronald de Sousa, *The Rationality of Emotion* (Cambridge, Mass.: The M.I.T. Press, 2001); Robert Solomon, "Emotions and Choice," in Solomon, ed., *What Is an Emotion?* (Oxford: Oxford University Press, 2003); Richard Lazarus, "Appraisal: The Minimal Cognitive Prerequisites of Emotion," in Solomon, *What Is an Emotion?*; James R. Averill, "Emotion and Anxiety: Sociocultural, Biological, and Psychological Determinants," in Amélie Oksenberg Rorty, ed., *Explaining Emotions* (Berkeley: University of California Press, 1980).

47. Martha Nussbaum, *Love's Knowledge* (Oxford: Oxford University Press, 1990), 41.

48. Martha Nussbaum, *Upheavals of Thought* (Cambridge: Cambridge University Press, 2001), 46.

49. Ibid., 47.

50. Ibid.

51. For other arguments to this effect, see de Sousa, *The Rationality of Emotion*, xv, 332; Barbara Koziak, *Retrieving Political Emotion* (University Park: Pennsylvania State University Press, 2000), 16, 155; Henry S. Richardson, *Practical Reasoning About Final Ends* (Cambridge: Cambridge University Press, 1997), 185–88; Patricia S. Greenspan, "Ambivalence and the Logic of Emotion,"

in Oksenberg Rorty, *Explaining Emotions*, 242; Michael Stocker, *Valuing Emotions* (Cambridge: Cambridge University Press, 1996), 3, 6; and see Cheryl Hall, "Passions and Constraint," *Philosophy and Social Criticism* 28(6) (2003): 727–48.

52. Nussbaum, *Upheavals of Thought*, 3.

53. Nussbaum, *Love's Knowledge*, 79.

54. Ibid.

55. Ibid., 81

56. Ibid.

57. For additional defenses of moral particularism, see Lawrence Blum, *Moral Perception and Particularity* (Cambridge: Cambridge University Press, 1994) and Koziak, *Retrieving Political Emotion*, 161. For accounts of emotion that connect it to general rules and a generalized standpoint, see Richardson, *Practical Reasoning*, 184, 188–89; Roger Scruton, "Emotion, Practical Knowledge, and Common Culture," in Oksenberg Rorty, *Explaining Emotions*, 526–27; and Stocker, *Valuing Emotions*, 191.

58. Nussbaum, *Love's Knowledge*, 68.

59. Ibid., 84.

60. Ibid., 92.

61. Ibid.

62. Ibid., 94.

63. Ibid., 93.

64. Ibid., 96.

65. Ibid.

66. Ibid., 79, 81.

67. Ibid., 79.

68. Nussbaum, *The Therapy of Desire: Theory and Practice in Hellenistic Ethics* (Princeton: Princeton University Press, 1994), 497, 499.

69. Nussbaum, *Love's Knowledge*, 97.

70. The expressivist dimensions of Hume's view seem to be at the heart of Nussbaum's rejection of it; see *Upheavals of Thought*, 136. She acknowledges, however, that Hume's own view is more complicated and "more plausible than some official statements suggest" (ibid., 25n7).

71. Nussbaum, *Love's Knowledge*, 78.

72. Ibid., 41.

73. Nussbaum, *Upheavals of Thought*, 60.

74. Ibid., 62, 64.

75. Ibid., 64.

76. Ibid., 61.

77. Ibid., 23.

78. Ibid., 77.

79. G.E.M. Anscombe, *Intention* (Oxford: Oxford University Press, 1963); and see John Bricke, *Mind and Morality* (Oxford: Oxford University Press, 1996), 25n13.

80. Bricke, *Mind and Morality,* 26; emphasis in original.

81. Ibid., 27.

82. It is worth noting here that affective states can operate below the level of conscious awareness, as commonly occurs with desires. We are not always fully aware of the desires that we have, or of the salience of some desires rela-

tive to others. But even when desires operate subconsciously, they can powerfully affect our thought and action. Nussbaum finds the notion of unconscious affects incoherent (*Upheavals of Thought*, 61), but there should be nothing mysterious about the subconscious existence of affect in this form (namely, conative states). One may not realize on the conscious level how much one cares about justice—until one sees videotape of protesters for a good cause being beaten by police officers. One's anger under such circumstances reveals an affective concern for justice that normally operates in the background of judgment, not fully conscious but nevertheless shaping one's decisions and actions. Unconscious affect simply comprises emotions and concerns that are not at the moment the subject of one's conscious attention.

83. This is an example of how emotions entail concerns, as discussed in the introduction.

84. Bernard Williams, "Internal and External Reasons," in *Moral Luck* (Cambridge: Cambridge University Press, 1986), 101.

85. Ibid.

86. Ibid.

87. Ibid., 111.

88. Ibid., 102.

89. Williams, "Persons, Character, and Morality," in *Moral Luck*, 13.

90. Ibid.

91. Williams, "Internal and External Reasons," 105.

92. Williams, *Ethics and the Limits of Philosophy* (Cambridge, Mass.: Harvard University Press, 1985), 200; see also Williams, "Morality and the Emotions," in Bernard Williams, *Problems of the Self* (Cambridge: Cambridge University Press, 1973), 223.

93. Williams, *Ethics and the Limits of Philosophy*, 67.

94. Ibid., 69.

95. Williams, "Internal and External Reasons," 105.

96. Ibid., 103.

97. Ibid.

98. Ibid., 107.

99. Ibid.

100. Ibid., 109.

101. Ibid., 104.

102. Williams, *Ethics and the Limits of Philosophy*, 69.

103. Williams rejected the ideal of impartiality in both its utilitarian and Kantian forms. For discussion of the former, see "A Critique of Utilitarianism," in J.J.C. Smart and B. Williams, *Utilitarianism For and Against* (Cambridge: Cambridge University Press, 1973), esp. 96, 116–17. For discussion of the latter, see "Persons, Character, and Morality," in *Moral Luck*, esp. 14, 18.

104. Williams, *Ethics and the Limits of Philosophy*, 114.

105. Ibid., 198.

106. Simon Blackburn, *Ruling Passions* (Oxford: Oxford University Press, 1998), 279–80.

107. Michael Smith, *The Moral Problem* (Malden: Blackwell, 1994), 5.

108. Ibid., 7.

109. Ibid., 11.
110. Ibid., 95.
111. Ibid., 95.
112. Ibid., 134–35.
113. Ibid., 135.
114. Ibid., 150.
115. Ibid., 156, 158–59.
116. Ibid., 173.
117. Ibid., 165.
118. Ibid., 179.
119. Ibid., 111, 112.
120. Blackburn, *Ruling Passions*, 118.
121. Ibid., 232; emphasis in original.
122. Ibid., 48.
123. Ibid., 49.
124. Ibid., 70.
125. Ibid.
126. Ibid., 123.
127. Ibid., 131.
128. Ibid.
129. Ibid., 2.
130. Ibid.
131. Ibid., 9.
132. Ibid.
133. Ibid.
134. Ibid., 14.
135. Ibid., 38.
136. Erving Goffman, *Stigma: Notes on the Management of Spoiled Identity* (New York: Simon and Schuster, 1963), 2 (cited in William Ian Miller, *The Anatomy of Disgust* [Cambridge, Mass.: Harvard University Press, 1997], 198).
137. Blackburn, *Ruling Passions*, 232–33.
138. Ibid., 308.
139. Ibid.
140. Ibid., 307–8.
141. Ibid., 232, 241, 253.
142. Ibid., 257–58.
143. Ibid., 258.
144. Ibid., 237.
145. Ibid., 206.
146. Ibid., 207.
147. Ibid., 205.
148. Ibid., 201–2.
149. Ibid., 210.
150. Ibid.
151. To be fair, the political dimensions of moral judgment and the political implications this view of judgment has for public deliberation are reasonably beyond the scope of Blackburn's project. His intended contribution is to moral

philosophy, not political theory. The present study, as should be clear, regards this contribution as valuable and seeks to elaborate for political theory the political implications of a similarly Humean view.

CHAPTER THREE
MORAL SENTIMENT AND THE POLITICS OF JUDGMENT IN HUME

1. For discussion, see Duncan Forbes, *Hume's Philosophical Politics* (Cambridge: Cambridge University Press, 1975), esp. 32–58; J. L. Mackie, *Hume's Moral Theory* (London: Routledge, 1980), esp. 14–30; David Fate Norton, "Hume, Human Nature, and the Foundations of Morality," in Norton, ed., *The Cambridge Companion to Hume* (Cambridge: Cambridge University Press, 1999), 150–58; and Knud Haakonssen, *Natural Law and Moral Philosophy: From Grotius to the Scottish Enlightenment (*Cambridge: Cambridge University Press, 1996).

2. David Hume, *A Treatise of Human Nature*, ed. L. A. Selby-Bigge (Oxford: Clarendon Press, 1968), 413, 463. Hereafter references to the *Treatise* will appear parenthetically in the text preceded by the letter "T."

3. David Hume, *An Enquiry Concerning the Principles of Morals* (LaSalle, Ill.: Open Court, 1966), 4; and see T 458. Hereafter references to the *Enquiry* will appear in the text preceded by the letter "E."

4. Although I accept Hume's assertion that reason as he defines it cannot motivate, in the coming chapters I argue for a revised conception of practical reasoning, in which cognitive and affective modes of consciousness (reason and passion, in Hume's terms) are more fully integrated. This understanding of practical reasoning is actually more compatible with Hume's own view than may at first appear, as should become clear in the course of the following discussion.

5. Immanuel Kant, *Grounding for the Metaphysics of Morals,* trans. James W. Ellington (Indianapolis: Hackett, 1981), 46 [442], 59 [460].

6. See A. J. Ayer, *Hume: A Very Short Introduction* (Oxford: Oxford University Press, 1980), 104. This interpretation is contested by others, such as Larry Arnhart, "The New Darwinian Naturalism in Political Theory," *American Political Science Review* 89 (2) (June 1995): 389; Annette Baier, *A Progress of Sentiments: Reflections on Hume's* Treatise (Cambridge, Mass.: Harvard University Press, 1999), 180; Donald Herzog, *Without Foundations: Justification in Political Theory* (Ithaca: Cornell University Press, 1985), 165; Terrence Penelhum, *David Hume: An Introduction to His Philosophical System* (Lafayette, Ind.: Purdue University Press, 1992), 137; Barry Stroud, *Hume* (London: Routledge, 2000), 182; and Jacqueline Taylor, "Hume and the Reality of Value," in Anne Jaap Jacobsen, ed., *Feminist Interpretations of David Hume* (University Park: Pennsylvania State University Press, 2000, 114–15.

7. Páll S. Árdal, *Passion and Value in Hume's* Treatise (Edinburgh: Edinburgh University Press, 1966), 45.

8. See, for example, Douglas Chismar, "Hume's Confusion About Sympathy," *Philosophy Research Archives* 45 (1988–89), esp. 245. For further discussion, see Robert J. Lipkin, "Altruism and Sympathy in Hume's Ethics," *Australasian*

Journal of Philosophy 65 (1) (March 1987); and Baier, *A Progress of Sentiments*, 147–51.

9. The cultivation of S1 is largely a matter of enhancing exposure to, or information about, the sentiments of increasingly wider classes of relevant persons. The intellect will have a role here. Hume thinks that one refines the faculty of moral sentiment (and increases the impartiality and refinement of one's moral judgments) by reading works of poetry and history, by viewing and thinking about other art forms, and by engaging in conversation and discussion with people from other cultures and walks of life. None of these activities would be possible without reason. At the same time, strengthening one's capacity to feel S2 for an increasingly extensive class of others may help make one more receptive to the operations of S1 in relation to them. So S2 may help to cultivate a more extensive faculty of S1. By the same token, as S1 brings the sentiments of others into our minds and hearts in ways that resonate with our own concerns, our capacity to feel S2 for a wider range of persons is likely to increase. This process is aided, again, by the intellect. Among other things, reason, as Hume defines it, helps us to identify similarities between our own concerns and those of others, and hence to identify with or care about them. But the cultivation of S2 also will need to involve practices of socialization and habituation, much as the cultivation of any moral or civic virtue does. Concern for others, especially relatively distant or unfamiliar others, needs to be nourished and encouraged if it is to develop.

10. Hume is somewhat ambiguous in this example as to whether the object of our value and esteem is the man's riches or the rich man himself. He sometimes seems to mean the former, saying that sympathy gives us "an esteem for power and riches, and a contempt for meanness and poverty" (T 362). Elsewhere, however, he suggests that the person of the rich man is the object of approbation, as sympathy with his pleasures and those of his expected beneficiaries generate esteem and respect for the man himself. He invokes the latter logic to explain the culture of deference surrounding the rich that was characteristic of eighteenth-century European societies, including his own (T 616). Our society, by contrast, values wealth but not necessarily the wealthy—or at least our esteem for the rich is far more ambivalent than what Hume describes. Our more democratic political order, which gives a stronger voice to the sentiments of the poor, causes our sympathy to extend in other directions. American society is not fully democratic, of course, and sympathy for the sentiments of the poor is still limited here, but American society is more democratic than eighteenth-century Britain. Comparison and self-interest also enter into the equation in ways that alter the effects of sympathetic communication. Even in Hume's time, an equally common response to perceiving the pleasures of the wealthy must have been envy and resentment. So the sentiments that inform our judgments of the wealthy are more complex than Hume's example of the rich man suggests, although this complexity is in principle compatible with the general method of judgment Hume describes. The example does point to one of the dangers of Humean judgment, however, which is that sympathy may be hindered by social inequalities, resulting in distorted judgments. This issue is addressed later in the chapter.

11. Jacqueline Taylor, "Hume on Luck and Moral Inclusion," Panel paper presented at the 2003 Annual Meeting of the American Political Science Association, Philadelphia, Pennsylvania.

12. David Hume, "Of the Standard of Taste," in Hume, *Essays: Moral, Political, and Literary* (Indianapolis: Liberty Fund, 1987), 247.

13. See George Kateb, *The Inner Ocean: Individualism and Democratic Culture* (Ithaca: Cornell, 1992).

14. It is perhaps worth noting that moral disapproval rests on a general aversion toward things that are produced specifically by human decisions and actions. The human cause is significant. We are generally averse to cancer, for instance, but we do not disapprove of it. Moral judgments apply only to human agents (whether individual or collective) as causes.

15. Aryeh Botwinick, *Ethics, Politics, and Epistemology: A Study in the Unity of Hume's Thought* (Lanham, Md.: University Press of America, 1980), 51, 59.

16. Sympathy is natural enough, Hume says, that it is "conspicuous in children, who implicitly embrace every opinion propos'd to them," and "also in men of the greatest judgment and understanding, who find it very difficult to follow their own reason or inclination, in opposition to that of their friends and daily companions" (T 316).

17. Annette Baier, *Moral Prejudices* (Cambridge, Mass.: Harvard University Press, 1995), 61–62. Michael Frazer elaborates this point: "Our uncorrected moral sentiments may lead to internal contradictions, Hume argues, because 'our situation, with regard to both persons and things, is in continual fluctuation, and a man that lies at a distance from us may in a little time become a familiar acquaintance' (T 3.3.1.15). The same vicious or virtuous act, which once harmed or benefited only those so distant from ourselves that we barely bothered to evaluate it, may thus come to our attention quite dramatically," giving rise to a new evaluation at odds with our previously held standards. Frazer, "The Enlightenment of Sympathy: Sentimentalist Political Philosophy from Hume to Herder" (Ph.D. diss., Princeton University, 2006), 78.

18. David Hume, "Of the Populousness of Ancient Nations," in *Essays*, 383, 385. See Frazer, "The Enlightenment of Sympathy," 79.

19. The standard of usefulness has an especially important role, which explains why Hume is often considered to be a utilitarian or proto-utilitarian thinker. See Ayer, *Hume: A Very Short Introduction*, 99–100; Jonathan Harrison, *Hume's Theory of Justice* (Oxford: Clarendon Press, 1981), viii; and Forbes, *Hume's Philosophical Politics*, 109. Yet the useful does not stand alone in moral judgment, according to Hume, but is "intermix'd in our judgments of morals" with what is immediately agreeable (T 590). For discussion of the nonutilitarian aspects of Hume's theory, see Annette Baier, *A Progress of Sentiments*, 199, 203; John B. Stewart, "The Public Interest vs. Old Rights," *Hume Studies* 21 (2) (November 1995): 171; and Sharon R. Krause, "Hume and the (False) Luster of Justice," *Political Theory* 32 (5) (October 2004): 634–38.

20. M. Jamie Ferriera, "Hume and Imagination: Sympathy and the Other," *International Philosophical Quarterly* 34 (1) (March 1994): 47.

21. Adam Smith, *The Theory of Moral Sentiments* (Washington: Regnery, 1997), part 1, section 1, chapter 3, paragraph 6.

22. Hume, "Of the Standard of Taste," 239.

23. Ibid., 240–41.

24. Ibid., 242.

25. Ibid., 246.

26. A sizable body of literature has emerged in recent years that makes a powerful case for value pluralism. Inspired by Isaiah Berlin's forceful defense of the idea in "Two Concepts of Liberty," a good deal of moral and political theory has since been carried out under this rubric. See, for example, William A. Galston, *Liberal Pluralism* (Cambridge: Cambridge University Press, 2002); Charles Larmore, *Patterns of Moral Complexity* (Cambridge: Cambridge University Press, 1987); John Kekes, *The Morality of Pluralism* (Princeton: Princeton University Press, 1993); Stuart Hampshire, *Morality and Conflict* (Cambridge, Mass.: Harvard University Press, 1983); Steven Lukes, *Moral Conflict and Politics* (Oxford: Clarendon Press, 1991); Michael Stocker, *Plural and Conflicting Values* (Oxford: Clarendon Press, 1990); Charles Taylor, "The Diversity of Goods," in Amartya Sen and Bernard Williams, eds., *Utilitarianism and Beyond* (Cambridge: Cambridge University Press, 1982); and John Gray, *Isaiah Berlin* (Princeton: Princeton University Press, 1996). Value pluralists differ about the sources of normativity and about the nature of moral judgment—and some would disagree with Hume's account of both—but there is convergence on the idea that moral values, although not merely relative to individuals or cultures, are nevertheless marked by a measure of plurality.

27. David Hume, "Of Commerce," in Hume, *Essays*, 265.

28. Hume, "Of the Populousness of Ancient Nations," in Hume, *Essays*, 383. See also Norman Kemp Smith, *The Philosophy of David Hume* (London: Macmillan, 1964), 45.

29. It is true that numerous cultures have instituted slavery, and this fact suggests that there may be something natural in the urge to dominate others, or to have somebody else do one's dirty work. Still, one cannot act on this desire, however common it may be, without generating grounds for the sentiment of disapproval because the experience of being enslaved is generally painful. Those who own slaves—like everyone else—would never want to be one, precisely because being enslaved thwarts basic human needs and obstructs so many human projects. Insofar as the slaveholder is willfully blind to the pain of his slaves, he lacks the virtue of humanity. Human nature as a standard in Hume does not include everything that comes "naturally" to human beings, then. It privileges common human concerns the satisfaction of which contributes to social coordination and does not systematically cause harm, or thwart other common human concerns, or demonstrate a want of humanity. Further discussion of this issue follows below.

30. Hume says, along these lines, that "justice, humanity, magnanimity, prudence, [and] veracity" are applauded "in all nations and ages" because they respond to fundamental human concerns. Hume, "Of the Standard of Taste," 228. See also John W. Danford, *David Hume and the Problem of Reason* (New Haven: Yale University Press, 1990), 104.

31. Hume, "Of the Dignity or Meanness of Human Nature," in Hume, *Essays*, 85.

32. See Paul Russell, *Freedom and Moral Sentiment: Hume's Way of Naturalizing Responsibility* (New York: Oxford University Press, 1995), 68; and Norton, "Hume, Human Nature, and the Foundations of Morality," 148.

33. Richard H. Dees, "Hume and the Contexts of Politics," *Journal of the History of Philosophy* 30 (2) (April 1992): 231.

34. David Hume, "A Dialogue," in P. H. Nidditch, ed., *David Hume: Enquiries Concerning Human Understanding and Concerning the Principles of Morals* (Oxford: Clarendon Press, 1998), 335.

35. Hume, *Enquiry Concerning Human Understanding*, section 10, part 2, paragraph 21, 127.

36. Along these lines, Hume refers in the *Enquiry Concerning the Principles of Morals* to the "necessary and infallible consequences of the general principles of human nature, as discovered in common life and practice" (E 66).

37. Hume, *Enquiry Concerning Human Understanding*, section 10, part 1, paragraph 4, 110–11.

38. The role of human nature in establishing evaluative standards speaks to the fact that Hume does connect "is" and "ought," contrary to some common interpretations of his comments at *Treatise* 3.1.1 (469–70). As Baier says, Hume has been wrongly "saddled by some commentators with 'Hume's law,' which says . . . that no sound inference or reasonable transition from *is* to *ought* can be made" (*A Progress of Sentiments*, 176–77). This is not what Hume meant to convey in the relevant passage. The point of the passage, as Stroud puts it, is rather that "because of the special character of moral judgments," transitions from "is" to "ought" cannot be perceived by reason alone (Stroud, *Hume*, 187). This reading squares with what Hume says in the paragraph immediately preceding: "Take any action allow'd to be vicious. . . . You never can find it [vice], till you turn your reflexion into your own breast, and find a sentiment of disapprobation, which arises in you, towards this action. *Here is a matter of fact; but 'tis the object of feeling, not of reason.* It lies in yourself, not in the object. So that when you pronounce any action or character to be vicious, you mean nothing, but that from the constitution of your nature you have a feeling or sentiment of blame from the contemplation of it" (T 468–69; emphasis added). For further discussion of this passage and the common misreadings of it, see A. C. MacIntyre, "Hume on 'Is' and 'Ought,' " in V. C. Chappell, ed., *Hume* (Notre Dame: University of Notre Dame Press, 1968), 242–64; John Rawls, *Lectures on the History of Moral Philosophy* (Cambridge, Mass.: Harvard University Press, 2000), 82–83; and Elizabeth Radcliffe, "Kantian Tunes on a Humean Instrument: Why Hume is Not Really a Skeptic about Practical Reasoning," in Rachel Cohon, ed., *Hume: Moral and Political Philosophy* (Aldershot: Ashgate/Dartmouth, 2001), 68.

39. This expressivism marks an important difference between the Humean approach and Martha Nussbaum's (self-described Aristotelian) account of emotion-inflected judgment. On her view, as we have seen in chapter 2 of this volume, emotions contribute to the "correct perception" of the moral meaning of a situation or "true ethical perception" (*Love's Knowledge* [Oxford: Oxford University Press, 1990], 79, 81). The emotions are "modes of vision or recognition" that allow us to see the ethical "nature of the practical situation . . . for

what it is" (ibid., 79). These remarks suggest that the function of judgment is to convey to us the intrinsic moral value that inheres in the world. That assumption is fundamentally at odds with Hume's insistence that moral value has no source other than human beings' common (and properly structured) responses to the world. The distinction drawn in this chapter between Hume and Aristotle thus parallels that between Blackburn and Nussbaum laid out in chapter 2 in this volume.

40. Samuel Scheffler, *Human Morality* (Oxford: Oxford University Press, 1992), 84, 61.

41. Kant, *Grounding for the Metaphysics of Morals*, 407–18 [22].

42. Hume, "Of the Standard of Taste," 235.

43. Ibid., 240

44. Ibid.

45. Ibid., 233–34.

46. Hume, *Enquiry Concerning Human Understanding*, section 10, part 1, paragraph 5, 112.

47. Hume, "Of the Standard of Taste," 239; emphasis in original. See Danford, *David Hume and the Problem of Reason*, 101–4.

48. Hume, "Of the Standard of Taste," 239.

49. Ibid., 567–68.

50. Ibid.

51. Ibid.

52. It is true that Hume characterized his project in the *Treatise* as that of an "anatomist" of ethics rather than a "painter" of practical morality (T 620). He understood himself to be explaining the general basis and operations of the moral sense rather than promoting a particular set of moral virtues. At the same time, however, he clearly saw a practical purpose for his moral anatomy. He explicitly means "to establish on [its basis] a science, which will not be inferior in certainty, and will be *much superior in utility* to any other of human comprehension" (T xxiii; emphasis added). Likewise, he insists that his "abstract speculations" about the nature of morality are "subservient to *practical morality*;" and he hopes that they "may render this latter science more correct in its precepts, and more persuasive in its exhortations" (T 621; emphasis in original). So even though the function of the *Treatise* is not to inculcate a particular set of virtues, it would be wrong to think that Hume had no practical purpose in mind in writing it. Along these lines, John Immerwahr has argued that "Hume saw his work as therapeutic as well as analytic," and that Hume was "a rhetorician dedicated to producing change, rather than an abstract philosopher preoccupied with understanding." John Immerwahr, "Hume on tranquilizing the passions," *Hume Studies* 18 (2) (1992): 308.

53. See Christine Korsgaard, *The Sources of Normativity* (Cambridge: Cambridge University Press, 1996), 56–67.

54. Ibid., 63.

55. Ibid., 65–66.

56. Baier, *A Progress of Sentiments*, 152–53; Jacqueline Taylor, "Humean Ethics and the Politics of Sentiment," *Topoi* 21 (2002): 176–77.

57. Stuart Hampshire, *Innocence and Experience* (Cambridge, Mass.: Harvard University Press, 1989), 18; cited in Taylor, "Humean Ethics," 176. See also Rawls, *Lectures on the History of Moral Philosophy*, 36, 50; and Jean Hampton, "Does Hume Have an Instrumental Conception of Practical Reason?" *Hume Studies* 21 (1) (April 1995): 57–74.

58. Or at least Hume did not work this out in his philosophical works. His *History of England* (Indianapolis: Liberty Fund, 1983) contains examples of what he had in mind, however. Some interpreters have even argued that the *History* offers the best view into Hume's concept of political judgment and his political theory more generally. See Danford, *Hume and the Problem of Reason*, 77, 88; Herzog, *Without Foundations*, 200; Donald Livingston, "On Hume's Conservatism," *Hume Studies* 21 (2) (November 1995): 158; and Andrew Sabl, "When Bad Things Happen from Good People (and vice versa): Hume's Political Ethics of Revolution," *Polity* 35 (1) (fall 2002): 73, 79.

59. Thus Mackie maintains that "my belief that an impartial spectator, for example, would condemn a possible action which I am contemplating will prevent me from performing it only if I also want to fit in with the spectator's system of approbation." Mackie, *Hume's Moral Theory*, 69. Yet the moral perspective is not a mere belief, which would indeed require an additional motivating desire to generate action. The moral perspective issues rather in the feeling of disapprobation (or approbation), grounded in direct passions, which is intrinsically motivating, as the following passages show.

60. For further discussion of the category of the immediately agreeable in Hume and the questions it raises, see Krause, "Hume and the (False) Luster of Justice," esp. 635–37.

61. Note that this is the basis of the sense of duty in Hume. See Radcliffe, "The Humean Sense of Duty," 396–97.

62. In fact, Radcliffe insists that the general appetite to good and aversion to evil, which Hume refers to when he is discussing the influencing motives of the will, "*is* the moral sense." Ibid., 397.

63. It is worth distinguishing this claim about the intrinsic motivational force of moral sentiment from the earlier discussion of why sympathy need not generate concern for others. Remember that although "my sympathy with another may give me the sentiment of pain and disapprobation" for any object that pains him, I may still be unwilling to "sacrifice any thing of my own interest, or cross any of my passions, for his satisfaction" (T 586). While sympathy conveys the pains of others to me it need not interest me in sacrificing myself for the purpose of relieving their pains. I can see that John's lie has harmed Robert but this perspective does not necessarily motivate me to come to Robert's aid; it cannot be equated with benevolence. The perception of the harm that results from lying does give me grounds and a motive to avoid engaging in this behavior, however. In part, this motive follows from the resonance that I am bound to feel (however slightly) with Robert's pain. I will want to avoid inflicting pain because, in light of the sympathetic communication of sentiments, I am likely to have to feel the pain I inflict, and I have a natural aversion to pain. In part, too, the motive to refrain from lying comes from the anticipa-

tory pain of self-disapprobation that I feel on contemplating my own lie, once I have judged lying to be wrong.

64. Radcliffe, "The Humean Sense of Duty," 384, 389.

65. Radcliffe, "Kantian Tunes on a Humean Instrument," 258.

66. Ibid., 259.

67. For examples of this view, see Elijah Millgram, "Was Hume a Humean?" *Hume Studies* 21 (1) (April 1995): 76; Hampton, "Does Hume Have an Instrumental Conception of Practical Reason?" 57, 72; and Korsgaard, "Skepticism about Practical Reasoning," *Journal of Philosophy,* 83 (1986): 5–25.

68. See Radcliffe, "Kantian Tunes on a Humean Instrument," 258.

69. Ibid., 249. Radcliffe notes that Baier's interpretation also supports the view that Hume has a theory of practical reasoning and moral deliberation. One of the points of Baier's discussion of Hume is to enlarge our conception of reason so as to make it socially and affectively engaged. Radcliffe, "Kantian Tunes," 267n33. Tito Magri also insists that Hume was not a skeptic about practical reason. See Magri, "Natural Obligation and Normative Motivation in Hume's *Treatise,*" *Hume Studies* 22 (2) (November 1996): 242.

70. See Korsgaard, *The Sources of Normativity*; Radcliffe, "The Humean Sense of Duty;" and Blackburn, *Ruling Passions* (Oxford: Oxford University Press, 2000).

71. It is true that on most Christian views what God commands is also held to be good for us. Hume may have had in view the natural law doctrine found in Grotius and Pufendorf, which derived from medieval Christianity. As one commentator has said, "for them moral obligation rests on natural law or on divine law. This law is addressed to us by God, who has legitimate authority over us as our creator; it is a dictate of divine reason or of divine will. In either case we are directed to comply on pain of penal sanctions. And while this law commands only what is, all things considered, good for us and human society, it is not in acting from it as for our good that we fulfill our obligation, but rather in acting from it as imposed by God and seeing ourselves as obedient to God's authority. Now here it is obvious that God's law when supported by sanctions can give us a motive for doing many things to which we have, in Hume's sense, no natural inclination. If we fear God's sanctions, as we must, then we have a motive of fear for not doing whatever God will punish." By contrast, Hume insisted that "no action can be virtuous, or morally good, unless there is in human nature some motive to produce it, distinct from a motive arising from its being sanctioned as a divine command." Rawls, *Lectures on the History of Moral Philosophy,* 56. In other words, Hume holds that nothing could be normative for us if it does not exercise a natural pull on our affections, independently of the influence of any external authority (T 518). Hume's insistence in this regard is part of a larger effort to forestall what he called the "monkish virtues" (E 108), self-abnegating dispositions that thwart natural human needs and purposes and undermine the gentle virtue of humanity. The monkish virtues not only make life unpleasant in themselves but also tend to create zealots and extremists, who then make others miserable and threaten to destabilize political society.

72. Kant, *Grounding for the Metaphysics of Morals,* 22 [411].

73. This term is used by Bernard Williams in "Internal and External Reasons," in Williams, *Moral Luck* (Cambridge: Cambridge University Press, 1981), 102.

74. Rawls's distinction between object-dependent, principle-dependent, and conception-dependent desires is relevant here. Rawls, *Political Liberalism*, 82–84. His typology of desire illuminates the variety of desires we can have depending on the amount and type of cognitive content. At the same time, however, Rawls's account differs fundamentally from the Humean approach by insisting that the normative authority of desires rests entirely on their cognitive content, or on "the principle to which the desire is attached," rather than on the desire itself (ibid., 82n31). Does the principle answer to reason? If so, then the desire carries normative weight in judgment and deliberation; if not, it carries no such weight. Like Rawls, Hume recognizes the importance of reflecting critically on the desires people happen to have, and this process of reflection will involve the intellect. The normative force of a particular desire held by some individual is not given simply by its psychological strength as this strength is felt by the individual herself. Instead, the normative force of the desire rests on its being endorsable from within the generalized perspective of moral sentiment and in its being consistent with human nature. Yet whether or not the desire is so endorsable will depend on the degree to which it supports fundamental human concerns, or is consistent with commonly held human desires. In this sense, the normative force of particular desires is indeed tied to their psychological strength, but only when seen (or felt) from a properly generalized point of view.

75. Our concerns contribute to the constitution of our characters and to our general dispositions in ways that are not always consciously felt, even when they carry motivational force. Hence we can sometimes find ourselves acting in ways that mystify us until, through reflection, we come to identify the unconscious concerns behind the action.

76. Williams, "Internal and External Reasons," 104.

77. Hume, "The Sceptic," in *Essays*, 170. See Richard H. Dees, "Hume on the Characters of Virtue," *Journal of the History of Philosophy* 35 (1) (January 1997): 60.

78. Hume, "The Sceptic," 171.

79. Rawls, *Lectures on the History of Moral Philosophy*, 42.

80. Ibid., 43.

81. Ibid., 48.

82. Dees, "Hume on the Characters of Virtue," 62.

83. Taylor, "Hume on Luck and Moral Inclusion" and "Justice and the Foundations of Social Morality in Hume's Treatise," *Hume Studies* 24 (1) (April 1998): 5–30; and see Sabina Lovibond, *Realism and Imagination in Ethics* (Minneapolis: University of Minnesota Press, 1983), 134–35.

84. Frazer, "The Enlightenment of Sympathy," 78.

85. Alexis de Tocqueville, *Democracy in America*, trans. Harvey C. Mansfield and Delba Winthrop (Chicago: University of Chicago Press, 2000), vol. 2, part 3, chapter 1, 535–39.

CHAPTER FOUR
AFFECTIVE JUDGMENT IN DEMOCRATIC POLITICS

1. Hume, "Of the Idea of a Perfect Commonwealth," in Hume, *Essays: Moral, Political, and Literary* (Indianapolis: Liberty Fund, 1987), 528; and "Of Public Credit," *Essays*, 355.

2. Hume, "Of the Coalition of Parties," in Hume, *Essays*, 499–500.

3. Hume, "Of the Populousness of Ancient Nations," in Hume, *Essays*, 416.

4. For the distinction between public deliberation as "opinion-formation" and public deliberation as "will-formation," see Jürgen Habermas, *Between Facts and Norms*, trans. William Rehg (Cambridge, Mass.: The MIT Press, 1996), 307–8. See also Nancy Fraser, "Rethinking the Public Sphere: A Contribution to the Critique of Actually Existing Democracy," in Craig Calhoun, ed., *Habermas and the Public Sphere* (Cambridge, Mass.: The MIT Press, 1993), 132–36 ; and Seyla Benhabib, "Toward a Deliberative Model of Democratic Legitimacy," in Benhabib, *Democracy and Difference: Contesting the Boundaries of the Political* (Princeton: Princeton University Press, 1996), 83–84.

5. James Scott, *Domination and the Arts of Resistance: Hidden Transcripts* (New Haven: Yale University Press, 1990); Judith Rollins, *Between Women: Domestics and Their Employers* (Philadelphia: Temple University Press, 1985).

6. On this point, see Jacqueline Taylor, "Humean Ethics and the Politics of Sentiment," *Topoi* 21: 184.

7. Hume, "Of Essay-Writing," in Hume, *Essays*, 534–35.

8. It is also worth noting that while Hume thought the extension of experience important to the refinement of moral sentiment, he did not have the democratic aspirations for moral sentiment that animate my own account. He wanted to move moral sentiment beyond prejudice and the limits of national taste but in the direction of a more hierarchical sense of refinement than in the socially egalitarian, even multiculturalist, direction I have in view.

9. Although at least one democratic theorist has argued recently that democracy itself, if properly understood, necessarily entails some ostensibly "liberal" mechanisms, which serve to constrain deliberative outcomes. See Corey Brettschneider, *Democratic Rights: The Substance of Self-Government* (Princeton: Princeton University Press, 2007). Brettschneider's analysis suggests that what has traditionally gone by the name of liberal democracy may be better characterized as democracy proper. I take no position on this issue here. For present purposes, what matters is that the political context of moral sentiment balance participatory rights with principled constraints on deliberative outcomes. I refer to this type of political context in the conventional way as "liberal-democratic."

10. Jean-Jacques Rousseau, *On the Social Contract*, trans. Judith R. Masters (New York: St. Martin's, 1978), 2:vi, 69.

11. Ibid., 69–70.

12. Ibid., 70.

13. Fraser, "Rethinking the Public Sphere," 123.

14. Ibid.

15. Iris Marion Young, "Activist Challenges to Deliberative Democracy," in James S. Fishkin and Peter Laslett, eds., *Debating Deliberative Democracy* (Malden: Blackwell, 2003), 118.

16. Lynn Sanders likewise argues for the value of "giving testimony" in democratic politics. Although she presents testimony as potentially compatible with public deliberation, she insists that it is distinct from deliberation. What is fundamental about giving testimony is "telling one's own story, not seeking communal dialogue." Lynn M. Sanders, "Against Deliberation," *Political Theory* 25 (3) (June 1997): 372. Sanders offers an important challenge to the often obfuscated influence of status and hierarchy in the standard accounts of democratic deliberation, and she is careful to make room for affect. Yet because her account eschews the aspiration to common ground, it is of limited use for public deliberation. It is, as her title suggests, an argument "against deliberation." So while she usefully reminds us of deliberation's limits, her view does not much illuminate the process of deliberation itself.

17. Does this mean that in order to articulate its claims successfully the gay community (to stick with the current example) must do so in a heteronormative vernacular? The claims to equal treatment will indeed need to engage elements in this vernacular but this does not mean that they are subjugated to it. In engaging the heteronormative vernacular, such claims also challenge and (if successful) ultimately transform it. This issue is discussed at greater length later in the chapter.

18. James Bohman, *Public Deliberation: Pluralism, Complexity, and Democracy* (Cambridge, Mass.: The MIT Press, 1996), 67.

19. Ibid.

20. Jane Mansbridge, "Everyday Talk in the Deliberative System," in Stephen Macedo, ed., *Deliberative Politics: Essays on* Democracy and Disagreement (Oxford: Oxford University Press, 1999), 217.

21. Ibid.

22. Ibid., 218–19.

23. Ibid., 227.

24. See, for instance, William A. Galston, "Diversity, Toleration, and Deliberative Democracy: Religious Minorities and Public Schooling," in Macedo, *Deliberative Politics*, 39–48. See also Jennifer Nedelsky, "Legislative Judgment and the Enlarged Mentality: Taking Religious Perspectives," in Richard Bauman and Tsvi Kahana, eds., *The Least Examined Branch: The Role of Legislatures in the Constitutional State* (Cambridge: Cambridge University Press, 2006), 93–124.

25. Included in the reciprocity requirement is the idea that justification must appeal to evidence that anyone can assess and to reasons that are accessible to all citizens, not limited (as through revelation) to a select few. See Amy Gutmann and Dennis Thompson, *Why Deliberative Democracy?* (Princeton: Princeton University Press, 2004), 4, 139.

26. Rawls, *Political Liberalism* (New York: Columbia University Press, 1993), 192.

27. Ibid., 193. Rawls borrows this definition from Ronald Dworkin, *A Matter of Principle* (Cambridge, Mass.: Harvard University Press, 1985), 191–92. Neutrality of aim is distinguished from "procedural neutrality" in that the latter,

on Rawls's definition, is given "by reference to a procedure that can be legitimated, or justified, without appealing to any moral values at all," or by appeal to "neutral values" (Rawls, *Political Liberalism*, 191–92). For further discussion of the meaning of "liberal neutrality," see, for example, Joseph Raz, *The Morality of Freedom* (Oxford: Clarendon Press, 1986); and Charles Larmore, *Patterns of Moral Complexity* (Cambridge: Cambridge University Press, 1987).

28. As we saw in chapter 3, sentiments shape moral judgments in two ways: (a) as the conditions of judgment (in the form of the horizons of concern within which moral judgment takes place); and (b) as inputs into the generalized standpoint (in the form of the sentiments of those affected) that gives rise to feelings of approval and disapproval.

29. Polygamy as a part of the Mormon religion has been restricted, for instance (*Reynolds v. United States*, 98 U.S. 145 [1878]). Similarly, religious rituals involving the use of illicit drugs have been proscribed (*Employment Div. Ore. Dept. of Human Res. v. Smith*, 494 U.S. 872 [1990]).

30. That is, polls currently show that while a majority of Americans opposes gay marriage (approximately 54 percent), most favor the legalization of homosexual relations between consenting adults (59 percent) and support equal rights for homosexuals in terms of job opportunities (89 percent). Clearly, one could not support these basic civil liberties for persons one believed brought serious harm to society. Thus I take it as implicit in the polling numbers that the weight of opinion in the United States recognizes that homosexuality in itself brings no harm to society, although it is true that most people continue to believe that gay marriage would bring some kind of harm to society—otherwise (presumably) they would not oppose it. These polling results are taken from Gallup's annual Values and Beliefs survey, conducted in May 2007, available online at http://www.galluppoll.com/content/?ci=27694.

31. Hume, "Of the First Principles of Government," in Hume, *Essays*, 32.

32. This is not to say that unaffected others cannot contribute anything to one's moral judgments and deliberations. Such people can bring in matters of fact of which we may have been unaware, or point out resemblances between an affected person's sentiments and our own, or help us think through the consequences of our actions and our judgments, or make us aware of sentiments we had not considered, and so on. In short, unaffected others can contribute information and perspective to our deliberative process, but their personal sentiments do not carry the same weight as those of affected parties. It is also worth noting that the degree to which any particular person is affected by the object under consideration (in the case at hand, gay marriage) may be contestable.

33. Rawls, *A Theory of Justice*, 121.

34. It is true that people are sometimes willing to undertake risky actions for purposes that are not empirically verifiable, and even though actions of this sort can be very destructive, they are also sometimes valuable. A faith-based sacrifice, which as a general matter would not meet the test for sound practical deliberation, may turn out to be socially beneficial. Think of the civilians in World War II who, acting in response to their religious faith, risked everything to help Jews escape the Nazis. While it would be wrong to deny

the value of the action in this case, it would also be a mistake to see it as indicative of a generally sound approach to practical deliberation. The mental and emotional states that constitute a "leap of faith" are not on the whole conducive to sound judgment and practical deliberation. As a general matter, we would not want moral and political life to be guided by a form of deliberation that regularly overrides or ignores empirical evidence and empirical considerations relating to consequences.

35. Cass Sunstein has shown that exposure to different views can sometimes generate polarization rather than mutual understanding. Under certain circumstances, "members of a deliberating group move toward a more extreme point in the direction indicated by members' predeliberative tendencies." Sunstein, "The Law of Group Polarization," in Fishkin and Laslett, *Debating Deliberative Democracy*, 81. Nevertheless, Sunstein presses the importance—and the possibility—of effective institutional correctives to this danger (ibid., 98).

36. Gutmann and Thompson, *Democracy and Disagreement*.

37. Lani Guinier, *The Tyranny of the Majority* (Cambridge, Mass.: Harvard University Press, 1994).

38. Alexis de Tocqueville, *Democracy in America*, trans. Harvey C. Mansfield and Delba Winthrop (Chicago: University of Chicago Press, 2000), vol. 1, part 2, chapter 8, 262.

39. Jeffrey Abramson, *We the Jury: The Jury System and the Ideal of Democracy* (Cambridge, Mass.: Harvard University Press, 2000), 5.

40. There are also good reasons to preserve the peremptory challenge in some form, above all the fact that its abolition would result in a much increased power on the part of trial judges to "mold the jury" (Ralph N. Jonakait, *The American Jury System* [New Haven: Yale University Press, 2003], 169). Without peremptory challenges, the only removal mechanism for potential jurors would be challenges for cause, and judges "have great control over whether for-case challenges are granted" (ibid.). Jonakait has recommended a compromise position that would permit each side three peremptory challenges in the selection of a twelve-person jury (ibid., 170). Under this rule, attorneys "would be unlikely to exercise the peremptories solely on racial and gender grounds, for their challenges would be quickly exhausted." At the same time, the important check on the trial judge's power to shape a jury would remain intact (ibid., 170–71).

41. On this view, as Abramson writes, "the primary qualification of good jurors is that they themselves know nothing beforehand about the case they are about to judge. Precisely because they bring no personal knowledge or opinions to the case, they can judge it with the distance and dispassion that marks impartial justice." Abramson, *We the Jury*, 17. Changes of venue and the voir dire process more generally allow judges to screen out persons who have been exposed to pretrial publicity, or who have experience or knowledge of matters pertaining to the case. Abramson makes a convincing case against ignorance as the main criterion of impartiality in *We the Jury*.

42. Valerie P. Hans and Neil Vidmar, *Judging the Jury* (Cambridge, Mass.: Perseus, 1986), 107–8.

43. Johnson has therefore argued that all defendants should be entitled to racially similar juries. Sheri Lynn Johnson, "Black Innocence and the White Jury," *Michigan Law Review* 83 (7) (June 1985): 1677–78, 1686.

44. James J. Gobert, "In Search of the Impartial Jury," *Journal of Criminal Law and Criminology* 79 (2) (Summer 1988): 297–98; Hans and Vidmar, *Judging the Jury*, 167; Jonakait, *The American Jury System*, 90–93.

45. Hans and Vidmar, *Judging the Jury*, 174–75; Reid Hastie, Steven D. Penrod, and Nancy Pennington, *Inside the Jury* (Cambridge, Mass.: Harvard University Press, 1983), 82, 92, 112, 115, 165, 228–29; Jonakait, *The American Jury System*, 95–104.

46. Robert Goodin, "Democratic Deliberation Within," in Fishkin and Laslett, *Debating Deliberative Democracy*, 70.

47. Martha Nussbaum, *Hiding from Humanity: Shame, Disgust and the Law* (Princeton: Princeton University Press, 2004), 13–15.

CHAPTER FIVE
PUBLIC DELIBERATION AND THE FEELING OF IMPARTIALITY

1. Citizens are authors of the law insofar as they contribute, if only indirectly, to decision making about the enactment of laws; they are the masters of the law to the extent that they are capable of criticizing existing laws and influencing the reform or revocation of laws when they deem it appropriate.

2. In what follows, we focus on the deliberation leading up to collective decision making, not on the institutional mechanisms that constitute the decision procedure itself.

3. As we have seen, this history of communicated sentiments is embodied in personal experience as well as in literature, art, and historical writings.

4. Benjamin Barber, "Foundationalism and Democracy," in Seyla Benhabib, ed., *Democracy and Difference* (Princeton: Princeton University Press, 1996), 354. Along these lines Ian Shapiro maintains that "we can be individually reflective" but not "individually deliberative" because "deliberation involves two or more persons." Shapiro, "Optimal Deliberation?" in James Fishkin and Peter Laslett, eds., *Debating Deliberative Democracy* (Malden, Mass.: Blackwell, 2003), 122. Shapiro's distinction here is problematic, however. First, while public deliberation clearly involves more than one person, there is no reason to insist that deliberation per se is similarly interactive. One can deliberate on one's own about what one ought to do, bringing different options and their probable consequences into view and weighing each in turn. Secondly, "reflectiveness" does not in itself capture the necessarily action-guiding quality of deliberation. One can be reflective about one's life or character without acting on one's reflections; indeed, the best time for such reflectiveness may be precisely the quiet moments of repose in which one is insulated from the demands of action.

5. Barber, *The Conquest of Politics* (Princeton: Princeton University Press, 1988), 199, 200.

6. Jürgen Habermas, "Three Normative Models of Democracy," in Benhabib, *Democracy and Difference*, 28. In a similar vein, Benhabib speaks of

"anonymous public conversations." Benhabib, "Toward a Deliberative Model of Democratic Legitimacy," in Benhabib, *Democracy and Difference*, 73–74. See also James Bohman, *Public Deliberation: Pluralism, Complexity, and Democracy* (Cambridge: The MIT Press, 1996), 179.

7. Gutmann and Thompson, *Why Deliberative Democracy?* (Princeton: Princeton University Press, 2004), 133.

8. Ibid., 134. Theories of deliberative democracy typically supplement the criterion of reciprocity with three others: publicity, accountability, and equal access. Publicity requires that reason-giving be public, while accountability holds that public officials who are empowered to make decisions for others must be held accountable to them, whether through elections or in some other way. Equal access means that all those bound by a decision have an equal opportunity to participate in the deliberative process and to bring issues forward for discussion (ibid., 135). Although I recognize the general value of these additional criteria, in what follows I bracket them for the purpose of focusing on reciprocity because this is where the moral sentiment model makes its distinctive contribution.

9. William Riker, *Liberalism Against Populism: A Confrontation between the Theory of Democracy and the Theory of Social Choice* (San Francisco: W. H. Freeman, 1982).

10. Bernard Manin, "On Legitimacy and Political Deliberation," *Political Theory* 15 (3) (August 1987): 351–52.

11. Joshua Cohen, "An Epistemic Conception of Democracy," *Ethics* 97 (1) (October 1986): 34; and see David Estlund, "The Insularity of the Reasonable: Why Political Liberalism Must Admit the Truth," *Ethics* 108 (2) (January 1998): 252-75.

12. Cohen, "An Epistemic Conception of Democracy," 34.

13. Gutmann and Thompson, *Why Deliberative Democracy?*, 16, 115.

14. Benhabib, "Introduction," in Benhabib, *Democracy and Difference*, 4.

15. John S. Dryzek, *Deliberative Democracy and Beyond: Liberals, Critics, Contestations* (Oxford: Oxford University Press, 2000), 76; see also Susan C. Stokes, "Pathologies of Deliberation" in Jon Elster, ed., *Deliberative Democracy* (Cambridge: Cambridge University Press, 1998), 123; and Adam Przeworski, "Deliberation and Ideological Domination," in Elster, *Deliberative Democracy*, 140.

16. Benhabib, "Toward a Deliberative Model of Democratic Legitimacy," 72.

17. Iris Marion Young, "Communication and the Other: Beyond Deliberative Democracy," in Benhabib, *Democracy and Difference*, 130, characterizing the view of Thomas Spragens in *Reason and Democracy* (Durham, N.C.: Duke University Press, 1990), 128.

18. Ronald Dworkin, *Sovereign Virtue* (Cambridge, Mass.: Harvard University Press, 2000), 365.

19. Jon Elster, "Deliberation and Constitution Making," in Elster, *Deliberative Democracy*, 109. Note that this requirement is at odds with Elster's own much-cited notion of "the civilizing force of hypocrisy," which he presents as an important support for democratic deliberation. This notion holds that "a desirable effect of publicity" is to force participants in deliberation to frame their arguments in "the language of reason" rather than narrow self-interest so that

they appear to be more public-spirited than they actually are. Publicity elevates (or rationalizes) the terms of debate even though it does not normally change the real motives of participants. As Elster puts it, "publicity does not eliminate base motives, but forces or induces speakers to hide them" (ibid., 111). Yet so long as the motives of participants are "passionate ones" they will undercut the integrity of deliberation, insofar as his definition requires that the motivating force of decisions be reason *as against* passion. In light of this inconsistency, James Johnson has argued that Elster's civilizing force of hypocrisy "hardly affords the robust moral resources to which advocates of deliberation aspire. It does not so much generate a 'reasoned agreement' as induce a conformity that is at once rather shallow and normatively suspect." Johnson, "Arguing for Deliberation," in Elster, *Deliberative Democracy*, 172.

20. Joshua Cohen, "Procedure and Substance in Deliberative Democracy," in Elster, *Democracy and Difference*, 100; and see Cohen, "Deliberation and Democratic Legitimacy," in James Bohman and William Rehg, eds., *Deliberative Democracy: Essays on Reason and Politics* (Cambridge, Mass.: The MIT Press, 1997), 74.

21. As Cheryl Hall notes, there is "little discussion in the literature of any difference between 'using reason' and 'giving reasons.' " She argues, along lines similar to those developed here, that "giving reasons requires making use of passion as well as reason." Hall, "Recognizing the Passion in Deliberation: Toward a More Democratic Theory of Deliberative Democracy," *Hypatia: A Journal of Feminist Philosophy* 22 (4) (Fall 2007), 93; and see also Hall, *The Trouble with Passion: Political Theory Beyond the Reign of Reason* (New York: Routledge, 2005). Although a central purpose of the present study is to show that practical reasoning incorporates both cognition and affect, in the discussion that follows I use the term "reason" as it is more commonly used by deliberative democrats to refer to a cognitive, as opposed to affective, mode of consciousness.

22. See Christine Korsgaard, *The Sources of Normativity* (Cambridge: Cambridge University Press, 1996).

23. Cohen, "Procedure and Substance in Deliberative Democracy," 100.

24. Cohen, "Democracy and Liberty," in Elster, *Deliberative Democracy*, 201.

25. Cohen, "Procedure and Substance in Deliberative Democracy," 100.

26. Or, as Korsgaard says, practical reason can generate conclusions in a way that does "not involve discerning relations between passions (or any preexisting sources of motivation) and those actions." Christine Korsgaard, "Skepticism about Practical Reason," in Elijah Millgram, ed., *Varieties of Practical Reasoning* (Cambridge, Mass.: The MIT Press, 2001), 106.

27. Cohen, "Democracy and Liberty," 200.

28. Ibid., 199.

29. Ibid., 201.

30. Ibid., 200.

31. Ibid., 199.

32. Ibid.

33. Cohen, "Procedure and Substance in Deliberative Democracy," 101.

34. Gutmann and Thompson, *Why Deliberative Democracy?*, 50–51. A related but more telling objection, which Gutmann and Thompson do not address

here, is that the arguments of marginalized groups will frequently *appear* to be less reasonable because they draw on ideas that are not yet a part of the shared horizon of concern that grounds public reason. See Krause, "Partial Justice," *Political Theory* 29 (3) (June 2001): 315–36.

35. Gutmann and Thompson, *Why Deliberative Democracy?*, 51.

36. Ibid., 50.

37. For similar treatments that recognize passion as a legitimate induce-ment to reasoned deliberation but do not develop the role of affect *within* deliberation, see for example, Jeffrey K. Tulis, "Deliberation Between Institu-tions," in Fishkin and Laslett, *Debating Deliberative Democracy*, 210; and Diego Gambetta, "Claro!: An Essay on Discursive Machismo," in Elster, *Deliberative Democracy*, 20. See also Michael Walzer, "Deliberation, and What Else?" in Ste-phen Macedo, ed., *Deliberative Politics: Essays on* Democracy and Disagree-ment (Oxford: Oxford University Press, 1999), 64: "issues on which citizens deliberate (or do not) arise through a political process that is largely nonde-liberative. It is through the mobilization of passions and interests that we are forced to address what is (only now) the 'question' of poverty, or corruption, or exploitation."

38. Iris Marion Young, *Justice and the Politics of Difference* (Princeton: Prince-ton University Press, 1990), 100.

39. Young, "Communication and the Other," 124.

40. James Johnson, "Arguing for Deliberation: Some Skeptical Conclu-sions," in Elster, *Deliberative Democracy*, 166.

41. Robert E. Goodin, "Democratic Deliberation Within," in Fishkin and Laslett, *Debating Deliberative Democracy*, 62–63.

42. Jane Mansbridge, "Everyday Talk in the Deliberative System," in Macedo, *Deliberative Politics*, 213.

43. Ibid., 225.

44. For a full statement of this critique, see Young, *Justice and the Politics of Difference*. Nedelsky comments on the fact that affect undercuts impartiality in Young. See Jennifer Nedelsky, "Embodied Diversity," in Nedelsky and Ronald Beiner, *Judgment, Imagination, and Politics* (Lanham, Md.: Rowman and Lit-tlefield, 2001), 231. Nedelsky's approach is closer to the one developed here in that she believes that affect can contribute to impartiality. Although she offers a stimulating and insightful presentation, however, she does not elaborate pre-cisely how affect serves impartiality. Additionally, the focus of her analysis is judicial deliberation rather the public deliberations of average citizens dis-cussed here.

45. Benhabib, "Toward a Deliberative Model," 83.

46. Ibid., 82–83. In other work, Benhabib offers a more nuanced account of the relationship between affective modes of consciousness and the generalized standpoint of moral judgment and public deliberation. Her influential critique of Rawls and Kohlberg, emphasizing the value of the "concrete other" within perspective-taking, is a case in point. Benhabib associates the perspective of the concrete other not only with particularity but also with affect. This perspec-tive "requires us to view each and every rational being as an individual with a concrete history, identity, and affective-emotional constitution," and generates

moral feelings of "love, care, sympathy, and solidarity" (Benhabib, "The Generalized and the Concrete Other," in Benhabib and Drucilla Cornell, eds., *Feminism as Critique* [Minneapolis: University of Minnesota Press, 1987], 87). Although she maintains that "our affective-emotional constitution . . . ought to be considered accessible to moral communication, reflection, and transformation," she says little about exactly how affect should figure in the moral standpoint, or how the practical rationality proper to deliberation incorporates feeling (94). Her account of the concrete other is intended to reveal "the ideological limits of universalistic discourse" but not to establish positive criteria for a viable alternative (92). In this respect, her account opens the door for the kind of further elaboration of affective impartiality offered here.

47. Mansbridge, "Everyday Talk in the Deliberative System," 225–26.

48. Nussbaum, *Hiding from Humanity: Shame, Disgust, and the Law* (Princeton: Princeton University Press, 2004),56, 69. The standard of appraisal she recommends is the "political conception" of justice found in Rawls's *Political Liberalism*. See Nussbaum, *Hiding from Humanity*, 62, 69.

49. Nussbaum, *Hiding from Humanity*, 14, 15.

50. Ibid., 36.

51. Richard A. Posner, "Emotion versus Emotionalism in Law," in Susan A. Bandes, ed., *The Passions of Law* (New York: New York University Press, 1999), 322. Posner is responding to Martha Nussbaum, " 'Secret Sewers of Vice': Disgust, Bodies, and the Law," in Bandes, *The Passions of Law*, 19–62.

52. Dryzek, *Deliberative Democracy and Beyond*, 52.

53. See also Bohman's valuable account of how reasons become publicly convincing. Bohman, *Public* Deliberation, 59–65.

54. Dryzek, *Deliberative Democracy and Beyond*, 53.

55. Ibid., 167.

56. Ibid., 52.

57. For statements of this concern, see William A. Galston, "Diversity, Toleration, and Deliberative Democracy: Religious Minorities and Public Schooling," in Macedo, *Deliberative Politics*, 43; Michael J. Sandel, "A Response to Rawls's Political Liberalism," in Sandel, *Liberalism and the Limits of Justice* (Cambridge: Cambridge University Press, 1982), 196; John Tomasi, *Liberalism Beyond Justice: Citizens, Society, and the Boundaries of Political Theory* (Princeton: Princeton University Press, 2001); and Lucas Swaine, *The Liberal Conscience: Politics and Principle in a World of Religious Pluralism* (New York: Columbia University Press, 2006).

58. See Stephen K. White, *Sustaining Affirmation: The Strengths of Weak Ontology in Political Theory* (Princeton: Princeton University Press, 2000), 47.

59. As we have seen in previous chapters, Rawls describes this kind of commitment in terms of principle- and conception-dependent desires. See *Political Liberalism* (New York: Columbia University Press, 1993), 82–86. It is true that there are some citizens in the United States today who lack these desires. Certain religious extremists, for instance, object to the constitutional principle of religious freedom and have no desire for it. They would prefer theocracy instead, or at least the rule of their own religion. There are those, too, who genuinely do not wish to see liberty and equality for African Americans. We shall

have more to say about public reason and the fact of diversity, but the main point here is that insofar as Americans do subscribe to the principles of public reason, their commitment is not only an intellectual one but also has affective valence.

60. Thus, as John Tomasi puts it, "the desire to be a good citizen must be shown to be a natural part of each person's good." Tomasi, *Liberalism Beyond Justice*, 79.

61. Richardson's notion of "extended reflective equilibrium" is relevant here, although it is intended to apply to questions of individual deliberation rather than public deliberation. Ethical reflection, he says, properly "incorporates emotionally informed perceptions of the particulars of the situation of action and emotionally guided awareness of one's commitments as elicited in response to the situation." These affective modes of consciousness contribute to considered judgments and can support "proper and 'reliable' judgment" about such matters as the Holocaust or the Bhopal disaster. Richardson, *Practical Reasoning about Final Ends* (Oxford: Oxford University Press, 1997), 188.

62. Young's example is as follows: "When asked to put themselves in the position of a person in a wheelchair, they do not imagine the point of view of others; rather, they project on to those others their own fears and fantasies about themselves." Young, "Asymmetrical Reciprocity: On Moral Respect, Wonder, and Enlarged Thought" in *Judgment, Imagination, and Politics*, 209.

63. Attentiveness to the sentiments of all affected may seem to be too demanding in politics. After all, laws and public policies affect lots of people. Taking them all into account will be challenging. But the idea that we should do so ought not be surprising. We already believe a version of this claim. For as liberal democrats, nothing could be more obvious to us than the notion that public decisions should take into account the *interests* of those affected. This is a requirement of freedom and equal respect. The point here is really no different. It is justified on the same basis, and its practical implementation is no more demanding.

64. Goodin, "Democratic Deliberation Within," 60.

65. If participants are attached to the process itself, as an embodiment of public values they care about, they will have grounds to be committed to the outcome of the process, whether they share in the specific concerns served by that outcome or not. Yet for a decision process to count as deliberative rather than merely aggregative it is important that participants internalize and respond to the claims of others rather than just register and count them. If the process is simply a matter of publicizing and aggregating the preferences of participants, then it is not a fully deliberative process. Under such circumstances, participants will not have been pushed to think and feel beyond the limits of their own private perspectives. To the extent that a process is genuinely deliberative such that outcomes are more than a mechanistic aggregation of unreflective, private sentiments, it will need to include uptake and engagement. In uptake and engagement, sympathy (in Hume's sense) makes available to participants the sentiments of others, facilitating genuine reflection on the values and concerns at hand. In this process, too, participants can come to

see how the concerns of others intersect with their own concerns. The intermingling of sentiments, in which the initial concerns of participants are broadened or refined in light of the expressed concerns of one another, makes this possible. This kind of reflection does not happen as much as it should in liberal democracies, but it does happen. Indeed, it would be difficult to explain social change and the reform of public opinion over time without reference to such intermingling of sentiments via sympathetic uptake and engagement.

66. Immanuel Kant, "To Perpetual Peace," in Kant, *Perpetual Peace and Other Essays,* trans. Ted Humphrey (Indianapolis: Hackett, 1983), 366 [124].

67. Equal respect requires that we consider these sentiments initially, filtering them out only on reflection in light of the concerns discussed below.

68. Democratic legitimacy is defined in various ways. See, for instance, the different views defended by Jeremy Waldron, *Law and Disagreement* (Oxford: Oxford University Press, 1999); Rawls, *Political Liberalism*; and Corey Brettschneider, *Democratic Rights: The Substance of Self-Government* (Princeton: Princeton University Press, 2007), esp. chap. 7. The present account, like that of Brettschneider, assumes a view of democratic legitimacy that balances sensitivity to an inclusive popular will with fidelity to more enduring, legally codified public values.

69. The moral value of one's purpose may well be enough to justify acts of civil disobedience or conscientious objection, however.

70. I do not mean to suggest here that no one could ever be satisfied with a life lived primarily in the domestic sphere, or to minimize the genuine satisfactions of such a life. But the fact that so many women took advantage of the new opportunities to work outside the home when these opportunities became available does suggest than a life confined to the domestic sphere is not for everyone, and, at least for many women, was not as fully satisfying as they themselves may once have thought.

71. Bohman, *Public Deliberation*, 64–65.

72. This point is pressed forcefully by Gutmann and Thompson in *Democracy and Disagreement* (Cambridge: Harvard University Press, 1996), esp. 73–79.

73. This is consistent with the principle of equal respect as deliberative equality, which requires that we be sensitive to the sentiments of all others and free of prejudice, but which (as we have seen) allows for principled distinctions in the weight accorded these sentiments within the generalized standpoint.

74. Aristotle, *Nicomachean Ethics*, trans. Hippocrates G. Apostle (Grinnell: Peripatetic Press, 1984), 1112b8–10.

75. See the interesting discussion by Bonnie Honig of moral dilemmas in the work of Bernard Williams. Honig, "Difference, Dilemmas, and the Politics of Home," in Benhabib, *Democracy and Difference*, 257–77.

76. Gutmann and Thompson, *Democracy and Disagreement*, 74.

77. Ibid.

78. Ibid., 80.

79. Under the program, poverty among the elderly dropped from 40 percent in 1959 to 12 percent in 1990. Margaret Weir, "Social Welfare and Poverty," in Donald C. Bacon, Roger H. Davidson, and Morton Keller, eds., *The Encyclopedia of the United States Congress* (New York: Simon and Schuster, 1995), 1850. See

also Donald Wolfensenberger, "Congress and Security," paper presented for the Congress Project Seminar on "Congress and the Politics of Aging," Woodrow Wilson International Center for Scholars, September 13, 2005, available online at www.wilsoncenter.org/events/docs/aging-essay-intro.pdf.

CHAPTER SIX
THE AFFECTIVE AUTHORITY OF LAW

1. Hamilton, Alexander, James Madison, and John Jay, *The Federalist Papers*, ed. Clinton Rossiter (New York: Mentor, 1961), no. 48.

2. Such a polity would be a form of despotism, the government that has fear as its animating principle. See Montesquieu, *De l'esprit des lois*, in *Oeuvres complètes*, 2 vols, ed. Roger Caillois, "Bibliothèque de la Pléiade" (Paris: Gallimard, 1949–1951), vol. 2, especially books 2–3.

3. Ronald Dworkin points out, for instance, that Bentham, the "first philosopher to present a systematic version of legal positivism," was inspired in this project by moral egalitarianism: "He hoped to undermine the political power of judges who claimed to have discovered law in natural rights or in ancient traditions beyond what Parliament, as the congress of the people, had explicitly declared." Ronald Dworkin, "Thirty Years On," *Harvard Law Review* 115 (April 2002): 1677. Legal positivists on the American bench such as Oliver Wendell Holmes and Learned Hand "appealed to positivism to support progressive economic and social legislation against conservative Supreme Court Justices who invoked supposed natural rights protecting established property to justify holding such legislation unconstitutional" (ibid.). Others have held that to recognize "a distinction between law and morality leads to an important moral advance because it leaves [us] free to oppose and disobey law on moral principles." Samuel M. Thompson, "The Authority of Law," *Ethics* 75 (1) (October 1964), 23.

4. Hans Kelsen, *The General Theory of Law and State* (New York: Russell and Russell, 1945), 419–37, and *What is Justice?* (Berkeley: University of California Press, 1957), 141, 144, 179, 198ff., 228–29, 258–61, 295–302; H.L.A. Hart, *The Concept of Law* (Oxford: Clarendon Press, 1961), 181–95; Joseph Raz, *The Authority of Law* (Oxford: Oxford University Press, 1979), 37–52, 129–32, and *Practical Reason and Norms* (Oxford: Oxford University Press, 1975), 162–70; and Ronald Dworkin, *Law's Empire* (Cambridge, Mass.: Harvard University Press, 1986), 35–37.

5. The traditional marginalization of affect within the study of law more generally is now being challenged. Legal scholars have recently begun to explore the relationship between the law and affective modes of consciousness such as passions and emotions in ways that fruitfully contest the traditional ideal of law as a bastion of impartial reason devoid of sentiment. See, for example, the essays collected in Susan A. Bandes, ed., *The Passions of Law* (New York: New York University Press, 1999); as well as Martha Nussbaum, *Hiding from Humanity: Shame, Disgust, and the Law* (Princeton: Princeton University Press, 2004); Jennifer Nedelsky, "Embodied Diversity and the Challenges to Law," in Ronald Beiner and Jennifer Nedelsky, eds., *Judgment, Imagination, and Politics*

(Lanham, Md.: Rowman and Littlefield), 229–56; and Kathryn Abrams, "The Progress of Passion," *Michigan Law Review* 100 (May 2002): 1602–20. For an earlier set of reflections on emotion in adjudication, see William J. Brennan, Jr., "Reason, Passion, and the Progress of the Law," *Cardozo Law Review* 10 (3) (1988): 3–23, and the various articles of response collected in that issue. Yet much as the scholarship on the authority of law has neglected the role of affect, this new work on law and emotion has tended to overlook the question of the law's authority. An important exception is John Deigh, "Emotion and the Authority of Law," in Bandes, *The Passions of Law*, 285–308. Deigh's argument is discussed at some length in what follows.

6. See Joseph Raz, *The Morality of Freedom* (Oxford: Clarendon, 1986), 28–31, 48–53; and Philip Soper, "Legal Theory and the Claim of Authority," *Philosophy and Public Affairs* 18 (3) (Summer 1989): 224–27.

7. John Locke, *A Letter Concerning Toleration* (Indianapolis: Hackett, 1983), 27.

8. See Soper, "Legal Theory and the Claim of Authority," 225–26.

9. Richard Posner, "Emotion versus Emotionalism in Law," in Bandes, *The Passions of Law*, 310. Along similar lines, Jennifer Nedelsky has argued that motivating change in our attitudes and actions requires more than rational reflection or the recognition of logical inconsistency: "it takes affect to change affect." See Nedelsky, "Embodied Diversity and the Challenges to Law," 251; see also 243.

10. Soper, "Legal Theory and the Claim of Authority," 225–26.

11. Ibid., 225.

12. It is perhaps worth emphasizing that practical authority is by no means fully independent of epistemic considerations. A legislature that makes too many mistakes of fact ultimately undercuts its authority. The point is that there is more to practical authority (in contrast to theoretical authority) than its success in accurately representing the world.

13. Hart, *The Concept of Law*, 80.

14. Ibid.

15. Ibid., 83–88.

16. Ibid., 81; emphasis in original.

17. Ibid., 86.

18. Ibid., 86–88.

19. Ibid., 87.

20. Ibid.

21. Ibid.

22. In a similar way, Deigh notes that although Hart's view ostensibly "excludes the thesis that the law's authority is conditioned on an emotional bond between law and its subjects," nevertheless "one can plausibly assume that some emotional bond to the law lies behind" the internal point of view. Deigh, "Emotion and the Authority of Law," 292, 305.

23. Raz, "Authority and Justification," *Philosophy and Public Affairs* 14 (1) (Winter 1985): 25; see also Raz, *Ethics in the Public Domain* (Oxford: Clarendon Press, 1999), 214.

24. Raz, *Ethics in the Public Domain*, 214.

25. Raz, "Authority and Justification," 19.

26. Raz, *Ethics in the Public Domain*, 214. See also Jules Coleman, "Authority and Reason," in Robert P. George, ed., *The Autonomy of Law* (Oxford: Oxford University Press, 1996), 309.

27. Raz, *Ethics in the Public Domain*, 214.

28. Raz, *Practical Reason and Norms* (Oxford: Oxford University Press, 2002), 31.

29. Raz, *Ethics in the Public Domain*, 333.

30. Rawls, *A Theory of Justice* (Cambridge, Mass.: Harvard University Press, 1971), 477–78.

31. Raz, *Practical Reason and Norms*, 34.

32. Ibid., 170.

33. Raz, *The Authority of Law*, 29.

34. Jeremy Waldron, *Law and Disagreement* (Oxford: Oxford University Press, 1999), 144. It should be noted that *Law and Disagreement* offers an account of the authority of legitimate, democratic law, not an account of the authority of law per se. In this respect, Waldron's view differs from those of Raz and Hart, who are both concerned to articulate the nature of law's authority in a more general sense.

35. Ibid., 117. Elsewhere Waldron speaks of the "felt need" among members of a society for the common framework that law represents. Waldron, *Law and Disagreement*, 102.

36. Ibid., 102.

37. Dworkin, *Law's Empire*, 225.

38. Ibid.

39. Ibid., 239.

40. Steven D. Smith, "Radically Subversive Speech and the Authority of Law," *Michigan Law Review* 94 (2) (November 1995): 358.

41. This is essentially the force of the objection raised against Dworkin by Richard D. Parker in "Democratic Honor: Liberal and Populist," *Harvard Civil Rights-Civil Liberties Review* 39 (2) (Summer 2004): 239–97. Bruce Ackerman's "dualist" approach to the interpretation of constitutional law represents an effort to mediate between the moralist approach (which he calls "foundationalism") and one that is more sensitive to democratic will. Bruce Ackerman, *We the People* (Cambridge, Mass.: Harvard University Press, 1991).

42. Dworkin, *Law's Empire*, 211. True community is both a condition and a consequence of law-as-integrity in the sense that the two are mutually reinforcing.

43. Ibid., 214.

44. Ibid., 211.

45. Ibid., 200.

46. Ibid., 201.

47. Ibid., 190. And see Leslie Green, "Associative Obligations and the State," in Justine Burley, ed., *Dworkin and His Critics* (Malden, Mass.: Blackwell, 2004), 271.

48. Dworkin, *Law's Empire*, 201; Green, "Associative Obligations and the State," 271.

49. Green, "Associative Obligations and the State," 271.

50. Deigh, "Emotion and the Authority of Law," 295.

51. Ibid.

52. Ibid.

53. Ibid.

54. Ibid., 296.

55. Ibid.

56. Ibid.

57. For an account of the ways that emotions can be socially constructed and the implications of this for the law, see Cheshire Calhoun, "Making up Emotional People: The Case of Romantic Love," in Bandes, *The Passions of Law*, 217–40; and Abrams, "The Progress of Passion," 1610–11.

58. Law's authority as a whole (or the authority of a legal system) can survive the occasional statute or judicial decision that is inconsistent with moral sentiment, but too many such laws will undermine the justification for respecting the law and hence will undercut its normative authority.

59. See Susan Moller Okin, *Justice, Gender and the Family* (New York: Basic, 1989); Martha Nussbaum, "Rawls and Feminism," in Samuel Freeman, ed., *The Cambridge Companion to Rawls* (Cambridge: Cambridge University Press, 2003), 488–520; and Susan Mendus, "The Importance of Love in Rawls's *Theory of Justice*," *British Journal of Political Science* 29 (1999): 57–75. For related discussion of the role of empathy in legal deliberation, see Lynne N. Henderson, "Legality and Empathy," *Michigan Law Review* 85 (June 1987): 1574–1653; and Susan Bandes, "Empathy, Narrative, and Victim Impact Statements," *University of Chicago Law Review* 63 (2) (Spring 1996): 361–412.

60. Simon Blackburn, *Ruling Passions* (Oxford: Oxford University Press, 2000), 9.

61. Ibid., 14.

62. Neil MacCormick attributes to Hart a belief in just such an "autonomous, rational, and discursive approach to moral questions." MacCormick, "The Concept of Law and *The Concept of Law*," *Oxford Journal of Legal Studies* 14 (1) (Spring 1994): 5.

63. Austin Sarat, "Authority, Anxiety, and Procedural Justice: Moving from Scientific Detachment to Critical Engagement," *Law and Society Review* 27 (3) (1993): 665–66.

64. Ibid., 647.

CONCLUSION
TOWARD A NEW POLITICS OF PASSION: CIVIL PASSIONS
AND THE PROMISE OF JUSTICE

1. David Hume, *A Treatise of Human Nature*. Ed. L. A. Selby-Bigge (Oxford: Clarendon, 1968), 621.

2. David Hume, *An Enquiry Concerning the Principles of Morals* (LaSalle, Ill.: Open Court, 1966), 30n1.

3. Ibid., 118.

4. John Rawls, *Political Liberalism* (New York: Columbia University Press, 1993), 28.

5. John Tomasi, *Liberalism Beyond Justice: Citizens, Society, and the Boundaries of Political Theory* (Princeton: Princeton University Press, 2001), 79.

Bibliography

Abizadeh, Arash. 2007. "On the Philosophy/Rhetoric Binaries: Or, Is Habermasian Discourse Motivationally Impotent?" *Philosophy and Social Criticism* 33 (4): 445–472.

Abrams, Kathryn. 2002. "The Progress of Passion." *Michigan Law Review* 100 (May): 1602–20.

Abramson, Jeffrey. 2000. *We the Jury: The Jury System and the Ideal of Democracy.* Cambridge, Mass.: Harvard University Press.

Ackerman, Bruce. 1991. *We the People: Foundations.* Cambridge, Mass.: Harvard University Press.

Anscombe, G. E. 1963. *Intention.* Oxford: Oxford University Press.

Árdal, Páll S. 1966. *Passion and Value in Hume's* Treatise. Edinburgh: Edinburgh University Press.

Aristotle. 1984. *Nicomachean Ethics,* trans. Hippocrates G. Apostle. Grinnell: Peripatetic Press.

Arnhart, Larry. 1995. "The New Darwinian Naturalism in Political Theory." *American Political Science Review* 89 (2) (June): 389–400.

Averill, James R. 1980. "Emotion and Anxiety: Sociocultural, Biological, and Psychological Determinants," in Rorty, *Explaining Emotions*, 37–72.

Ayer, A. J. 1980. *Hume: A Very Short Introduction.* Oxford: Oxford University Press.

Bacon, Donald C., Roger H. Davidson, and Morton Keller, eds. 1995. *The Encyclopedia of the United States Congress.* New York: Simon and Schuster.

Baier, Annette. 1996. *Moral Prejudices.* Cambridge, Mass.: Harvard University Press.

———. 1999. *A Progress of Sentiments.* Cambridge, Mass.: Harvard University Press.

Bandes, Susan, 1996. "Empathy, Narrative, and Victim Impact Statements," *University of Chicago Law Review* 63 (2) (Spring): 361–412.

———, ed. 1999. *The Passions of Law.* New York: New York University Press.

Barber, Benjamin. 1988. *The Conquest of Politics.* Princeton: Princeton University Press.

———. 1996. "Foundationalism and Democracy," in Benhabib, *Democracy and Difference*, 348–60.

Barry, Brian. 1995. "John Rawls and the Search for Stability," *Ethics* 105 (4) (July): 874–915.

———. 1995. *Justice as Impartiality.* Oxford: Oxford University Press.

Bauman, Richard, and Tsvi Kahana, eds. 2006. *The Least Examined Branch: The Role of Legislatures in the Constitutional State.* Cambridge: Cambridge University Press

Baynes, Kenneth. 1995. "Democracy and the *Rechsstaat:* Habermas's *Faktizität und Geltung,*" in White, *The Cambridge Companion to Habermas*, 201–32.

Beiner, Ronald. 1983. *Political Judgment*. Chicago: University of Chicago Press.

Beiner, Ronald and Jennifer Nedelsky, eds. 2001. *Judgment, Imagination, and Politics*. Lanham, Md.: Rowman and Littlefield.

Benhabib, Seyla. 1987. "The Generalized and the Concrete Other," in Benhabib and Drucilla Cornell, eds., *Feminism as Critique*. Minneapolis: University of Minnesota Press, 77–95.

———, ed. 1996. *Democracy and Difference*. Princeton: Princeton University Press.

———. 1996. "Toward a Deliberative Model of Democratic Legitimacy," in Benhabib, *Democracy and Difference*, 67–94.

———. 2001. "Judgment and the Moral Foundations of Politics in Hannah Arendt's Thought," in Beiner and Nedelsky, *Judgment, Imagination, and Politics*, 183–204.

Bennett, Jane. 2001. *The Enchantment of Modern Life*. Princeton: Princeton University Press.

Bickford, Susan. 1996. *The Dissonance of Democracy: Listening, Conflict, and Citizenship*. Ithaca: Cornell University Press.

Blackburn, Simon. 2000. *Ruling Passions: A Theory of Practical Reasoning*. Oxford: Oxford University Press.

———. 1992. *Essays in Quasi-Realism*. Oxford: Oxford University Press.

Blum, Lawrence A. 1994. *Moral Perception and Particularity*. Cambridge: Cambridge University Press.

Bohman, James. 1996. *Public Deliberation: Pluralism, Complexity, and Democracy*. Cambridge, Mass.: The MIT Press.

———, and William Rehg, eds. 1997. *Deliberative Democracy: Essays on Reason and Politics*. Cambridge, Mass.: The MIT Press.

Botwinick, Aryeh. 1977. "A Case for Hume's Nonutilitarianism." *Journal of the History of Philosophy* (October): 423–35.

———. 1980. *Ethics, Politics, and Epistemology: A Study in the Unity of Hume's Thought*. Lanham, Md.: University Press of America.

Brader, Ted. 2006. *Campaigning for Hearts and Minds: How Emotional Appeals in Political Ads Work*. Chicago: University of Chicago Press.

Brennan, William J. 1988. "Reason and Passion." *Cardozo Law Review* 10 (37): 3–23.

Brettschneider, Corey. 2007. *Democratic Rights: The Substance of Self-Government*. Princeton: Princeton University Press.

Bricke, John. 2000. *Mind and Morality: An Examination of Hume's Moral Psychology*. Oxford: Oxford University Press.

Burley, Justine, ed. 2004. *Dworkin and His Critics*. Malden, Mass.: Blackwell.

Calhoun, Cheshire. 1999. "Making up Emotional People: The Case of Romantic Love," in Bandes, *The Passions of Law*, 217–40.

Calhoun, Craig, ed. 1993. *Habermas and the Public Sphere*. Cambridge, Mass.: The MIT Press.

Capaldi, Nicholas. 1995. "Hume as Social Scientist," in Tweyman, *David Hume: Critical Assessments*.

Chappell, V. C. 1968. *Hume*. New York: Anchor.

Chismar, Douglas. 1988–89. "Hume's Confusion about Sympathy," *Philosophy Research Archives* 15: 237–246.

Cocks, Joan. 1989. *The Oppositional Imagination: Adventures in the Sexual Domain.* London: Routledge.

Cohen, G. A. 2003. "Facts and Principles." *Philosophy and Public Affairs* 31 (3): 211–45.

Cohen, Joshua. 1986. "An Epistemic Conception of Democracy," *Ethics* 97 (1) (October): 26–38.

———. 1996. "Procedure and Substance," in Benhabib, *Democracy and Difference*, 95–119.

———. 1997. "Deliberation and Democratic Legitimacy," in Bohman and Rehg, *Deliberative Democracy*, 67–92.

Cohon, Rachel, ed. 2001. *Hume: Moral and Political Philosophy.* Aldershot: Ashgate/Dartmouth,

Coleman, Jules. 1996. "Authority and Reason" in George, *The Autonomy of Law*, 287–320.

Connolly, William E. 2002. *Neuropolitics: Thinking, Culture, Speed.* Minneapolis: University of Minnesota Press.

Cottle, Charles E. 1979. "Justice as an Artificial Virtue in Hume's *Treatise*." *Journal of the History of Ideas* 40: 457–66.

Crawford, Neta. 2000. "The Passion of World Politics: Propositions on Emotion and Emotional Relationships." *International Security* 24 (4) (Spring): 116–56.

Damasio, A. R. 1994. *Descartes' Error: Emotion, Reason, and the Human Brain.* New York: HarperCollins.

Danford, John W. 1990. *David Hume and the Problem of Reason.* New Haven: Yale University Press.

Davie, William. 1985. "Hume on Morality, Action, and Character." *History of Philosophy Quarterly* 2 (3) (July): 337–48.

———. 1988. "A Personal Element in Morality," *Hume Studies* 14 (1) (April): 191–205.

Dees, Richard H. 1992. "Hume and the Contexts of Politics." *Journal of the History of Philosophy* 30 (2) (April): 219–42.

———. 1997. "Hume on the Characters of Virtue." *Journal of the History of Philosophy* 35 (1) (January): 45–64.

Deigh, John. 1999. "Emotion and the Authority of Law: Variations on Themes in Bentham and Austin," in Bandes, *The Passions of Law*, 285–308.

de Souza, Ronald. 2001. *The Rationality of Emotion.* Cambridge, Mass.: The MIT Press.

Dryzek, John S. 2000. *Deliberative Democracy and Beyond: Liberals, Critics, Contestations.* Oxford: Oxford University Press.

Dworkin, Ronald. 1985. *A Matter of Principle.* Cambridge, Mass.: Harvard University Press.

———. 1986. *Law's Empire.* Cambridge, Mass.: Harvard University Press.

———. 2002. "Thirty Years On." *Harvard Law Review* 115 (April): 1655–87.

Elster, Jon. 1998. "Deliberation and Constitution Making," in Elster, *Deliberative Democracy*, 97–122.

Elster, Jon, ed. 1998. *Deliberative Democracy*. Cambridge: Cambridge University Press.

Estlund, David. 1998. "The Insularity of the Reasonable: Why Political Liberalism Must Admit the Truth," *Ethics* 108 (2) (January): 252–75.

Ferriera, M. Jamie. 1994. "Hume and Imagination: Sympathy and the Other." *International Philosophical Quarterly* 34 (1) (March): 39–57.

Fisher, Philip. 2002. *The Vehement Passions*. Princeton: Princeton University Press.

Fishkin, James and Peter Laslett, eds. 2003. *Debating Deliberative Democracy*. Malden, Mass.: Blackwell.

Forbes, Duncan. 1975. *Hume's Philosophical Politics*. Cambridge: Cambridge University Press.

Fraser, Nancy. 1993. "Rethinking the Public Sphere: A Contribution to the Critique of Actually Existing Democracy," in Calhoun, *Habermas and the Public Sphere*, 109–42.

Frazer, Michael. 2006. "The Enlightenment of Sympathy." Ph.D. diss., Princeton University.

———. 2007. "John Rawls: Between Two Enlightenments," *Political Theory* 35 (6) (December 2007): 756–80.

Freeman, Samuel, ed. 2003. *The Cambridge Companion to Rawls*. Cambridge: Cambridge University Press.

———. 2003. "Congruence and the Good of Justice," in Freeman, *The Cambridge Companion to Rawls*, 277–315.

Galston, William A. 1999. "Diversity, Toleration, and Deliberative Democracy: Religious Minorities and Public Schooling," in Macedo, *Deliberative Politics*, 39–48.

———. 2002. *Liberal Pluralism*. Cambridge: Cambridge University Press.

Gambetta, Diego. 1998. "Claro!: An Essay on Discursive Machismo," in Elster, *Deliberative Democracy*, 19–43.

George, Robert P., ed. 1996. *The Autonomy of Law*. Oxford: Oxford University Press.

Gilligan, Carol. 1982. *In a Different Voice: Psychological Theory and Women's Development*. Cambridge, Mass.: Harvard University Press.

———. 1995. "Moral Orientation and Moral Development," in Held, *Justice and Care*, 31–46.

Gobert, James J. 1988. "In Search of the Impartial Jury." *Journal of Criminal Law and Criminology* 79 (2) (Summer): 269–327.

Goffman, Erving. 1963. *Stigma: Notes on the Management of Spoiled Identity*. New York: Simon and Schuster.

Goodin, Robert E. 2003. "Democratic Deliberation Within," in Fishkin and Laslett, *Debating Deliberative Democracy*, 54–79.

Goodwin, Jeff, James M. Jasper, and Francesca Polletta, eds. 2001. *Passionate Politics: Emotions and Social Movements*. Chicago: University of Chicago Press.

Gray, John. 1996. *Isaiah Berlin*. Princeton: Princeton University Press.

Green, Leslie. 2004. "Associative Obligations and the State," in Burley, *Dworkin and His Critics*, 267–84.

Greenspan, Patricia S. 1980. "Ambivalence and the Logic of Emotion," in Rorty, *Explaining Emotions*, 223–50.

Guinier, Lani. 1994. *The Tyranny of the Majority: Fundamental Fairness in Representative Democracy.* New York: The Free Press.

Gutmann, Amy and Dennis Thompson. 1996. *Democracy and Disagreement.* Cambridge, Mass.: Harvard University Press.

———. 2004. *Why Deliberative Democracy?* Princeton: Princeton University Press.

Haakonssen, Knud. 1989. *The Science of a Legislator: The Natural Jurisprudence of David Hume and Adam Smith.* Cambridge: Cambridge University Press.

———. 1996. *Natural Law and Moral Philosophy: From Grotius to the Scottish Enlightenment.* Cambridge: Cambridge University Press.

Habermas, Jürgen. 1996. *Moral Consciousness and Communicative Action.* Trans. Christian Lenhardt and Shierry Weber Nelson. Cambridge, Mass.: The MIT Press.

———. 1996. "Three Normative Models of Democracy," in Benhabib, *Democracy and Difference*, 21–30.

———. 1999. *Between Facts and Norms.* Trans. William Rehg. Cambridge, Mass.: The MIT Press.

———. 1999. "Citizenship and National Identity," in Habermas, *Between Facts and Norms*, Appendix II, 491–516.

———. 2001. *The Inclusion of the Other.* Trans. Ciaran Cronin and Pablo De Greiff. Cambridge, Mass.: The MIT Press.

———. 2001. *Justification and Application.* Trans. Ciaran Cronin. Cambridge, Mass.: The MIT Press.

Hall, Cheryl. 2003. "Passions and Constraint," *Philosophy and Social Criticism* 28 (6): 727–48.

———. 2005. *The Trouble with Passion: Political Theory Beyond the Reign of Reason.* New York: Routledge.

———. 2007. "Recognizing the Passion in Deliberation: Toward a More Democratic Theory of Deliberative Democracy," *Hypatia: A Journal of Feminist Philosophy* 22 (4) (Fall): 81–95.

Hamilton, Alexander, James Madison, and John Jay. 1961. *The Federalist Papers*, ed. Clinton Rossiter. New York: Mentor.

Hampshire, Stuart. 1983. *Morality and Conflict.* Cambridge, Mass.: Harvard University Press.

———. 1989. *Innocence and Experience.* Cambridge, Mass.: Harvard University Press.

Hampton, Jean. 1995. "Does Hume Have an Instrumental Conception of Practical Reason?" *Hume Studies* 21 (1) (April): 57–74.

Hans, Valerie P., and Neil Vidmar. 1986. *Judging the Jury.* Cambridge, Mass.: Perseus.

Harrison, Jonathan. 1981. *Hume's Theory of Justice.* Oxford: Clarendon.

Hart, H.L.A. 1961. *The Concept of Law.* Oxford: Clarendon.

Hastie, Reid, ed. 1993. *Inside the Juror: The Psychology of Juror Decision Making.* Cambridge: Cambridge University Press.

Hastie, Reid, Steven D. Penrod, and Nancy Pennington, eds. 1983. *Inside the Jury.* Cambridge, Mass.: Harvard University Press.

Held, Virginia. 1993. *Feminist Morality: Transforming Culture, Society, and Politics.* Chicago: University of Chicago Press.

———, ed. 1995. *Justice and Care.* Boulder, Colo.: Westview.

Henderson, Lynne N. 1987. "Legality and Empathy." *Michigan Law Review* 85 (June): 1574–1653.

Herzog, Don. 1985. *Without Foundations: Justification in Political Theory.* Ithaca: Cornell University Press.

Honig, Bonnie. 1996. "Difference, Dilemmas, and the Politics of Home," in Benhabib, *Democracy and Difference*, 257–77.

Hume, David. 1966. *An Enquiry Concerning the Principles of Morals.* LaSalle, Ill.: Open Court.

———. 1968. *A Treatise of Human Nature.* Ed. L. A. Selby-Bigge. Oxford: Clarendon Press.

———. 1983. *The History of England.* 6 vols. Indianapolis: Liberty Fund.

———. 1987. *Essays: Moral, Political and Literary.* Indianapolis: Liberty Fund.

———. 1998. *Enquiries Concerning Human Understanding and Concerning the Principles of Morals.* Ed. P. H. Nidditch. Oxford: Clarendon.

Immerwahr, John. 1992. "Hume on Tranquilizing the Passions." *Hume Studies* 18 (2): 293–314.

———. 1992. "Hume's Revised Racism." *Journal of the History of Ideas* 53 (3) (July–September): 481–86.

Ingram, Attracta. 1996. "Constitutional Patriotism." *Philosophy and Social Criticism* 22 (6) (1996): 1–18.

Jacobson, Anne Jaap, ed. 2000. *Feminist Interpretations of David Hume.* University Park: Pennsylvania State University Press.

Johnson, James. 1998. "Arguing for Deliberation," in Elster, *Deliberative Democracy*, 161–84.

Johnson, Sheri Lynn. 1985. "Black Innocence and the White Jury." *Michigan Law Review* 83 (7) (June): 1611–1708.

Jonakait, Ralph N. 2003. *The American Jury System.* New Haven: Yale University Press.

Kant, Immanuel. 1981. *Grounding for the Metaphysics of Morals.* Trans. James W. Ellington. Indianapolis: Hackett.

———. 1983. *Toward Perpetual Peace and Other Essays.* Trans. Ted Humphrey. Indianapolis: Hackett.

Kateb, George. 1992. *The Inner Ocean: Individualism and Democratic Culture.* Ithaca: Cornell University Press.

Kekes, John. 1993. *The Morality of Pluralism.* Princeton: Princeton University Press.

Kelsen, Hans. 1945. *The General Theory of Law and State.* New York: Russell and Russell.

———. 1957. *What Is Justice?* Berkeley: University of California Press.

Kemp Smith, Norman. 1964. *The Philosophy of David Hume.* London: Macmillan.

———. 1967. "The Naturalism of Hume," in Portens, MacLennan, and Davie, *The Credibility of Divine Existence: The Collected Papers of Norman Kemp Smith.*

Kolin, Andrew. 1992. *The Ethical Foundations of Hume's Theory of Politics*. New York: Peter Lang.

Korsgaard, Christine. 1996. *The Sources of Normativity*. Cambridge: Cambridge University Press.

———. 2001. "Skepticism about Practical Reason," in Millgram, *Varieties of Practical Reasoning*, 103–26.

Koziak, Barbara. 2000. *Retrieving Political Emotion:* Thumos, *Aristotle, and Gender*. University Park: Pennsylvania State University Press.

Krause, Sharon. 2001. "Partial Justice." *Political Theory* 29 (3) (June): 315–36.

———. 2004. "Hume and the (False) Luster of Justice." *Political Theory* 32 (5) (October): 628–55.

———. 2005. "Desiring Justice: Motivation and Justification in Rawls and Habermas." *Contemporary Political Theory* 4 (4) (November): 363–85.

———. 2006. "Brains, Citizens, and Democracy's New Nobility." *theory and event* 9 (1).

Larmore, Charles. 1987. *Patterns of Moral Complexity*. Cambridge: Cambridge University Press.

———. 1996. *The Morals of Modernity*. Cambridge: Cambridge University Press.

Lazarus, Richard. 2003. "Appraisal: The Minimal Cognitive Prerequisites of Emotion," in Soloman, *What Is an Emotion?*, 125–30.

LeDoux, Joseph. 1996. *The Emotional Brain*. New York: Simon and Schuster.

Lipkin, Robert J. 1987. "Altruism and Sympathy in Hume's Ethics." *Australasian Journal of Philosophy* 65 (1) (March): 18–32.

Livingston, Donald W. 1995. "On Hume's Conservatism." *Hume Studies* 21 (2) (November): 151–64.

Locke, John. 1983. *A Letter Concerning Toleration*. Indianapolis: Hackett.

Lovibond, Sabina. 1983. *Realism and Imagination in Ethics*. Minneapolis: University of Minnesota Press.

Lukes, Steven. 1991. *Moral Conflict and Politics*. Oxford: Clarendon.

MacCormick, Neil. 1994. "The Concept of Law and *The Concept of Law*." *Oxford Journal of Legal Studies* 14 (1) (Spring): 1–23.

Macedo, Stephen, ed. 1999. *Deliberative Politics: Essays on Democracy and Disagreement*. Oxford: Oxford University Press.

MacIntyre, A. C. 1968. "Hume on 'Is' and 'Ought,'" in Chappell, *Hume*, 240–64.

———. 1984. *After Virtue*. Notre Dame, Ind.: University of Notre Dame Press.

Mackie, J. L. 1980. *Hume's Moral Theory*. London: Routledge.

Magri, Tito. 1996. "Natural Obligation and Normative Motivation in Hume's *Treatise*." *Hume Studies* 22 (2) (November): 231–53.

Manin, Bernard. 1987. "On Legitimacy and Political Deliberation." *Political Theory* 15 (3) (August): 338–68.

Mansbridge, Jane. 1999. "Everyday Talk in the Deliberative System," in Macedo, *Deliberative Politics*, 211–42.

Marcus, George E. 2002. *The Sentimental Citizen: Emotion in Democratic Politics*. University Park: Pennsylvania State University Press.

Marcus, George E., W. Russell Neuman, and Michael Mackuen. 2000. *Affective Intelligence and Political Judgment*. Chicago: University of Chicago Press.

Marcus, George E., W. Russell Neuman, and Michael Mackuen. 2007. *The Affect Effect*. Chicago: University of Chicago Press.

Markell, Patchen. 2000. "Making Affect Safe for Democracy? On 'Constitutional Patriotism.' " *Political Theory* 28 (1) (February): 38–63.

McCarthy, Thomas. 1994. "Kantian Constructivism and Reconstructivism: Rawls and Habermas in Dialogue." *Ethics* 105 (1) (October): 44–63.

McDermott, Rose. 2004. "The Feeling of Rationality: The Meaning of Neuroscientific Advances for Political Science." *Perspectives on Politics* 2 (4) (December 2004): 691–706.

Mendus, Susan. 1999. "The Importance of Love in Rawls's *Theory of Justice*." *British Journal of Political Science* 29 (1999): 57–75.

Miller, William Ian. 1997. *The Anatomy of Disgust*. Cambridge, Mass.: Harvard University Press.

Millgram, Elijah. 1995. "Was Hume a Humean?" *Hume Studies* 21 (1) (April): 75–93.

———, ed. 2001. *Varieties of Practical Reasoning*. Cambridge, Mass.: The MIT Press.

Minow, Martha, and Elizabeth Spelman. 1988. "Passion for Justice." *Cardozo Law Review* 10 (37): 37–76.

Montesquieu, Charles de la Brède et de. 1949–51. *De l'esprit des lois*, in Montesquieu, *Oeuvres complètes*. 2 vols. Ed. Roger Caillois. Bibliothèque de la Pléiade. Paris: Gallimard.

Moon, J. Donald. 1995. "Practical Discourse and Communicative Ethics," in White, *The Cambridge Companion to Habermas*, 143–66.

Moore, James. 1976. "Hume's Theory of Justice and Property." *Political Studies* 24 (2) (June): 103–19.

Mounce, H. O. 1999. *Hume's Naturalism*. New York: Routledge.

Nagel, Thomas. 1986. *The View from Nowhere*. New York: Oxford University Press.

Nedelsky, Jennifer. 2001. "Embodied Diversity and Challenges to Law," in Beiner and Nedelsky, *Judgment, Imagination, and Politics*, 229–56.

———. 2006. "Legislative Judgment and the Enlarged Mentality: Taking Religious Perspectives," in Bauman and Kahana, *The Least Examined Branch: The Role of Legislatures in the Constitutional State*, 93–124

Noddings, Nel. 1984. *Caring: A Feminine Approach to Ethics*. Berkeley: University of California Press.

Norris, Andrew. 1996. "Arendt, Kant, and the Politics of Common Sense." *Polity* 29 (2) (Winter): 165–91.

Norton, David Fate, ed. 1999. *The Cambridge Companion to Hume*. Cambridge: Cambridge University Press.

———. 1999. "Hume, Human Nature, and the Foundations of Morality," in Norton, *The Cambridge Companion to Hume*, 148–81.

Nussbaum, Martha. 1990. *Love's Knowledge*. Oxford: Oxford University Press.

———. 1994. *The Therapy of Desire: Theory and Practice in Hellenistic Ethics*. Princeton: Princeton University Press.

———. 2002. *Upheavals of Thought*. Cambridge: Cambridge University Press.

———. 2003. "Rawls and Feminism," in Freeman, *The Cambridge Companion to Rawls*, 488–520.

———. 2004. *Hiding from Humanity: Shame, Disgust, and the Law*. Princeton: Princeton University Press.

Okin, Susan Moller. 1989. *Justice, Gender and the Family*. New York: Basic.

———. 1989. "Reason and Feeling in Thinking about Justice." *Ethics* 99 (2) (January): 229–49.

Parker, Richard D. 2004. "Democratic Honor: Liberal and Populist." *Harvard Civil Rights-Civil Liberties Review* 39 (2) (Summer): 291–315.

Penelhum, Terence. 1992. *David Hume: An Introduction to His Philosophical System*. West Lafayette, Ind.: Purdue University Press.

Pitson, A. E. 1989. "Projectionism, Realism, and Hume's Moral Sense Theory." *Hume Studies* 15 (1) (April): 61–92.

Plamenatz, John. 1958. *The English Utilitarians*. Oxford: Blackwell.

Popkin, Richard H. 1980. "Hume's Racism," in Watson and Force, *The High Road to Pyrrhonism*, 251–66.

———. 1992. "Hume's Racism Reconsidered," in Popkin, *The Third Force in Seventeenth-Century Thought*, 64–75.

———, ed. 1992. *The Third Force in Seventeenth-Century Thought*. Leiden: E. J. Brill.

Portens, A., A. MacLennan, and G. Davie, eds. 1967. *The Credibility of Divine Existence: The Collected Papers of Norman Kemp Smith*. New York: Macmillan.

Posner, Richard. 1999. "Emotion versus Emotionalism in Law," in Bandes, *The Passions of Law*, 309–29.

Przeworski, Adam. 1998. "Deliberation and Ideological Domination," in Elster, *Deliberative Democracy*, 140–60.

Radcliffe, Elizabeth. 1996. "How Does the Humean Sense of Duty Motivate?" *Journal of the History of Philosophy* 34 (3) (July): 383–407.

———. 2001. "Kantian Tunes on a Humean Instrument: Why Hume is Not Really a Skeptic about Practical Reasoning," in R. Cohon, *Hume: Moral and Political Philosophy*, 59–84.

Raphael, D. D. 1980. *Justice and Liberty*. London: Athlone.

———. 1980. "Justice and Utility (I & II)," in Raphael, *Justice and Liberty*, 157–89.

Ramachandran, V.S. 1998. *Phantoms in the Brain: Probing the Mysteries of the Human Mind*. New York: William Morrow.

Rawls, John. 1971. *A Theory of Justice*. Cambridge, Mass.: Harvard University Press.

———. 1993. *Political Liberalism*. New York: Columbia University Press.

———. 1995. "Reply to Habermas." *Journal of Philosophy* 92 (3) (1995): 132–80.

———. 2000. *Lectures on the History of Moral Philosophy*. Cambridge, Mass.: Harvard University Press.

———. 2001. *Justice as Fairness: A Restatement*. Cambridge, Mass.: Harvard University Press.

Raz, Joseph. 1975. *Practical Reason and Norms*. Oxford: Oxford University Press.

———. 1979. *The Authority of Law*. Oxford: Oxford University Press.

Raz, Joseph. 1985. "Authority and Justification." *Philosophy and Public Affairs* 14 (1) (Winter): 3–29.

———. 1986. *The Morality of Freedom*. Oxford: Clarendon.

Raz, Joseph. 1999. *Ethics in the Public Domain*. Oxford: Clarendon.

Richardson, Henry S. 1997. *Practical Reasoning About Final Ends*. Oxford: Oxford University Press.

Riker, William. 1982. *Liberalism Against Populism: A Confrontation Between the Theory of Democracy and the Theory of Social Choice*. San Francisco: W. H. Freeman.

Rollins, Judith. 1985. *Between Women: Domestics and Their Employers*. Philadelphia: Temple University Press.

Rosenblum, Nancy, ed. 1989. *Liberalism and the Moral Life*. Cambridge, Mass.: Harvard University Press.

Rorty, Amélie Oksenberg, ed. 1980. *Explaining Emotions*. Berkeley: University of California Press.

Rousseau, Jean-Jacques. 1978. *On the Social Contract*. Trans. Judith R. Masters. New York: St. Martin's.

Ruddick, Sara. 1989. *Maternal Thinking: Toward a Politics of Peace*. Boston: Beacon.

Russell, Paul. 1995. *Freedom and Moral Sentiment: Hume's Way of Naturalizing Responsibility*. New York: Oxford University Press.

Sabl, Andrew. 2002. "When Bad Things Happen From Good People (and vice versa): Hume's Political Ethics of Revolution." *Polity* 35 (1) (Fall): 73–90.

Sandel, Michael J. 1982. *Liberalism and the Limits of Justice*. Cambridge: Cambridge University Press.

Sanders, Lynn. 1997. "Against Deliberation." *Political Theory* 25 (3) (June): 347–76.

Sarat, Austin. 1993. "Authority, Anxiety, and Procedural Justice: Moving from Scientific Detachment to Critical Engagement." *Law and Society Review* 27 (3): 647–71.

Scanlon, T. M. 1982. "Contractualism and Utilitarianism," in Sen and Williams, *Utilitarianism and Beyond*, 103–28.

———. 1998. *What We Owe to Each Other*. Cambridge, Mass.: Harvard University Press.

Scheffler, Samuel. 1992. *Human Morality*. Oxford: Oxford University Press.

Scott, James C. 1990. *Domination and the Arts of Resistance*. New Haven: Yale University Press.

Scruton, Roger. 1980. "Emotion, Practical Knowledge, and Common Culture," in Rorty, *Explaining Emotion*, 519–36.

Sen, Amartya, and Bernard Williams, eds. 1982. *Utilitarianism and Beyond*. Cambridge: Cambridge University Press.

Shapiro, Ian. 2003. "Optimal Deliberation?" in Fishkin and Laslett, *Debating Deliberative Democracy*, 121–37.

Smith, Adam. 1997. *The Theory of Moral Sentiments*. Washington: Regnery.

Smith, Michael. 1994. *The Moral Problem*. Malden, Mass.: Blackwell.

Smith, Steven D. 1995. "Radically Subversive Speech and the Authority of Law." *Michigan Law Review* 94 (2) (November): 348–70.

Solomon, Robert. 1995. *A Passion for Justice*. Lanham, Md.: Rowman and Littlefield.

———. 2003. "Emotions and Choice," in Solomon, *What Is an Emotion?*, 224–35.

———, ed. 2003. *What Is an Emotion?* Oxford: Oxford University Press.

Soper, Philip. 1989. "Legal Theory and the Claim of Authority." *Philosophy and Public Affairs* 18 (3) (Summer): 209–37.

Spragens, Thomas. 1990. *Reason and Democracy*. Durham, N.C.: Duke University Press.

Steinberger, Peter J. 1993. *The Concept of Political Judgment*. Chicago: University of Chicago Press.

Stewart, John B. 1963. *The Moral and Political Philosophy of David Hume*. New York: Columbia University Press.

———. 1995. "The Public Interest vs. Old Rights." *Hume Studies* 21 (2) (November): 165–88.

Stocker, Michael. 1990. *Plural and Conflicting Values*. Oxford: Clarendon.

———. 1996. *Valuing Emotions*. Cambridge: Cambridge University Press.

Stokes, Susan C. 1998. "Pathologies of Deliberation," in Elster, *Deliberative Democracy*, 123–39.

Stroud, Barry. 2000. *Hume*. London: Routledge.

Sunstein, Cass. 2003. "The Law of Group Polarization," in Fishkin and Laslett, *Debating Deliberative Democracy*, 80–101.

Swaine, Lucas A. 2006. *The Liberal Conscience: Politics and Principle in a World of Religious Pluralism*. New York: Columbia University Press.

Taylor, Charles. 1982. "The Diversity of Goods," in Sen and Williams, *Utilitarianism and Beyond*, 129–44.

———. 1995. "Cross-Purposes: The Liberal-Communitarian Debate," in Taylor, *Philosophical Arguments*. Cambridge, Mass.: Harvard University Press, 181–203.

Taylor, Jacqueline. 1998. "Justice and the Foundations of Social Morality in Hume's *Treatise*." *Hume Studies* 24 (1) (April): 5–30.

———. 2000. "Hume and the Reality of Value," in Jacobson, *Feminist Interpretations of David Hume*, 107–36.

———. 2002. "Humean Ethics and the Politics of Sentiment." *Topoi* 21: 175–86.

———. 2003. "Hume on Luck and Moral Inclusion." Panel paper presented at the annual meeting of the American Political Science Association, Philadelphia, Pa.

Thompson, Samuel M. 1964. "The Authority of Law." *Ethics* 75 (1) (October): 16–24.

Tocqueville, Alexis de. 2000. *Democracy in America*. Trans. Harvey C. Mansfield and Delba Winthrop. Chicago: University of Chicago Press.

Tomasi, John. 2001. *Liberalism Beyond Justice: Citizens, Society, and the Boundaries of Political Theory*. Princeton: Princeton University Press.

Tronto, Joan. 1994. *Moral Boundaries: A Political Argument for an Ethic of Care*. New York: Routledge.

Tulis, Jeffrey K. 2003. "Deliberation Between Institutions," in Fishkin and Laslett, *Debating Deliberative Democracy*, 200–211.

Tweyman, Stanley, ed. 1995. *David Hume: Critical Assessments*. New York: Routledge.

van Holthoon, F. L. 1993. "Adam Smith and David Hume: With Sympathy." *Utilitas* 5 (1) (May): 35–48.

Waldron, Jeremy. 1999. *Law and Disagreement*. Oxford: Oxford University Press.

Walzer, Michael. 1999. "Deliberation and What Else?" in Macedo, *Deliberative Politics*, 58–69.

———. 2003. "Passion and Politics." *Philosophy and Social Criticism* 28 (6): 617–33.

———. 2004. *Passions and Politics*. New Haven: Yale University Press.

Warren, Mark E. 1995. "The Self in Discursive Democracy," in White, *The Cambridge Companion to Habermas*, 167–200.

Watson, Richard A., and James E. Force, eds. 1980. *The High Road to Pyrrhonism*. San Diego: Austin Hill.

Weir, Margaret. 1995. "Social Welfare and Poverty," in Bacon, Davidson, and Keller, *The Encyclopedia of the United States Congress*, 1841–52.

West, Robin. 1997. *Caring for Justice*. New York: New York University Press.

White, Stephen K., ed. 1995. *The Cambridge Companion to Habermas*. Cambridge: Cambridge University Press.

———. 2000. *Sustaining Affirmation: The Strengths of Weak Ontology in Political Theory*. Princeton: Princeton University Press.

Whitman, Walt. 1950. "Song of Myself," in Whitman, *Leaves of Grass and Selected Prose*. Ed. John Kouwenhoven. New York: Modern Library.

Williams, Bernard. 1985. *Ethics and the Limits of Philosophy*. Cambridge, Mass.: Harvard University Press.

———. 1986. *Moral Luck*. Cambridge: Cambridge University Press.

———. 1996. "History, Morality, and the Test of Reflection," in Korsgaard, *The Sources of Normativity*, 210–218.

Wolfsenberger, Donald. 2005. "Congress and Security." Paper presented for the Congress Project Seminar on "Congress and the Politics of Aging," Woodrow Wilson International Center for Scholars, September 13, 2005, available online at www.wilsoncenter.org/events/docs/aging-essay-intro.pdf.

Young, Iris Marion. 1990. *Justice and the Politics of Difference*. Princeton: Princeton University Press.

———. 1996. "Communication and the Other: Beyond Deliberative Democracy," in Benhabib, *Democracy and Difference*, 120–36.

———. 2001. "Asymmetrical Reciprocity: On Moral Respect, Wonder, and Enlarged Thought," in Beiner and Nedelsky, *Judgment, Imagination, and Politics*, 205–28.

———. 2003. "Activist Challenges to Deliberative Democracy," in Fishkin and Laslett, *Debating Deliberative Democracy*, 102–20.

Index